HOOSIER GERMAN TALES
small & TALL

HOOSIER GERMAN
TALES

SMALL &
TALL

by,
and with the help of,
all these folks and many others
who came long before us . . .

Jerome Alles–Victor Baumgart–Joe Becher–Chris Betz
Evangeline C. Bockstahler–Lester Bockstahler–Fritz Bockstege–C. R. Borneman
Norbert Bufka–Wilford C. Butt–Lillian Doane–David Dryer–Martina Eckert
Rock G. Emmert–Angela S. Etherton–John Bernard Flodder
Peter Freeouf–Georgine Leininger Gallagher–Joseph R. Gogel–Ray E. Hall
Jane Leitshuh Harnett–Frances Himes–Louis Hoelker–William A. Hoelker
Bob Hoffman–Antonius Holtmann–Ilse Horacek–Phyllis Johanneman
Dorothy Keiser Campbell–Gerhard Klemm–Bill and Pat Koch
Norbert Krapf–Elfrieda Lang–James Madison–Jeanne Melchior–Mary Joe Meuser
Carl Eugene Miller–Mrs. Ernest B. Miller–Lora Naffe
Marilyn Nathan–Elmer E. Peters–Ellen Klingman Pettay–Roger Pfingston
Nan Schenck Polley–Kari Points–Joan Quante–Betty Lou Randall–Mrs. G. M. Rogers
Donald M. Royer–L. C. Rudolph–Ralph Ruppel–Ruth Noerr Scanland
Sheryl Schaefer–James Schloot–George Schricker–Marcia and Arthur Schwenk
Clifford H. Scott–William Selm–Kay Smith–Bob Steffe–Bernadette Stenger
Melvin H. and Jo Ann Roberts Sundermann
Irvin ("Mugs") and Genevieve Langferman Waechter–Henry Wahl
Emma Wallpe–Herman B Wells–Sr. Adele Weyer–Corina Christian Wilhelm
Scott Wiseman–Leander C. Wollenmann–Justine Ziegler–James Ziegler.

Eberhard Reichmann
Editor

German-American Center
&
Indiana German Heritage Society, Inc.
INDIANAPOLIS

GERMAN-AMERICAN CENTER
and
INDIANA GERMAN HERITAGE SOCIETY, INC.

Deutsches Haus-Athenaeum, 401 East Michigan Street
Indianapolis, Indiana 46204

Volume 3

This publication was supported by
Wilhelm Bilgram — Evangeline C. Bockstahler — Ernestine Dillon
Martha B. Enyart — Jim Exner — William A. Hoelker
Susan Kessler — Rosalind Brown McCart
Robert A. and Lee M. McDougal — Glenn E Montgomery
Helen Moore — Joan Quante — Ruth Noerr Scanland
Kate B. and Robert R. Sturgeon — Richard C. Vonnegut, Sr.
Henry Wahl — Carol Weil

Ferdinand Historical Society
German Language Video Center & Heidelberg Haus Indianapolis
Klemm's German Sausage and Meat Market Indianapolis

Research was supported by an Indiana Heritage Research Grant
from the Indiana Humanities Council

Cover design and illustrations by R. L. Robertson

Printed in the United States of America
by Indiana University Printing Services

Produced and distributed by NCSA LITERATUR
Green Valley, Nashville, Indiana 47448

*From Lots of Hoosier Germans
to the Great State of Indiana
with Love
on Its 175th Anniversary
(1816-1991)*

ACKNOWLEDGMENTS & CREDITS

This book is the result of a cooperative effort extending over seven years. Thanks to all fellow contributors. It was their encouraging input that made this collection possible. The research of my students in the Hoosier German seminars at Indiana University-Bloomington and Indianapolis also opened many a forgotten door to the past. My wife Ruth promptly rescued me every time I screamed at the computer. Elfrieda Lang and Cecilia Wahl lent their eagle eyes to the proof reading process.

I am also grateful for an Indiana Heritage Research Grant from the Indiana Humanities Council, and for the contributions of our donors. Both institutional and individual support is essential for the preservation of our heritage.

Thanks are also due to the following authors and publishers for granting reprint permissions:

The Abbey Press, St. Meinrad, IN, for selections from Fr. Albert Kleber's *Ferdinand, Indiana, 1840-1940. A Bit of Cultural History* (1940);

AP News Features, New York, NY, and *The Herald-Times*, Bloomington, IN, for "Same Christmas Card Exchanged for 50 Years" (Dec. 24, 1986);

Ronald L. Baker and Indiana University Press, Bloomington, IN, for selections from Ronald L. Baker's and Donald Carmony's meritorious book on *Indiana Place Names* (1975), and from Ronald L. Baker's *Hoosier Folk Legends* (1982);

Ellsworth Barnard and Northern Michigan University Press, Marquette, MI, for two episodes from *Wendell Willkie, Fighter for Freedom* (1966);

Carol Burke and Purdue University Press, West Lafayette, IN, for "Finding His Sister," in: *Plain Talk* (1983);

Concordia Publishing House, St. Louis, MO, for selections from G. E. Hageman's *Friedrich Konrad Dietrich Wyneken. Pioneer Lutheran Missionary of the Nineteenth Century* (1926);

Fred D. Cavinder and Indiana University Press, Bloomington, IN, for the Studebaker brothers' contract in the *Indiana Book of Records* (1985);

Herald Printing Co., Jasper, IN, for the 1991 Strassenfest brochure picture used in the cover design;

Indianapolis News, for Anton Scherrer's "Unscrambling the Muellers in Indianapolis," and Wayne Guthrie's "Huntingburg Named for Good Hunting" (Aug. 1976);

Maurice V. Miller for a selection from "The Early Artists in Brown County," in: Dorothy Birney Bailey, *Brown County Remembers* (1986), Revere Press;

Lawrence Moll and *The Message*, Evansville, for "The Raid on the Taverns" (1973);

Owen Litho Service, Inc., Spencer, IN, for the "Eli Schoppell" selection from *Tales of Pioneers, History of Owen County* (1962);

Herman Pattee and *The Fulton County Historical Society Quarterly*, for an episode of "Kewanna Characters and High Jinks," vol. 62 (1986);

Linda Robertson and Walsworth Publishing Co., Marceline, MO, for the "Roann" story in the *Wabash County History, Bicentennial Edition 1976;*

Patricia Zimmerman, for the Hulman brothers selection, in: Dorothy J. Clark, *Terre Haute, Wabash River City* (1983), Windsor Publications, Inc., Chatsworth, CA.

Eberhard Reichmann

Dear Reader

Welcome to the world of old-time *Hoosier German Tales*. Our *Tales*—we use the term under the protection of poetic license—are stories and legends, poems, memoirs and thoughts, anecdotes and jokes, all of and by, and/or about, the Hoosier Germans. We began collecting these tales in 1984. Some of them came from interviews, others were written down from memory by some seventy contributors, and a third group was discovered in old Indiana German-language and English-language newspapers, in family, church, school, town and county histories, in monographs and other print sources.

Ours is a collection "by the people for the people," who for the most part are speakers of English only. In that respect it should be of interest to note that—not just in the Amish communities—we still have bilingual Hoosiers, who in the fourth generation (!) in Evansville, Jasper, Ferdinand, Oldenburg, Indianapolis, Fort Wayne, and many other places, still speak German. In order to capture a bit of the flavor of surviving German-American dialects, some of our twenty-seven chapters feature both German and English versions, notably those devoted to two Dubois County characters who have become legends, Ed Meyer (XXV) and Father Basil Heusler (VI). The fictitious Ed Meyer and the very real Fr. Basil are both embedded in the strong Dubois County German-American tradition.

The thematic organization of our book evolved naturally as the collection grew. The criteria for inclusion of texts were fairly logical: There had to be a Hoosier German-American connection in the plot, the character(s) and/or the narrator. Items had to reflect—and with a certain charm or punch—how life was experienced and perceived, how some folks came to Indiana, how they worked and saved, drank and smoked, goofed off and cussed, how they married and raised kids, how they struggled *mit Englisch* and mixed the languages, how they prayed and celebrated, how priests and preachers fit in, how wars affected them and—you name it. It stands to reason that many items, especially those dealing with language, are closely tied to the German-American experience; others, less parochial, are simply all-Hoosier, all-American, all-human. This reflects the actual situation of German Americana and most other ethnic cultures. Many things we do or are used to in America are still colored by their ethnic origins, while others have become so much part and parcel of the main stream that their origins have long been forgotten.

In the *Notes* each entry of the collection is identified as to originator or contributor, and/or bibliographical source.

We are fond of these tales, for they are like a precious heirloom that is passed on from generation to generation. They capture laughter and smiles, and fun and folly of yesteryear, and also worries, fears and tears, and good and bad and evil—a real mirror of life, without embellishment. They are dear to our hearts, for they are a vital part of our heritage, that historical dimension of our identity.

The 333 plus tales we present to you now should really be only the beginning of an all-out effort at *preserving* the tales that are locked in the memory of folks like you and me. When Jeanne Melchior from Jasper sent me some stories her grandfather used to tell, she noted with regret the irretrievable loss of others: "There were other stories too—The Fox and the Wolf, Ghosts in the Attic, The Night that Mr. Death Came for Granpa's Father. But we have only fragments and a memory of windy fire-lit nights, and Granpa taking slow puffs on his pipe, his voice heavy with German accent, intoning 'Back when I was a little fella . . .'"

Dear Reader, we know you have a good story or two you could have shared with us, but you probably didn't know about our project. It is not too late to preserve and to share them. Write them first on the blank pages of this book, copy them and send them to our attention at the German-American Center. Nothing would please us more than getting flooded with hundreds of new items that would lead to an even bigger volume, like *More Hoosier German Tales*. We firmly believe that this is possible, and you know why? The "Dutchmen"—of various generational vintage—make up a sizeable body in Indiana: One third of all Hoosiers, to be approximately precise, trace part or all of their roots to places in the German-speaking lands of Europe. That's why . . .

And now have fun with *our* tales and with the ones *you* will write for your family and your extended family, the Hoosier folks—with or without a German "accent."

Eberhard Reichmann

German-American Center, Indianapolis
German-American Day, October 6, 1991

viii

CONTENTS

I.

THE LONG, LONG WAY TO INDIANA

Family Treasures.

(1) The stowaway trunk of Harmon Henry Keiser (I.2.); present custodian is great-granddaughter Monteen Bugher, Carmel. *Courtesy Dorothy Keiser Campbell.*

(2) August Brandt's trunk was on the first ship with immigrants landing at New Orleans after the Civil War; present custodian is grandson Henry Lang, Mount Vernon. *Courtesy Elfrieda Lang.*

1. The Forefather Arrives

He stumbles off the ship America,
parts from the people who
speak the only language he's
ever known, and leads a wife
and six children toward the middle
of a dark continent. Eight
pairs of shoes shaped by
the contours of cobbled
Bavarian streets must soon
begin to fall evenly upon
uncultivated ground. Like
a startled rabbit, the woman
cocks her ears for the pealing
of distant churchbells.
The children cling to the man's
overcoat like cockleburrs.
A sailor whose eyes blink
back to the vineyards patching
the banks of the Main River,
he knows he must learn to
navigate this foreign land
by foot. He stares at
the bark of trees he's never
seen, flinches at the songs
of birds he's never heard.
He worries about laying seed
in the soil in the spring.
He sucks in his breath,
puts down one foot at a time.

2. The Trunk Called "Germany"

The trunk called "Germany" is old, but young
In the hearts of the grandchildren to whom it has come.
Its history is pleasant to all who will hear
Of the things it experienced so ancient and queer

'twas made by a youth while in dreams of a life
In far away America, for in Germany was much strife.

The son of a peasant, in love with a maid,
The parents knowing nothing of the plans that were laid.

In the hours of the night it came to its form
After the day's labor had been suffered and borne.
For the news of the marriage had come to those
Who because of their wealth had occasion to oppose.

Then the maid's parents decided to mend
The life of their daughter, so they planned to send
The young husband away for three long years
To serve in the army of Germany's sires.

These plans seemed good, but at last they learned
That all was fruitless, for the tide had turned,
The ship was leaving, and there on the deck
Stood the young wife, her thoughts a wreck.

For in yonder distance it was plain to see
That loved ones were astonished, and the mystery
That surrounded them all was now to unfold
For the secrets of the two had never been told.

Must have been hard to look back at the home land
And wave to the parents who did not understand.
There register that picture that all through life
To be the memories and dreams of this young wife.

But the word she had given was sacred to her,
And nothing on earth could stamp out or blur
The love that existed in the hearts of them
Who had left all, for their love to defend.

'twas thoughts of the trunk and what it contained
That kept up courage, for he had not remained
On Germany's soil, but was a stowaway
In the old trunk, the treasure of today.

This lone traveler and the key she possessed,
Was his only dependent, for no one guessed
What the trunk contained, and after each meal
To the hull of the ship she would quietly steal,

There to deliver both food and drink
Tell of their progress, and their plans to link,
To mark the way, for by night in the dark
He must be relieved, and from the trunk impart.

This duty was performed till the distance spanned
The coast-waters passed and the laws of the land
Had no control of the trunk and its charge,
And the trunk was unlocked, he was at large.

With this accomplished, the next thing to do
Was to get employment and work his way through.
So he went to the Captain and there in the court
These words were heard, "Produce your passport."

Proudly she stepped to the Captain's side
And unfolded the document that there defied
The laws of the army, and the Captain's report
Could be made clear, for she had his passport.

Seven long weeks of toil with the ropes
That held the sails that carried the hopes
Through stormy sea and wind and gale,
Ever remembering he must not fail.

At last they landed on America's coast,
Their prayers had been granted and the most
Of their possessions of earth's values, you see,
Was the old antique trunk, called "Germany."

I often wonder what I would have done
If under such conditions I were the one
To come to a new country, and there to ascend
Up life's rugged pathway, without even a friend.

But God was their master, and in one year
They had located friends who had come here
Some years before, and with their aid
Life would be pleasant, the gloom would fade.

They started their home all by hand
Near the small town called "Poland."

The house was of logs, and the only settee
Was the old antique trunk called "Germany."

As years passed by and the possessions increased
The farm was enlarged and poverty ceased.
Happiness reigned, and the dreams of their life
Were coming true for husband and wife.

Eleven children were born to increase their joy.
But time has elapsed, and only one boy
And mother of nine is here to tell
Of the old trunk we love so well.

Its years are one hundred, its form is antique,
Interior plain, a secret place to keep
All one's valuables, for in those days
The banks were few and quite a long ways.

I hope it will always have a home with those
Of some of the relatives when my life shall close,
Because it was one of the party of three
Of our past ancestors from Germany.

3. George Bauman's Vow on the High Seas

One group of eleven families left their homes in Paffenweiler, Baden, on March 25, 1847, to come to the United States. When during their first week on the Atlantic a storm of unusual violence threatened to wreck their sailing vessel, George Bauman, a stonecutter, made a vow that, if they should land safely, he would erect a stone crucifix near the church of the place where he should settle. As of old our Lord calmed the troubled sea of Galilee, so here this mental vision of the Crucified became an assurance of safety to the battered vessel. They landed safely at New Orleans on June 15. Arrived at Jasper, Mr. Bauman, with the cooperation of Mr. Heim of Tell City, Indiana, and of Frank Beck of Jasper, fulfilled his vow in 1848, Joseph Gramelspacher helping them financially in the execution of their pious design. Reverent hands worked on that large stone cross near the south entry to the church grounds.—A storm had been the occasion of the erection of the cross, and, in 1928, another storm wrecked it; but in 1932 Messrs. Harry Melchior and Otto J. Blessinger replaced it with a new one in pious memory of the faith of

6

George Bauman; however, on the new cross the stone figure of our Lord was replaced by one made of metal.

4. A Stormy Crossing

When Elizabeth Denzer was crossing the ocean from Germany, they ran into a severe storm. Much water poured into the ship. Elizabeth, soaking wet, went to her cabin to change clothes. She heard the captain cry out, "We are lost! We are lost!" Elizabeth cried out, "Oh, Mother of God, don't let me drown without any clothes on!" A brave sailor climbed up high and turned a sail and saved the ship.

5. From New York to Fort Wayne (1840)

An interesting incident—one which pictures the perils of the times—is given in connection with the coming of Daniel Nestel to Fort Wayne. Mr. Nestel was the father of the midgets, Charles and Eliza Nestel, known throughout the world as "Commodore Foote" and "The Fairy Queen."

Mr. Nestel was a native of Carlsbronn, Prussia, born in 1818. When he arrived at New York he had eight cents of his money left. He walked nearly the entire distance to Fort Wayne, accompanied by Fred Foellinger, who had come with him from Europe. When within about thirty miles of Fort Wayne the young men camped for the night, after having walked all day with no food but unripe nuts found in the woods. The wolves prowled about them, and, fearing they might be destroyed, Mr. Nestel carved these words in the bark of a small tree:

D. Nestel and Fred Foellinger,
died from hunger
and eaten by wolves.

The sentiment of the "epitaph," like many another, failed to record the facts, for the wanderers found themselves alive the next morning and managed to reach the town. For twenty-six years Mr. Nestel was a blacksmith in Fort Wayne, and later traveled with his son and daughter.

6. Arrival in St. Leon (1864)

It was a hot day in July of 1864. Aloys Bischoff had gone to the store in St. Leon to get some supplies. As he stepped out he saw a big wagon rolling up the road in a cloud of dust. Aloys told the folks in the store: *"Da kommen ein paar Deutsche."*

To his great surprise these Germans turned out to be Johann Adam Stadtmiller and his wife Maria Eva—Aloys' sister—holding her four-month old child, and there was also his beloved mother, Eva Maria Bischoff, and his brothers Leonhard and Adam, and his dear sister Hanna.

What a happy reunion! He took them to his home where they stayed until they established their own.

7. Thanks to Two Black Sheep

It wasn't always easy for newcomers from the old country to locate the farms of their relatives. One day these folks arrived in Evansville and took a wagon north to Knox County. But from Vincennes on the instructions they had gotten didn't help much anymore. One thing they knew: their relatives had two black sheep in their herd. Some people along the way knew where such a herd existed, and so the relatives were found.

8. The Immigrant and the Gambler (1872)

When my Great-Grandpa Wilhelm Klingman from Baden arrived in New York harbor in 1872, he didn't have enough money to buy a train ticket to Ohio to join his brother; neither could he speak English yet. On the waterfront he met a German gambler wearing a red vest who loaned him the train fare. As soon as Wilhelm reached Ohio, he borrowed money from his brother and sent it to the German gambler in the red vest. By return mail he received a letter treasured by our family. The gambler wrote, "I have loaned money to many German immigrants over the years, but you are the only one who ever repaid me."

And so, at age 18, Great-Grandpa set a standard of integrity for generations yet unborn.

9. The Welcoming Committee in Mishawaka (ca. 1880)

Somehow some of the Huemmer family had made their way from Kircheich, Germany, to Mishawaka, Indiana. Once settled, these Huemmers sent for the rest of the family giving them orders to take a train on the New York-Chicago line once they reached New York City.

The trains on that line went right through the center of Mishawaka; unfortunately, most of them normally didn't stop. In fact, the trainmen didn't even now where Mishawaka was. Thus, the newly arrived Huemmers, who probably didn't even know where Indiana was, much less Mishawaka, had to arrange something with their settled-in relatives. Sure enough, when the train approached Mishawaka, a Huemmer was there to flag it down with a white flag so that the travel-weary immigrants wouldn't miss their stop. And thus the Huemmer family was reunited.

10. A Youthful Traveler Headed for South Bend (1881)

About a year ago William Henninger and his wife came to this city (South Bend) from Germany and began working for the Walworth Mfg. Co. As soon as he got a little money ahead, he sent some to Germany to pay for his six year old daughter's passage. The money got lost and he sent it a second time. But not getting any confirmation he supposed that the second shipment was also lost.

Saturday evening a little girl arrived here, consigned to Dr. Piepenbrink. It was Henninger's little daughter, who had made the trip from Germany to here all alone. She showed want of care, but will be all right in a few days.

11. The Greenhorn (1883)

On the 17th of June, 1883, I arrived in Indianapolis. At the station I had a hard struggle with a Negro dray driver in trying to make him understand that I wanted my baggage taken to the Circle House Hotel. At last he grinned and motioned for me to hop on the driver's seat, but the idea of riding in broad daylight through the city next to a Negro driver was totally at variance with my German *Weltanschauung*. I preferred to walk and follow the dilapidated vehicle.

Since leaving the French steamer "Normandie" at New York, I had been alone. The few acquaintances I had made during the ocean trip vanished quickly in the hustle and bustle of the great American metropolis. My first unpleasant experience in the Land of the Free occurred with a cab driver who demanded five dollars for taking me the short distance from the French pier to the Belvedere Hotel. I refused to pay the exorbitant charge and held on to my baggage. Finally, with the aid of the hotel clerk, the claim was settled for $1.50, about three times the amount of the regular fare.

As I entered the barber shop of the hotel for a shave, the barber quickly recognized in me a freshly imported "greenhorn." Although he too had all the earmarks of a German, he professed to have no knowledge of the language. Putting his hand through my hair, he intimated that I needed a haircut. I nodded in my embarrassment. After he had finished his job, he mumbled something I did not understand, but stupidly I nodded again. As a result I suffered the torture of a shampoo and was rudely shocked when the barber smashed a raw egg on top of my head. That performance was followed by a face massage, and then a grinning Negro boy pushed a box in front of me and proceeded to shine my shoes. What a strange world America seemed to be. At last, released from the chair, the barber smilingly handed me a ticket for $2.65, and then I overheard him say, in German, to his partner that he had gotten every cent out of that "greenhorn." I was dumfounded. In old Ulm I used to pay fifteen pfennig (four cents) for a shave, and here in New York within a short hour I had spent ten marks and sixty pfennig in a barber shop. With my cab fare of six marks, I had already paid out a fortune. I was afraid of New York and left the city the same evening.

At the steamer landing, an agent of the Erie Railroad, who spoke German, had sold me a ticket to Indianapolis. I left New York at 6 p.m. and arrived at Hamilton, Ohio, at 10 o'clock the next evening, much too late to make connection with the train to Indianapolis. There I stood, all alone with bag and baggage, on the dimly lit platform in front of a wooden shed, called Erie Junction. It was raining. Not a soul was visible. A few Negroes passed, but I did not know how to talk to them. I was perplexed, almost in despair.

Then I discovered a well-lighted house near the junction. I dragged my luggage toward it. As I came nearer I noticed that the house was surrounded on three sides by railroad tracks. Over the front entrance I could read the sign, "Saloon." I entered. At the bar stood three rough-looking fellows, presumably railroaders, with big schooners of beer before them. They looked at me curiously. One of them must have made some witty remark about me, because they laughed uproariously. The floor of the cheaply furnished room was covered with sawdust. There was a pool table at one end. I counted eight spittoons around it. The rest of the room was crowded with chairs and tables and more spittoons. From the ceiling and around the gas fixtures dangled strips of fly paper with thousands of dead flies. The air was thick with the foul stench and haze of tobacco smoke, almost obscuring the walls and the brightly colored chromos of Rigi, Pilatus and other Swiss scenery. Above the fireplace hung a large old, fashioned cuckoo clock and on the mantelpiece stood carved wooden ornaments. They looked to me like old friends.

The proprietor came to my table, asking what I wanted. He spoke German, that peculiar Swiss-German, sounding like the noise of a rip-saw whenever the letters "ch" appeared in a word. He was a corpulent, short-set man with a sandy, scrubby beard. His prominent nose glimmered in all colors of the rainbow. In the old country they call such a nose a "Kupferbergwerk," a copper mine. My host looked tough and uncanny, but his kindly blue eyes were in direct contrast to his gruff, uncouth manner. He was shabbily dressed and wore no coat or collar.

I told him of my predicament, that I had missed the train to Indianapolis, and asked whether he could give me shelter for the night. While I was talking to him, the door of an adjoining room near our table was slightly opened and a woman behind it listened to our conversation. Without answering my question, my host went into that room, and after whispering to the woman, supposedly his wife, for some time, he returned to tell me that I could stay. The three ruffians at the bar watched us intently and laughed noisily when the proprietor, Joe Naegli, came with a railroad lantern to take me to my room on the second floor. It did not look inviting.

As soon as I was alone I made a careful inspection. The first thing I noticed was that the key to the door was missing. In one of the closets I discovered a large assortment of formidable implements, hammers, saws, files, wrenches, a sledge hammer and a crowbar. Cautiously I moved the washstand, holding a large porcelain basin and pitcher, in front of the door, turned out the light and undressed. Lying down on one side of the huge creaking bed, I put my money and watch under the pillow, and beside me my revolver and big jackknife that some friend in Ulm had advised me to take along. I tried to sleep, but the switch engines under the window of my room puffed to and fro, continuously whistling, tooting and ringing bells. Up from the barroom came a boisterous noise. I felt that those fellows were still talking about me. While I was tossing around in bed, my mind wandered back to the stories I had read about the Nihilists at St. Petersburg, the Apaches of Paris, the Maffia of Sicily, the vendettas of Corsica, the sinister slums of London and Berlin. My surroundings looked suspicious; I was afraid.

After midnight I heard steps ascending the stairway; the man and the woman were whispering. The man stumbled and the woman scolded. I knew my time had come. Noiselessly I slipped out of bed, revolver in hand and the jackknife next to me. On one side of the washstand I took a correct military position, right knee up, left knee down. I remembered my army instructions that in ambush one is to remain motionless and not shoot until the aim is sure. I waited. Nothing happened. My right knee began to tremble in the strained position. I heard a door slam and a woman's voice. After minutes of waiting that seemed hours, I crawled back to bed. The switch engines seemed to have gone to sleep and so did I. Someone knocked at my door and called that it was time to get up. I was startled. The sun shone brightly into my room. It was 9 o'clock. The train to Indianapolis was due in forty-five minutes. Hurriedly I washed and dressed.

Entering the barroom, I noticed a table covered with white linen and on it rolls, honey, butter, fruit and coffee. Joe Naegli, who had looked so rusty the night before, was smoothly shaven and wore a collar and tie; his wife, Barbara, wore a fresh apron over her neat house dress. While I was eating my breakfast they informed me that they had lived in America for over twelve years, that Joe came from Rorschach in Switzerland, and Barbara from Friedrichshafen. When I told her that I had just directly come from Ulm, she was delighted. I asked for my bill for room and breakfast. Barbara protested; she wouldn't think, she said, of accepting money from one of her countrymen. I insisted on paying at least for the breakfast and laid a silver dollar on the table; Joe was ready to take it, but his wife would not let him. As I left for the station, the kind woman gave me a box with sandwiches and fruit for my trip. I thanked both heartily for their hospitality. Walking to the station, the thought came to me that good people can be found in every corner of the world.

12. A Fish out of Water (1883)

Toward evening on the day of my arrival at Indianapolis, I called at the residence of distant relatives (southeast corner of Tennessee and North Streets). The lady of the house and her three daughters were engaged in a game of croquet in the garden adjoining their home. Introducing myself with a polite bow, a feeling of awkwardness crept over me, as mother and daughters continued their game, paying only cursory attention to their visitor. One of the girls remarked, hitting her ball with emphasis, "Everytime a German comes to Indianapolis, he expects to find a job in father's business." Fortunately, the arrival of the father, whom I had met the year before at Goeppingen (Wuerttemberg), eased the situation. The next morning I joined the army of clerks in the wholesale department of Charles Mayer & Company, in which firm William Haueisen was partner and a most active executive. That firm, founded in 1840, had given many Germans a start in business. Young men with good education would always find employment, not only for sentimental, but also for economic reasons. In order to gain a foothold, those immigrants would work long hours at a minimum wage.

Entering the retail store of Charles Mayer & Company, I doffed my hat at the door, as was customary throughout Germany. If one bought a cigar in a cigar store there, good form required that such transaction be performed bareheaded. I remember, years after, on a visit to Munich, I entered a cigar store. Immediately the clerk said to me, "You prefer fresh cigars, being an American." I asked him how he knew. "Because," he answered, "you are keeping on your hat." My walk through the Charles Mayer store, hat in hand, caused great merriment among the clerks behind the show cases. The girls giggled. In an instant they recognized in me one of the new fledglings.

Quite soon I began to realize that a German unacquainted with the English language was considered a sort of a comical figure. During those first "greenhorn" days, all nimbus of vanity as a Latin and French scholar, as an ex-soldier of the preferred class, as a near-cashier of a bank, flickered away in the barber shop of New York, in the saloon at Hamilton, Ohio, and at the first reception in Indianapolis. I felt myself shriveling up, reduced in age at least ten years (to an eighth grader). I was like a fish out of water.

13. Instant Immigrant Wedding in Crawfordsville (1897)

Emilie Jahnke, having arrived from Bremen, Germany, recently arrived in Crawfordsville, where after only thirty minutes she was wedded to Wilhelm Laube, whom she had never seen before. Laube is also a German, but he has lived in the area for several years. He sought a wife through a German newspaper, and Emilie responded resolutely. The new-fledged couple traveled perfectly happily to their new home close to Hillsboro.

14. Doctor Meets Son for First Time—in Dale (1906)

Dr. Felix Maslowsky of Mariah Hill (Spencer County) came to Dale last Saturday to meet his son, a young man about 21 years of age who had just arrived from Germany. Strange to say, he had never seen him before, nor had the young man ever seen his father.

The doctor formerly lived in Germany, where he was educated and first practiced medicine. Some time before he came to this country he married a young German lady. Hoping to do better in America in the practice of medicine he crossed the Atlantic, leaving his young wife for the time with friends on the other side. The doctor decided to remain in this country, but his wife never came over. Shortly after he left for America a boy was born to Mrs. Maslowsky. The boy grew to manhood and then determined to come over and visit his father.

The father and son met for the first time on the street near the hotel in Dale on Saturday. They seemed to know each other on sight, and embraced and kissed each other as affectionately as would a fond parent and a tender hearted son who had been separated for a year or two only.

15. Finding His Sister

My father didn't have any money, and he came to America to get away from the standing army in Germany. He had a sister here in America. And he was hungry, and he knocked on a lady's door and spoke German. She became very frightened and closed the door. So then he tried another door, and the lady said, "Well, I think you're speaking German, and I think there's a man that mends shoes who speaks German." She told him where to go. So he went to see this man who spoke German and was fed, and they got along beautifully. This man knew my father's sister in this country. That was surely a coincidence. And he got them together.

16. How Fred Klemm Decided between Cincy and Indy

Fred had learned the stone mason trade in Germany. But he had a yearning for distant places, so he had himself hired as a sailor. He had been to a number of American ports before he made up his mind to live in this country. When he finally went ashore as an immigrant, he had saved enough money to buy him a car to drive to Cincinnati, his destination. At one point, however, and it was already pretty dark, Fred must have missed a turn and was no longer headed for Cincy, but for Indy instead. Now you must know that Fred was a stubborn Dutchman. He didn't need a quarter to do heads-or-tails. He just said to himself, "I've gone too far already, I might as well forget about Cincinnati," and on he went to Indianapolis. He didn't regret it. He got a good job as a mason with the construction of the War Memorial, and many Indy house numbers done in stone speak of his skill to this day.

II.

PLACE NAMES

". . . when all of a sudden the door was swung open" (II.4.)

1. Gone to the Bloomin' Town

I wish I had a picture of her—the mother of old Bartholomew Wahl—as she stood there that morning with the squirrel rifle clasped firmly in her hands. At the time her son was not old, maybe only ten or eleven, almost a century and a half ago.

Less than a dozen miles to the north and a little east lay the wooded slopes which were to become Indiana University's main campus. And just to her left ran a road but slightly traveled at the time.

She stood immobile, a tall gaunt figure clad in grey homespun. Between her and the cabin behind nodded goldenrod burnished under the touch of a September sun. But she was oblivious of such beauty now, for her eyes were riveted upon a large boulder, beneath which Barty had told her he had seen a big rattlesnake wriggle but a moment before.

She heard horse hoofs approaching but she did not turn her head nor did her glance waver from the rock when a cheery voice called out:

"Howdy, Mam. My name's Williams. Just come over from the land office in Vinceenes. I've been down in the clearin' a looking for the Carter brothers. Someone told me I might git 'em to help me build my cabin. Know whar they be?"

"Nope," answered the woman, her eyes still glued to the rock. "But I reckon they've gone to that bloomin' town to git drunk! It's quite a ride up that way." And she jerked her head to the north.

Williams rode off in the direction she had indicated, but before getting out of ear shot, he heard the faint crack of a squirrel rifle and smiled.

As he kept riding northward, he is said to have asked all he met: "How do I git to that bloomin' town?" And not long afterwards, what had once been an Indian village, and early was designated simply as "Monroe County Post Office" began to be called Bloomington.

2. Tampico, Jackson County

I heard this about sixty years ago. In the early days Tampico was called "Pico." It was the trading point for the German settlement ten miles east of Brownstown. Well, one of these old Germans that got his English pronunciation fouled up when he got excited or mad went to Pico to get some large spikes to use in building his barn. After driving all the way to Pico, he was told that they had no spikes that large. He became very angry and cried, "Well tam (damn) Pico anyhow; I will trade in Brownstown."

After that they started calling Pico "Tampico."

3. Roann, Wabash County

One story says that Elijah Hackleman, the surveyor, named it to honor two young ladies who cooked his meals while he stayed at Tavern, Beckner's one eighth of a mile south of present Roann. The girls' names were Ann Beckner and Ann Roe.

Another story tells of Ann Beckner's rowing on the river. A wild storm was blowing her off her course. Her father stood on the bank shouting, "Row, Ann, row, Ann, row!" Or if you like, you may prefer to believe that the Indians were chasing her, as another story goes. Since the Indians in the area at that time, 1853, were friendly, that story may be discounted...

4.-5. Santa Claus, Spencer County.

4. Under the Influence

One story goes:"Santa Claus . . . was founded by German pioneers on Christmas Eve in 1852 during a village meeting to find a name for their settlement. Snow was very deep and travel was almost impossible. When all of the settlers arrived, they began proposing names, but none suited them, when all of a sudden the door was swung open, and there stood a man dressed in a Santa Claus costume. They were all pretty drunk and ready for anything, so one of them suggested it be named Santa Claus and thus it was named Santa Claus, Ind."

5. . . . Or a Child's Clue?

. . . Appropriately, it was a child who provided the inspiration in naming this community after Santa Claus. Going into the late fall months of 1852, there was no Santa Claus community. Residents of the area had spent months trying to select a name for the community, but none of those suggested carried universal appeal. For some time it seemed "Wyttenbach", the surname of the circuit-riding reverend, would gain ultimate approval as the tiny town's name.

Then on Christmas Eve, as the congregation gathered at the church for yet another meeting, the sound of bells was heard outside. "Santa!" a jubilant child rang out, "it's Santa Claus!" "That's it!" shouted one of th elders. "Why not call it Santa Claus!" The residents all agreed, and the town of Santa Claus was born.

6. Huntingburg, Dubois County

Nothing makes a nimrod happier than to find a good, productive place to try his skill. That traditional love was responsible for both the founding and the naming of the thriving little city of Huntingburg at Ind. 45 and 64 in the southern part of Dubois County.

That same affection and connotation persisted, and before consolidation the nickname borne by Huntingburg High School's athletic teams was the Happy Hunters.

But, back to the beginning. It harks to the time of about 1836 when Col. Jacob Geiger, an avid hunter from Louisville, 60 miles east, came to that area to hunt bear. What he found there—good hunting, fertile valleys, rolling hills and beautiful groves and forests—pleased him so much that he bought large acreages from the Federal government near what is now Huntingburg. In the following year he laid out and platted the town . . . Huntingburg, bespeaking the successful hunting he had experienced.

As one historian put it, "The town gained its name from an early hunting expedition made from a sister state.". . .

Geiger was an unusual character who never failed to attract the attention of anybody seeing him for the first time. Not very large, spry and extremely courtly toward the ladies, he wore his hair in a queue and invariably carried a gold-headed cane. That cane was the bane of many youngsters in the community who feared it and the colonel himself. He had no patience with loafers. If he saw a lad loafing he would yell at him: "Run, you little devil. Go home. Your mother wants you.". . .

7. Holland, Dubois County

The early settlers around Holland were nearly all Germans and were called Dutchmen by the Hoosiers because they wore wooden shoes and talked about digging turf and cutting grass for hay in Holland (Netherlands), to earn some extra money to come to America. From 1857 to 1859, the Holland neighborhood was talking and planning to have a voting place and a Post Office. Henry Kunz decided to plot a town. . . Some called the place Kunztown, the younger boys called it Coontown, and one day while they were surveying, some of these younger boys came to see what was going on and someone said that they had come over to see if they could earn a little extra money like their parents did when they went to Holland to get money to come to America. So there it was—"Holland." The town little realized that the name would stick; they had the Holland Post Office. . . .One of the largest milk processing corporations in the

19

state is located at Holland and is using the windmill and wooden shoes as its trademark.

8. Nigger Hill

This German farming family decided to move from the Bluegrass to the Hoosier state. When they sold their land, they told their slave that she was free to go.

The first night on their journey north the farmer noticed something moving right near their camp site. He looked to find out what it was, but it had vanished in the dark. The next night, when the camp fire was going strong, the watchful farmer saw a figure slowly moving toward them. This time he had his gun ready and commanded, "Come with your hands up or I'll shoot!" A sobbing voice answered him, "It's me, Master." "For God's sake, what are you doing here?" the farmer wanted to know. She said, "I wants to stay with you." Meanwhile the whole family were on their feet and they were all agreed that their freed slave would be more than welcome to stay with them.

They built their new Indiana homestead on a hill. When the neighbors learned that there was a "nigger woman" with them, they started to call the Dutchman's place "Nigger Hill."

9. Dutchman's Bridge, Vigo County

Seven and a half miles south of town (Terre Haute) there's an old covered bridge called the Dutchman's Bridge because when it was built there was a Dutch family in a covered wagon on a rainy night; they spent the night in the bridge, and the woman delivered a baby that night. It's haunted because in the early 1930s when the KKK was very active in Indiana they hung a nigger down there, and a man and a woman who lived down there started through the bridge on the opposite end of the hanging. When they came to the dead man the horse reared, and they took off some other way.

10. The *Teufelseckers* in Dubois County

The unruly element that had become disastrous to Ferdinand in 1849 re-asserted itself off and on also later. There were especially several families that formerly lived over toward St. Anthony and that had the reputation of being of a rough and pugnacious disposition; so much so, that that section of the parish was popularly dubbed the *Teufelseck*—Devil's Corner. Anton Drach with his numerous family lived back there. Drach was desirous of having similar minded neighbors. One time a *Teufelsecker* who was according to old Drach's liking died comparatively young; Drach expressed his regrets, "If for once a regular fellow comes to live, the Devil gets him." It is still remembered how on the occasion of picnics, back in the 1860s, some *Teufelseckers*, at times with their faces masked, would frighten the women and children by galloping into the crowd. When two Egler boys, who hailed from that section of the parish, began to study for the priesthood, some oldtimers shook their heads: "Can anything good come from the *Teufels Eck*?

11. Mariah Hill, Spencer County

. . . Father Ulrich, under the date of September 17, 1857, obtained the bishop's permission to build a church. The church was dedicated in 1858 to Mary, Help of Christians, whence both the church and the town were called with the beautiful name of *Maria Hilf*. On the feast of the Annunciation in 1859, Ferdinand, the mother church, organized a grand procession to Maria Hilf, a distance of eight miles; a beautiful statue of the Blessed Virgin was to be escorted to the daughter church. About one thousand persons, together with the priest, took part. . .

Later, when an application was made to have a post office in the village, the Post Office Department, not knowing what to make of this German name, assigned *Mariah Hill* as the official name of the post office.

III.

NAMES AND NICKNAMES

". . . Unscrambling the Muellers in Indy" (III.3.)

1. Hu Had de Schbelling Broplem?

Surely, farmer Johann Wallpe had some spelling problems with his native German (which farmer and non-farmer "don't"?), but never with his own name. And when he landed in New York in 1852 and all the way to Oldenburg, it sure was W-a-l-l-p-e. Soon after his arrival in Indiana he found him a wife. But before they could get married he had to go to the court house in Brookville for a marriage license. He put it in his pocket and didn't look at it until he got home. My, that clerk sure made a mess with his name. Johann Wallpe was now a Walbye. But so what, it was only a marriage license.

In 1854 he was ready to become an American citizen. Like the first clerk, this one that filled out the naturalization papers apparently also relied only on his ear when he wrote Johann's last name on that solemn document: *W-e-o-l-p-e*. Now wait. The clerk had to write the name twice on it, but he must have had some afterthought (or no thought at all), or he just couldn't spell. The second spelling of poor Johann's proud family name was again: "*W-a-l-b-y-e*. Well, Johann didn't mind it too much. When he read the whole thing through slowly, he found, much to his surprise, that he was now born in "the Kingdom of Aldinsburg in Prussia. "It took about sixty years before this name mess was harmoniously resolved. On his Catholic memorial card—he died in 1913—the one side in English has him as *John Wallpe*, the other in German says *Johann Wallpe*.

2. A Name Change and Inheritance in the Old Country

Not long after arriving from Germany and spending a while at his brother's place in Ohio, Wilhelm Klingmann got the "Indiana fever" and moved to Howard Twp. in Howard County. There he found sweet Maria Anna Troyer and married her on Christmas Day of 1873. As time went by, Wilhelm and Maria Anna—she had been born here—decided to follow the trend of the times and "Americanize" their names to William ("Bill") and Mary Ann Klingman. Later, Bill was to lose an inheritance from the family in Germany, because he could not prove he was Wilhelm Klingmann.

3. Anton Scherrer Unscrambling the *Muellers* in Indy

In a conscientious effort to clean up everything I know about this lavish town of ours (Indianapolis), I've now reached the point where there is nothing left to do but clear up the mystery of the Muellers.

Sixty years ago when I was a kid, Indianapolis had so many men blessed with the name of Mueller that the only way to tell them apart was to identify them by their trades.

For example, the Mr. Mueller whose privilege it was to supply Indianapolis with cheese was never referred to as Edward (his baptismal name), but always as "Kaese Mueller" which, in case you have to be told, was the German equivalent of "Cheese Mueller."

It was that way all along the line. Ferdinand A. Mueller was always called "Apotheker Mueller" for the obvious reason that he ran a drug store; Emil Mueller was known as "Schneider Mueller" because he was a tailor by profession, and John A. D. Mueller was "Treppen Mueller" because he happened to be a stair builder, a trade involving a knowledge of higher mathematics which few men had the patience to learn at the time. Indeed, it was more in the nature of a God-given gift which probably accounts for the fact that Treppen Mueller figured out most of the intricate runs of the incredible stairways that identified the mansions of Indianapolis in the later half of the Nineteenth Century.

The same semasiological system came in mighty handy, too, when we had to differentiate between Charles G. Mueller and Charles M. Mueller. Charles G. was called "Architect Mueller" because that happened to be his business. As for Charles M., he was always pointed out as "Uhren Mueller" because—sure, because he tinkered with clocks and watches.

Fool-proof as it appears, the system was far from perfect. In support of which I cite the difficulty we had back in the Nineties when we discovered that Treppen Mueller (John. A. D.) had five sons (William, John, Henry, Frederick and Albert) who were associated with him in the stair-building business. Obviously, the system wasn't elastic enough to cover both father and sons who elected to pursue the same profession. And that's probably why I, for one, never got Treppen Mueller's sons straightened out sufficiently to address them by their baptismal names even to this day. For some reason, a boy of my generation always profited by talking to a man blessed with the name of Mueller.

I still remember the afternoon, for instance, when Mother sent me to Kaese Mueller's store—the one saturated with a robust Rabelaisian smell which was more or less of an accepted institution on E. Washington St. at the time.

When I arrived, the proprietor—a smallish man of considerable girth and a face as pink as that of a baby—was out on the sidewalk receiving a consignment of cheese, the shipping directions of which revealed that they had come straight from Switzerland. They were as big as cart wheels, and I distinctly recall that Mr. Mueller had a cane in his hand. He used it to tap each cheese before he was ready to accept it.

The curious sight must have made my eyes pop, I guess. Otherwise, Mr. Mueller wouldn't have taken time off to explain to a little boy that he tapped the cheese to make sure that the holes in them were of the right size to suite his clientele. He said people were awful funny that way and questioned the authenticity of the Swiss cheese if it didn't have the right-sized perforations.

The Russians, he said, demanded a small hole; the South-Americans a medium-size hole, and the people of the United States, as big a hole as they could get for their money. The Swiss were so slick, said Mr. Mueller, that they could build a cheese with any size hole the trade demanded.

The cane Kaese Mueller used that afternoon was nothing more than an ordinary walking stick. In his hands, however, it turned into a divining rod which when tapped against the cheese produced sounds responding to their specific densities, with the result that he was able to deduce the size of the hidden holes. Of course, Mr. Mueller was gifted with a mighty good ear to catch the nuances.

That evening at the supper table, after observing that his dessert was provided with holes bigger than pin pricks, Father pronounced my purchase a genuine Swiss cheese. Indeed, he used the occasion to instruct Mother to stick with merchants of Kaese Mueller's integrity.

4. They Called Him Argonaut

Friedrich Wilhelm Kruger and his wife Anna Marie made the big journey to America in the cold of February 1846. On the 26th Anna Marie gave birth to a boy. He was baptized by the captain of the German immigrant vessel "Argonaut." And to remember this highly unsusual place of birth, they gave baby Georg Friedrich the middle name Argonaut.

5. They Named Her Corina

"My mother's name was Cora Blank."

"Your name *Corina* is rather unusual. Did your name come from your mother's name *Cora*?"

"Well, I should say yes. But it is the name of a cigar, and it sounded a lot like my mother's, so Dad thought that was a good name."

"Was that the brand he smoked?"

"Yes."

6. Kids Play "Kraut" Names

One rainy summer afternoon, my brother, two sisters and myself, along with two neighbor girls were sitting in our kitchen fretting about the rain, "Mom, what can we do?" "Why, we could make up funny names for everyone," she said, "like Lester could be *Sammy Sauerkraut*. That set the tone, and all of us ended up with a "krauty" name:

sister Irene	*Molly Schlobbergorgen*
sister Bernice	*Jemima Hanswurst*
myself Ruth	*Henrietta Hasenpfeffer*
neighbor girl	*Susie Schmierkaese*
neighbor girl	*Wilhelmina Pumpernickel*

That made us forget the rainy afternoon, but we have never forgotten these names. In fact, we still and often refer to each other in this manner—one of the links to our childhood.

7. The "Fuenfzig Thaler Schneider" of Oldenburg

One evening a crowd of town-folk stared bewilderedly up at a phantom-like light that moved from clock-room to bell-chamber, high up in the church steeple. Everyone was sure that it was a ghost. Then a certain tailor, in solemn protestation of his fear, cried out: "Nothing doing! I wouldn't climb up into that belfry for fifty dollars." Hence "Fuenfzig Thaler Schneider."

8. "Pankuchen" Ben

Ben Dahmus was a carpenter and fix-it-man. When people invited 'm for dinner and asked 'm what he liked, he usually opted for "pancakes." So he got his nickname, "Pankuchen Ben."

IV.

LANGUAGE—GOOD AND BAD
(geseasoned mit sum wery gemixte pickels)

"Bilingual Bird" (IV.1.)

Notiz: go first tu Number 11.
fuer Explaneischn
& iesier Wershn

Wer nit höre will muß fühle!

Ihr amerikaneist Euch ä wenig zu schnell. Drauße habt Ihr „Deutsch-land, Deutschland über Alles", „Hamburg ist än schönes Städtchen" un annere patriotische Lieder gesunge, un kaum seid Ihr a paar Monat im Land so singt Ihr „Wie wohnt go hohm till Morning" un „Hehl Kolombia be Okschen of be Okschen", aber des schafft nit!—Ihr seid nit mehr mit „nem Glas Bier zufriede, es muß ä „Kocktehl" oder „Komm und Tschery" oder „Brändy Smäsch" sein, sunst geht's nit!—Des muß annersch werde. Ihr müßt die gute alte deutsche Männers bei-behalte un vor Allem geb' ich Euch den Abweiß: Bresörwt die deutsche Länguitsch! Ich bin jetzt scho beinoh vierzig Jahr in sele Kontry, aber in alle Sochieties un Logdshes wozu ich belonge thu, wird bloß die deutsche Länguitsch gejuhßt.—Wenn in bene Mietings ä Resoluschen gepäßt wird oder einer ä Moschen macht, muß es uf Deutsch gesche oder die Members werde gefeint. Nur allß Deutsch gesproche Jungens—Euer Englisch versteht doch kei Mensch, ganz von meiner Persönlichkeit abgesehe—„Si bohnt thinkt so—yes!" Bloß um Euch zu zeige, daß ich auch uf Englisch grob werde kann, wenn's sein muß. Aber für heut muß ich schließe denn ich muß noch vor Dinner ä Slieping-Lauitsch kaufen, weil ich Kumpany expekte thu, also geh ich schnell zu

BORN & CO.,

97 und 99 Oft Washington Str.

wo ich sie schuhr am billigsten und gegen leichte Abzahlungen laufen kann.

1. Bilingual Bird (1895)

In Columbus lives a lady by the name of Augusta Busch who owns a parrot that speaks both German and English.

2. The Language of God

Cecilia's mother tells of church-going as a child. When they entered the church everything was in German. After services and again outside the language was English.

So-o-o it was obvious to Mama that German was the language of God.

3. Confirmation in English or in German? (1918)

When Elfrieda Lang was to be confirmed in 1918, her father told her grandmother that the service was not going to be in German but in English. That shocked the staunch Dutch woman. "Oh no," she said, "if it isn't done in German, Elfrieda will never get to heaven!"

P.S. On Confirmation Sunday they had the worst downpour in ages. And grandmother knew why.

4. Why the Christian Rudolph Family Dropped German

My uncle William Rudolph was the oldest child of the Christian Rudolph family at Portersville, Dubois County, and so the first child of the family to attend public school. He went to school speaking German and came home crying because he could not communicate. For his parents that settled the matter. From then on it was English only in the house and none of the younger children learned German.

5. Three Generations Speaking German

For three generations the Klingman family remained literate in both English and German. Records of their church, family, and threshing rings were kept in both languages: one paragraph in German and the next in English—no duplicate entries. I was the first generation not to be bilingual—because my mother was Scotch-Irish and didn't speak German well, and because I was born after World War II, during which the Germans in our community had suffered much discrimination.

Although my grandfather, Andrew Elmer Klingman, was born in Indiana and spoke English perfectly, I have reason to believe that German was more important to him. When Grandpa was dying at 89, he lapsed into a coma. Nurses and doctors were unable to rouse him. But when Daddy would visit him and speak German to him, Grandpa would return to consciousness, converse with Daddy in German for a while, and then switch to English to talk to the rest of us. When we would leave the room, Grandpa would lapse into a coma again—until Daddy returned and spoke German to him.

6. What Kind of Heating for St. Joseph's in Jasper?

In the beginning no provision had been made for heating the church. After several years, a number of parishioners expressed the desire that some type of heating system should be installed. Some said *Dampf-Heizung* (steam heating) should be used, while a large number in their Pennsylvania English-German favored *Shteem-Heizung*—also steam heating. Father Fidelis was not familiar with the English language and, therefore, under the impression that the Pennsylvania *Shteem* was something quite different from the German *Dampf*, said, "*Dampf, das lass ich mir gefallen. Aber Shteem, da bin ich dagegen*" (I am satisfied with *steam*, but I am opposed to *Shteem*). The question was settled and *steam* heating was installed.

7. Deaf Mother Remembers Produce Peddler

My mother who had grown deaf over the years would often speak aloud her thoughts and rememberings of her "hearing days" as she went about her duties in the kitchen. She usually spoke German, the language in which she had kept on thinking.

One time she talked about the old vegetable and fruit peddler. The man had become too old to do much farming. With his remaining horse he put out a large garden and orchard. In the summer he loaded up his produce on the spring wagon, hitched up Jack, the old and swaybacked horse, and peddled his wares in the towns near about, ringing a bell and calling out. That one summer, as my mother remembered, she could hear him coming:

"Birne, Bohne, Wassermelona!" ("Pears, beans, water melons!"). he loudly called, then in a lower voice, "Giddapp Jack." And Jack would go to the next house and stop. Again the man would shout, *"Birne, Bohne, Wassermelone!*—Giddap, Jack!" So Jack stopped automatically at each house and advanced at "Giddap Jack" until out of ear shot.

8. Wie geht's?

When Bill Hoelker worked for his father in the Oldenburg General Store, he always made it a point to greet Frau Pauline Baeumer with a smiling *Wie geht's?*, 'cause he got a kick out of her predictable response: *"So langsam und wackelig wie eine Gans"* (As slowly and wabbly as a goose).

9. Lady Loves Limburger

That lady—oh, did she love her Limburger cheese!—that lady went to a store in town and bought her a good chunk of her favorite. She wanted to be sure that the heavenly smell wouldn't escape from the wrapping, so she put some old string around it. By the time she got on the trolley the string broke. And while she was trying to wrap that Limburger again, she stuck her finger in it by accident. And, of course, the broken string was of no use to her any more. So figuring that the man next to her would surely understand German, too, she asked him, *"Mister, haben ein Bindfaden?"* (=thread). "No," he replied, "I haven't been fart'n."

10. At the Barbershop

Lizzie and Heini went to the city for a day. Heini told Lizzie that he's getting him a haircut. Lizzie said she's going to get her hair fixed, too, and she'd meet him later at that barbershop. When she was done, she went over there, but she didn't see no Heini. So she asked the English-speaking barber, *"Wo 'sch mei' Heini?"* "No," said the barber, "we only give shaves and haircuts."

11. An Indianapolis Ad in "Gemixte Languitsch" (ca. 1900)

Notíz: Ve have tuu wershns of sis item. First, de original Born & Co. ad vitch is probabli tuu diffikult for ju. Sekund, a wershn dat is ein little more getranslated fuer iesier readen. Ve rekommend ju start mit de iesier wershn hier, not mit de one on page 30, ja.

If You Don't Want to Listen You Must Bear the Consequences

You Americanize yourselves a bit too quick. Over dere you used to sing "Deutschland, Deutschland ueber Alles," "Hamburg is a Nice Little Town," and other patriotic songs, and you've hardly been here for a couple o' months and you're singing "Wie wohnt go hohm till Morning" n' "Hehl Kolombia de Tschem of de Ohschn," but that ain't de ding to do!—You're no longer satisfied with a glass o' beer, it's got to be a "Kocktehl" or a "Tomm und Tscherry" or a "Brandy Smash, osserwise you're not happy!—Dat's gotta be changed. You must stick to your gute alte German manners and above all take dis advice from me: **Presorwt die deutsche Languitsch!** It's nearly forty years dat I've been in dis here country, but in all Sosseieties 'n Lodsches to which I belong, only de German Languitsch is being gejuhst.—When in dem Meetings a Resoluschen gets gepassed or if one macht a Mohschen, it must be done in German or the

Members get gefeint. You jus' keep on speaking German, boys—Nobody understands your Englisch anyway, my Personality excluded—"Ei dohnt tink so—yes!" Just to show you dat I can talk pretty tuff also in Englisch, if nessessary. But I've got to stop at dis point, for I still have to buy a Slieping- Launsch before Dinner, because I do Kumpany expeckte, derefore I go quickly to

B O R N & C O.,
97 and 99 East Washington St.
where I can schuhr get de beste Preis und easy terms.

12. Stop de Musik!

There was dancing the night before *Christi Himmelfahrt* (Ascension Day) and it went on beyond midnight. One mother was worried about the desecration of the holy day. She ran over into that music hall and shouted, *"Stop de Musik! Tomorrow ist Christi Himmelfahrt, and tomorrow ist now!"*

13. Apology not Accepted

This old *Weibsbild*—call her an old woman—was on a trolley. And as she was getting off, this young fellow being in a hurry stepped on her long dress and ripped it quite a bit. He was embarrassed and offered his apology, "I beg y'r pardon." She shouted back at him, *"I pfeif dir auf dei bakin' powder. Du hast mir de Rock verrissa!"* (I don't give a hoot for your baking powder, you ripped my dress).

14. Girl Uses Bad Language

There was that girl. She'd cuss and swear so bad that her parents didn't know what to do about it anymore. So they called the minister. He came and he took the girl for a good talking under the trees behind the house. There was a lot of birds, and for some reason they just loved to unload their droppings on the minister's hat. Everytime that happened he said, "Praise the Lord," and then wiped it off. After the third time the girl got so upset with him and said, "What the hell do you mean with your *Praise the Lord?*" The minister said, "I am praising the Lord that cows don't have wings."

15. Three Oldenburg Krauts at a Yankee Revival

These three lively young Oldenburgers heard about a big religious revival going on about ten miles NW at "Buene"—its real name being Buena Vista. So on their horses they went and arrived in due time to join the crowd in an open air assembly.

After the preacher's fire & brimstone sermon ended, it came to be time for requests to the Lord from the faithful for various needs such as good health, good crops, of a personal nature, etc., etc. The boldest of the Krauts arose to do the same—and remember, this was the period when food stuffs came in bulk:

"Oh Lord, give me a barrel of flour,
Oh Lord, give me a barrel of sugar'
Oh Lord, give me a barrel of salt,
Oh Lord, give me a barrel of pepper—Oh, God damn no, that's too much pepper!"

Sensing the rising anger of the crowd for such blasphemy, they quickly mounted their steeds for a fast getaway back to Oldenburg.

16. Rabbits in the Garden

A family friend was a physician at Auburn, Ind. He had a farm with a German family who did the farming. One day the doctor was visiting the farm with the tenant. Herr Doktor was admiring the garden. The tenant was complaining about rabbits eating produce. This is what he said, "Dese are de most God-hellish rabbitz I ever dambed see'd. Ain't no more fitten to be rabbitz in spite a hell!"

17. Shocked at the Burley Que

Some of the IU Halls of Residence employees went to Naptown (Innaapolis)—heck you know what I mean—to see a Burley Que. A lady was telling about it: "Dem wimmen wuz prancin' 'round on that stage and they didn't even have no Brazils on."

18. The Woman's Illness

When we were living at the farm, a neighbor woman was quite ill. At the country store I inquired as to her health. The answer was, "She's mighty poorly. She's layin' atwixt ammonia fever and tuberlocis."

19. Diarrhea

That girl was so much in love with Fritz. Since she was expecting him over at the house, she wanted to have it all spick- and-span for him. So she cleaned and cleaned everything. When she was done, she got a terrible diarrhea and the house smelled awful. So she took the pine spray and gave every room a couple of real good shots. When the door bell rang, she dropped the spray behind the sofa. It was Fritz alright. He took a sniff or two and shook his head. That made her quite nervous and she asked him, "Is there anything wrong, honey?" Fritz said, "Hm, smells like somebody shit under the Christmas tree."

V.

PIONEER PRIESTS AND PREACHERS
AND IN N' OUT OF CHURCH

". . . a good saddle was a missionary's only comfort . . ." (V.2.)

1.-4. Pioneer Priest: Fr. Joseph Ferneding (1802-1872)

1. On Horseback

One time on a trip to Lawrenceburg, while crossing Tanner's Creek which was filled with floating ice, his horse shied. Father was forced to land on a little pan of floating ice which fortunately came to a halt on a little sand barrier in the creek. For ten hours he was in this precarious condition when his companion, Anton Walliser, the founder of New Alsace, succeeded in rescuing him.

2. Riding Again

At another time his horse got caught in the quick sand near the Wabash River. Father, seeing that he could not save the horse, unfastened the saddle, and throwing it to safety he jumped to solid land. A good saddle was a missionary's only comfort since he spent most of his day and night in it. When he arrived at the nearest inn, which was a great distance away from the scene of his escape from death, weary from carrying the heavy saddle, he met a Methodist minister whom he knew. The minister, after hearing Father's story about his horse, asked him if he gave the horse the last sacraments, to which Father replied, "No, I left him die like a Methodist."

3. Breaking the Ghost's Knuckles

There was a group of people at New Alsace who objected strongly to the coming of a Catholic priest. Hoping to frighten Father Ferneding away, they tried various ways of molesting him, especially at night. One time when Father was gone, some dressed as ghosts walked about on an old burial place nearby making a weird noise. Finally a bolder member of the party came to an open window of the log cabin where Father's sister Catharine was trying her best to be calm. In a fright she released the window, and it came down with a bang on the man's knuckles breaking them.

4. Night Visitors

Upon being aroused by a knocking one night, Father Ferneding took his lantern, went to the door, and upon opening it he was commanded by the parties in the dark to raise the lantern to his head and then lower it to his feet. Father bravely complied, whereupon he heard them say, "He has no horns or cloven feet." Then they asked him to marry them.

5.-8. Caring for Lutherans in Adams and Allen County: Friedrich Conrad Dietrich Wyneken (1811-1876)

5. A Perilous Night

On one occasion Pastor Wyneken set out on foot to visit some families. Night came, but believing himself headed in the right direction he kept on. Suddenly he found himself at the edge of a wide expanse of water. The whole region seemed flooded. He surveyed the situation and noticed that logs floated in the water. He figured that if he jumped from one to the other, he might easily reach the other side. He succeeded for a while, but soon discovered that the logs moved at each jump. Darkness had fully enveloped him by this time and made the going dangerous. Not far from his position he spied the trunk of a tree and beyond it others, which seemed to offer a chance of reaching dry ground. He made another attempt and landed on the large log. By the time he had regained his balance, he found that the shock of the jump had moved the log away from the rest of them, and he seemed to be in the middle of the pool. There was nothing left for him to do but to wait until daylight. In order not to fall off, he laid himself flat on the log and wholly exhausted he quickly fell asleep with his arms and legs hanging in the water. Daylight finally aroused him from his sleep, and he was able to escape from the swamp without much further difficulty, continuing on his way.

6. The Drunkard

One day a hardened sinner came to Pastor Wyneken to announce himself for communion. Wyneken looked him sharply in the eye for a few moments and declared abruptly, "You cannot go to Communion!"

"Why not?" asked the man, taken aback. Because you are a drunkard," was the blunt reply.

"What! I a drunkard!" the man returned indignantly. "How do you know? Who told you that? I'll fix that liar! I want to know who told you that!

"All right," remarked Wyneken calmly. "A man told me that who ought to know, and you will not be able to contradict him either."

"Is that so! Who is it?"

"Come over there, and I'll show him to you," said Wyneken and took the man by the arm and led him before a mirror. "Now look at him. That man with that red nose and that bloated face told me about it. Now look that man straight in the eye and deny it if you can."

Then, after a few moments, he said to the man in a most affectionate manner: "My dear friend, you are a creature of God. He created you in His image. He redeemed you with the precious blood of His Son. And you, whom God so highly honored and prized, thrust yourself like the swine into the mire and filth of sin and wallow in it."

Turning pale and trembling from head to foot, the man relented and repented of his sin, asking Wyneken whether there was any help for a man like him.

"Oh, indeed," Wyneken assured him. "Take a seat. There is help for you, too." Then he proceeded to explain to him the grace of God in Christ Jesus and in simple language told him to repent of his sin and to trust in the merits of his Savior. And as the man turned to go, Wyneken called after him, "Oh, I almost forgot. You may go to Communion."

7. The Non-believer

Wyneken soon became a well-known figure in those places where he carried on his work. Everybody knew the German preacher, and they knew where he stood. Many a gibe came his way, but he was never at a loss for a reply, and the shots went home, like this one:

"Say, preacher," said one to him, "do you really believe what you preach? I don't believe it," with emphasis on the personal pronoun.

"Then be sure to continue therein," replied Wyneken. "And when the devil has you by the collar and drags you into hell, then shout as loud as you can, 'I don't believe it! I don't believe it!'" With that he straddled his horse and rode off, leaving the man to stand in the road. But a few days later he who had spoken so wisely came back to the store where the encounter had occurred and inquired for Wyneken, "That man made me uneasy. I must speak to him again." They did meet again, and the scoffer became a believer.

8. Herr Pastor and His Trousers

Of his personal appearance and dress, Wyneken thought little. . . Not much fashion was in vogue then among his settlers, and he had very little money to spend on clothing anyway. Neither did his parishioners.

The women came to church in calico dresses and sunbonnets and the men usually appeared in shirt sleeves and jeans. Wyneken tried to preserve his only black suit for ministerial functions, but we can understand that the wear and tear of a frontiersman's life would not give it much of a chance. For a while Wyneken wore jeans like his country people, and he often preached in them, even though they were patched at the knee. His people thought nothing of this. In rainy weather he often wore a wide cape of some green material. And for a long while he wore a pair of bright yellow trousers. These trousers are famous, and they deserve a place here. Their history is as follows.

He had gone to nearby Decatur to make a few purchases. He stopped at a store whose proprietor, besides being a Romanist, was a drunkard. He knew Wyneken very well, for he had received many a talking-to from the preacher. Wyneken stepped into the store, the man was busy cutting a piece of yellow material, generally known as English leather. Wyneken, whose trousers were worn and frayed, observed him waiting on his customer, and probably his eyes betrayed his thoughts. At any rate, the shopkeeper suddenly turned to him and asked, "Would you like to have a piece of this cloth?" "No," replied Wyneken, "I have no money." "Well, if I gave you enough for a pair of trousers?" "I don't want any present from you," declared Wyneken bluntly. "Is that so! Why not?" rejoined the shopkeeper. "Because in that way you could stop my mouth, and I would not be able to admonish you for your drinking." "Is that it?" laughed the dealer. "Well, here is the cloth. Now scold me as much as you like."

Wyneken was nonplussed. It seemed like an answer to his prayer, and he took the gift as from God. When he reached home, he took the piece of cloth to a tailor in the village and had a pair of trousers made from it. And he was inordinately proud of them. He wore them everywhere. What pleased him most was that they would last a long time. But the deacons of his church were differently impressed by their sight. In fact, they were shocked. "Where in the world did our pastor get these trousers?" they asked. They soon found out much to their chagrin where the cloth for them had come from. They quickly got together, loaded a wagon with corn, drove to Decatur, and dumped it in front of the man's store.

"What are you doing there? I didn't order that corn!" protested the dealer indignantly. "That is the money for our pastor's trousers! We won't have you say that you had to support our pastor!" was the parting shot as they hastily drove off.

However, though their financial pride had been satisfied, they still had to endure the sight of these trousers. Wyneken wore them in town and country. And everybody knew that the preacher never had any money and that he could not invest in any better garb. But one of his deacons, Ernst Voss, was bound to get rid of those trousers. He quietly called upon all the members of the church and succeeded in collecting forty dollars to get the pastor a suit of clothes which would be more presentable. That was a very large sum of money in those days, and it took him some time to gather it. So we can imagine the joy he experienced when he brought the money to the pastor and urged him to buy himself a decent suit of clothes with it. But during the deacon's visit a poor woman called on the pastor and told him of her trouble and dire need. Her husband had been ill a long time, the rent had not been paid for months, and the landlord, she said, would not wait much longer, and she had no money to buy food for her children. It was a pitiful tale. Voss listened for a while and then left, feeling that he was an intruder. He figured that he had done his duty and felt sure that the pastor would use the money to clothe himself.

The members of the church waited patiently to see the pastor appear in the new suit. But nothing happened. He still wore the same outfit. Voss, of course, was in an embarrassing position. Had he delivered the money to the pastor? What had become of it? Finally the good deacon became uneasy and took occasion to approach the pastor to find out what he had done with the money and whether the suit was not yet ready. "New suit?" asked Wyneken. "What new suit? Where shall I get the money for a new suit of clothes?" "But," replied the dumbfounded deacon, "didn't I bring you forty dollars which had been collected for this very purpose? And now you say you have no money?"

"Well, you see, this is how it happened," remarked Wyneken naively. "Do you remember that woman who came to me and related her sorrow and dire need, weeping bitterly? I gave her the money because she needed it more than I. What is the matter with my clothes? They are good enough."

When Voss started to protest, Wyneken cut him short with the remark: "Now, don't make so much ado about nothing. God can give me twice as much money in return and a new pair of trousers in the bargain, if I need them." "Well, that is what you say," replied the discouraged deacon.

"Is that so! You doubt it? You are a fine Christian! Don't you know that the first article of the Creed says: I believe that God provides me with all that I need to support this body and life, richly and daily?"

Voss said nothing. Disappointment was written all over his face. What was to be done with a man like that? But he kept his thoughts to himself as they walked to the village together. As they passed the post-office, the postmaster called through the door, "Hey, Wyneken! Here is a letter for you!" "Where from?" he asked, surprised and happy; for letters then were not so common as they are now. "From Germany!" returned the postmaster as he handed him the letter. Wyneken noticed immediately that it was from his relatives. As he opened the letter, his eyes fell upon a draft of eighty dollars, which his brother had sent him "in order that you might not starve in the wilderness."

Turning to Voss with the money in his hand, he remarked gleefully, "See there, you doubting Thomas!" As they went down the street, they passed a tailor shop. The proprietor of the shop stood in the door, evidently on the lookout for the preacher, for as soon as he spied him, he hailed him with, "Pastor, step in a minute, will you please?" As soon as Wyneken was inside he turned to him and said, "Look here. I have a fine pair of trousers here which were made for a man out in the country. He is a man just like you. You would do me a great favor if you would try them on before I'll send them there. I could then tell whether they will fit him."

Wyneken did not like the idea at all. He refused. Why should he try on another man's trousers? The tailor, however, was not put off so easily and insisted that he try them on. Finally he yielded under protest. He went to a secluded part of the store and put on those trousers. As he stepped out into the light, the tailor remarked, "Well, how do you like them? It's a fine piece of goods. Just the kind of trousers for a pastor." "That may be," said Wyneken, "but they are not suitable for a man like me. As long as I have been pastor here, I have never had any like them. And I have no use for them now."

"Good! The trousers are yours, pastor. You are to keep them. They were made for you, and—they have been paid for!"

Wyneken protested vehemently. Angrily he went to the corner to get his old trousers—those beloved, comfortable yellow trousers. Alas, they had mysteriously disappeared! A conspiracy! Chagrined, he thanked the good man for his present and left the store with his friend Voss. As they parted outside and shook hands, Wyneken remarked to his deacon, who was overcome with emotion, "Well, my dear Voss, what have you to say now?"

Such is the famous story of the "immortal" yellow trousers. These days in Indiana Wyneken often declared in later life to have been the happiest of his life. He gave everything away. But he was satisfied and happy. How many of us can say the same thing of themselves today?

9. What It Cost to Build St. John's on the White Creek in Bartholomew County

In 1844 the Evangelical-Lutheran North Germans who had moved from Cincinnati to the White Creek wilderness built their second house of worship. The church records tell us about the "building materials" and their cost:

3 Gallen Branntwein (3 gallon of whiskey)	0.94
Boats [!] oder Dielen (boards or flooring)	0.56
Fenster fresen (window framing)	1.50
Hengade (hinges)	0.50
Glass (Glass)	0.96
ein Schloss (a lock)	1.00
ein Kirchenbuch (a church record book)	0.75
Papier (paper)	0.10
Dielen (flooring)	0.43
Glass (glass)	0.10
Brief an die Gemeinde (letter to congregation)	<u>0.18</u>
	$ 7.03

10.-12. At St.Peter's Lutheran Church, Harrison County: Fire and Firewater

10. Firefighter Rev. Firnschild

The church roof once caught on fire. This happened during the pastorate of the Rev. Firnschild. He climbed the bell rope to the belfry with buckets of water, took them out on the roof and extinguished the flames.

11. Supplies of the Supply Preacher

An unnamed supply preacher carried a bottle of whiskey with him during the cold winter months when he was traveling between St. Peter's and New Salisbury. While preaching he stuffed his bottle in the top of his boot where it lay neatly concealed from view during the service.

12. Frequent Trips to the Attic

While studying his sermons, Rev. Fismer often climbed to the corners of his attic in the old log parsonage. You know why.

13. The "Glennites" and "Henkelites" at Mount Solomon Lutheran Church in Harrison County (1840s)

In December 1841 the Rev. Peter Glenn took charge of the congregation. Membership at this time numbered seventy-six. In 1843 it was about one hundred and forty-six. The growth was there. But under his pastorate—he made the chills go down your spine when he was preaching—the congregation became divided. The one party followed him, the other followed the Rev. Eusebius Henkel. The former were called "Glennites" or "New Lutherans," because they liked the "new measures," revivals and the mourner's bench, and they also shared Rev. Glenn's strong stand on doing away with slavery, that unchristian institution. The latter were called "Henkelites" or "Old Lutherans" because of their conservatism. A law suit ensued over the church property which resulted in the Henkelites holding it.

The Glennites went about a mile east of Mount Solomon and built a church and called it Luther's Chapel. They say during the dedication on June 13, 1844 Rev. Glenn pointed toward Mount Solomon and said, "Old Mount Hickla is going to blow up!" Of course, it didn't, but the two parties kept on disliking each other.

One member of Mount Solomon made whiskey, and when a visitor came along he'd ask him, "Are you a Glennite or a Henkelite?" If the visitor was a Henkelite he'd be offered a drink, but if he said he was a Glennite he didn't get any.

Another one of the Old Lutherans so disliked the New Lutheran Rev. Glenn that one day, when he had caught a black racer snake, he took it to an outbuilding and drove a nail through its tail and let it hang alive. It lived some thirty days. He was much accustomed to exhibit his serpent to all who called at his residence, and always he would speak of it as a "Glennite."

14.-15. Methodist Stories from Santa Claus and Environs

14. Preacher, Watch Out!

From 1858 to 1860, Louis Mueller was a preacher at the German Methodist Episcopal Church of Santa Claus in Spencer County. Here is what happened to him:

"Once I called on a conservative Catholic woman in the vicinity. I spoke with her about her religious life. During the course of the conversation she became so angry that she set upon me with a fire poker the size of a broom stick. I took to flight but I saw that I could not untie and mount my horse before she overtook me. I ran, closed the door and held it shut from the outside. She tried with all her strength to open the door but did not succeed. She then started to come out of the window. When I saw that, I untied my horse and swung into the saddle. Scarcely had I done so before she was upon me. I called to the children that they must not follow her example, and I hoped that she would repent or she would have to spent many years in Purgatory. She cursed frightfully, and since she could not reach me, she called out and wished that a cloud burst of rain would fall on me before I got home. If she repented, I do not know.

Six weeks later I called on her again. This time. as we talked quietly and openly, three drunken men entered and set upon me like inquisitors. Who knows what might have happened to me had the women not protected me and pushed the beasts through the door."

15. Helping out the Lutherans

"Once I had a preaching appointment 8 miles south west of the Salem Congregation. A good Lutheran advised me to preach the gospel from the Calendar. I did so. Only Lutherans lived there and they had no preacher. One Sunday I came ten minutes late, and there stood a so-called preacher who had appeared during the week. He preached on the story of Nicodemus. He raved shamefully about the Methodists. When he had finished I asked his permission to make a few remarks. This was granted to me. I asked for proof of several assertions the pastor had made and asked him to answer several questions. Then he first recognized who I was. Proof and answers he was not able to give, so the fellow became abusive. I then challenged hime to a debate in 14 days, on his text and on "rebirth". He accepted the chance to debate and hopefully suggested that I study diligently, since so far as he knew all Methodist preachers lacked learning. I replied that that was my business and I thought that with a country tramp such as he was I could finish with him without study. When I returned after 14 days, no opponent was there. I preached on the story of Nicodemus and after I had finished inquired about my opponent. An old man said, "He bought, on credit, $40.00 worth of clothing from a widow and had then taken 'French leave'. Herr Pastor, you gave him the correct title."

16. "Fear Ye Not Them that Kill the Body"

Even so beloved a man as Father Isidor (Hobi) had his enemies at Ferdinand. The vulgar character of these was shown in various ways; they even defiled his porch during the night. Further, on the night of December 2, 1860, an anonymous letter was placed at his door suggesting that he leave town because some forty or fifty men had conspired against his life. The writer claimed that he had been designated by lot to kill Father Isidor, but that he could not do that and that by this letter he wished to apprise the pastor of the danger in which he was. Of course Father Isidor went calmly about his duties on the next morning. On the night following, Father Isidor had a sick call into the very district of his principal opponent—evidently the writer of that letter. As the pastor was going along in the moonlight, he suddenly saw a man with a gun approaching. There was no sense in turning either back or aside. When the two were face to face, the uncanny fellow merely asked whether Father Isidor had seen a dog. No. He had seen none—up till then. On one other night someone, whose name was well known, shot through Father Isidor's window.

17. Ferdinand's Father Eberhard Stadler

". . . There was a man who had authority in that town; and Ferdinand needed it. Many years ago I was a traveling salesman. One day, as I drove into the town, a rough fight was going on at the main intersection. When the affair seemed to become quite serious and I was thinking about a sheriff, one of the bystanders called out, 'Holt'n Pfoarra' (Fetch the pastor). After a little while I heard, 'Der Pfoarra kommt!' With everybody else I looked up the hill toward the church and saw a black-robed figure coming down with a firm step. 'Was ist da wieder los?' (What's going on here again?). But there no longer was anything 'los.' At the word, 'Der Pfoarra kommt,' the fighters tugged here and there at their clothes and tried to look unconcerned."

18. What Happened to the Rev. Wirz?

In the spring of 1853, a certain clergyman from Switzerland asked to be received into the Diocese of Vincennes and was actually accepted, and was appointed pastor of the Celestine parish. The priest, Rev. Wirz disappeared presumably having left for America, but there was no record that the disappeared Father Wirz from Switzerland ever arrived in America.

In the beginning of September of 1854, a man by name of Wirz presented himself to the Bishop of Vincennes and was immediately sent to assume his duties at Celestine. There was something suspicious about this man, because of the fact that he never signed his name to baptismal, funeral, or any other kind of church records, but always some other wording in distorted writing. Twenty-two months later he disappeared suddenly without leaving any address.

By chance a passport was found that contained the name of Michael Spichting, a teacher from the vicinity of the disappeared Father Wirz in Switzerland. This was the man who probably played the part of the priest. The Benedictines of St. Meinrad began an investigation, but before they got very far the false Wirz "flew the coop" and no one ever heard of him again.

19. Church Robbers

It happened at St. Maurice, Decatur County, in the 1890s. One night, the Rev. John B. Unverzagt (whose name means *undaunted, undismayed, unabashed, fearless, intrepid, bold, stout-hearted, resolute, indomitable—* take your pick) saw a light in the church. There was no mistake about it! Sacrilegious robbers were at work in the church. He aroused the whole town and, when everybody was ready they entered to "nab" the fellow! They found a candle burning which the Rev. Father had forgotten to extinguish when he left the church after his night prayers.

20. Lenten Rule: Wurst = Meat

The parish priest instructed his parish members on the Lenten rules. One member questioned why they can't eat *Wurst* (sausage). But the priest insisted: *"Wurst ist das selbe wie Fleisch"* (Sausage is the same as meat).

Shortly after this incident the priest asked this same man to bring him a load of firewood. He gladly responded with a thought of revenge in mind. He brought in a load of sawdust instead of firewood. And when the priest saw that, he exclaimed: *"Joseph, ich wollt' Feuerholz. Das ist kein Feuerholz* (I wanted firewood. This is no firewood). Joseph stated: *"Herr Pfarrer, Sie hab'n uns g'sagt, Wurst ist das selbe wie Fleisch; genauso ist dann*

Saegmehl auch Feuerholz (Rev. Father, you told us sausage is the same as meat; then, likewise, sawdust is also firewood).

21. Napping During the Sermon

Pastor John went to great length to make a nice sermon. One certain old gentleman who always sat in the last pew in church slept as usual through the sermon. Pastor John asked, "How many of you want to go to heaven? Whoever so, please stand." All stood up except this same old gentleman. The Pastor said, "Please be seated," and he continued by asking, "How many people want to go to hell? Whoever so, please stand." By now the old gentleman was awake and stood up all alone and said, "Pastor John, I don't know what we are voting for, but it looks like it's only the two of us in favor of it."

22. Generous Tithing

A parish priest noticed an unusual great tithing in the Sunday collection. After several Sundays had passed he instructed the ushers to keep an eye open as to who this generous person was. Finally they realized it was a little old lady dropping a $100 bill in the collection basket.

Father made a special effort one Sunday after Mass to greet his parishioners. When the little old lady came along, Father said to her, "Frau Schmidt, you are so very generous. Isn't it a big sacrifice on your part? She replied, "Oh, not really. My son sends me money." Father asked, "What does your son do?" "Oh, he's a vet. He has two cat houses, one in New York and one in Florida."

23. Help Not Appreciated

Herr Meier had two blackened eyes. On Tuesday he met Herr Mueller, his friend, in town. Herr Mueller questioned, "How come you've got two black eyes?" Herr Meier said, "Oh, last Sunday in church I was in back of this heavyset woman whose dress was tucked between her big buns. This bothered me so bad, so I reached up and pulled it out. She reached around with her right arm and hit me in the right eye. I figured, gosh, if this bothers her so bad, I'll just try to pull it back where it was, when wham, to my surprise, she hauled off with her left arm and, would you believe me, she made my left eye black, too. I sure didn't pray much."

24. Gossip Confessed

An old woman went to confession. She said she had spread some gossip about another woman. The priest told her to take a feather pillow up on a hill on a windy day and cut the pillow open and let the feathers fly in the wind, then come back. She did as she was told and returned. The priest said, "Now go and gather up the feathers." "But that's impossible," she said. He said, "It's just as possible for you to gather up the feathers as it would be for you to undo the wrong that was done by your gossip."

VI.

FATHER BASIL HEUSLER AT ST. JOSEPH'S DOWN IN JASPER

". . . throw a quarter in the offering box n' then grab you two dimes!" (VI.9.)

The legendary Father Basil served St. Joseph's parish in Jasper from 1898 to 1942. *Courtesy Claude Eckert.*

1. Good Connections to Heaven

The Feast of St. Joseph was celebrated on March 19. The factories closed, the band played. But it rained and rained. At 8:45 it was time for Father Basil to lead the solemn procession. When he appeared in the doorway, the clouds lifted and the sun shined for the procession.

2. *Argument gebeichtet* / Argument Confessed

Da kommt die Lizzie und will beichte' gehe'. Da hat sie abgereddelt und hat gesagt: "Ich und da Martin, mir h'en an Argument g'hat."
Pfarrer: "He, wer hat gewonne'?"

Lizzie comes and wants to go to confession. She rattled off her sins and said: "I and Martin, we had an argument."
Father: "Hey, who won?"

3. *Verlobung* / Engagement

Da Pfarrer Basil ist mit mir aus 'em Office g'gange. Und da sind zwei g'sesse ganz nah bei'nander auf die grosse lange Bank.
Pfarrer: "He, du! Ich glaub, die zwei h'en es im Sinn."

Father Basil walked out of the office with me. Two lovers were sitting close together on the big long bench.
Father: "Hey, you! I think those two have it in mind."

4. *s' Aufgebot* / Banns

Zwei Leut komme' zum Aufgebot im Pfarrer Basil sei' Office. Pfarrer: "Wolle' Ihr heirate' oder misse' Ihr? Es ist besser Kinde' habe' solche Weg, als wie gar keine habe' wolle'."

Two people come to Fr. Basil's office to have their intended marriage announced in church. Father: "Do you want to get married or do you have to? It's better to have children that-a-way, than not to want any at all."

5. A First Communion "Accident"

It was First Communion Sunday and Katie had her four-year-old grandson with her, the older one was making his First Communion. When Katie went to communion the younger grandson got away from her and went up there and got communion too. Katie almost had a heart attack. That afternoon she couldn't stand it no more. So she went to Father Basil.

Pfarrer: Ja, was ist denn los?
Katie: Heit war Komm'ion.
Pfarrer: Das weiss ich.
Katie: Mei kleiner Enkel, er ist erst vier, ist au zur Komm'ion g'gange. Er ist mir davong'loffe.
Pfarrer: Ja, lebt er noch?
Katie: Sure.
Pfarrer: Na geh heim! Sei ruhig!

Father: Well, what's the matter?
Katie: Today was Communion Sunday.
Father: I know that.
Katie: My little grandson, he's only four, he also went to Communion. He ran away from me.
Father: Well, is he still alive?
Katie: Sure.
Father: Then go home! Calm down!

6. Father Basil Recommends Dentist

Prof. Loepker came to see which dentist Father Basil would recommend.

Father: *Dr. Schneider.*
Professor: *Is das a gute Dentist?*
Father: *Ja, a gute Dentist—aber* a damned fool!

7.-10. *Kanzelsprich'* / Pulpit Talk

7. What the Squeaking Door Tells

When the front door was opened it squeaked. One day while Father Basil was giving a sermon the door squeaked. Father said: *"Geh' just 'naus. Ich weiss, du musst gehe'."* / "Go on out. I know you have to go (to the. . .)."

8. *Lange Predigt* / **Long Sermon**

"Und du da drunne, brauchst net uf die Uhr gucke. Wenn du a Roast in da Ofe hast, es geht doch verbrenna. Ich bin schon lang net fertig!"

"And you down there, you needn't look at your watch. If you've got a roast in the oven, it's gonna burn anyways. I ain't gonna be done for a long time!"

9. *Opferbox un' Geld wechsla* / **Off'ring Box n' Making Change**

"Du, John, schmeiss' amol a vertel Thale in die Opferbox und dann grab dich zwei zeh' cent Stick!"

"You, John, why don't you throw a quarter in the offering box n' then grab you two dimes."

10. *Katz' in da Kirch'* / **Cat in the Church**

"Und einmol hat der grosse Gott in der hoche Himmel, hat amol g'sproche' und hat g'sagt: 'Jemand nehm selle Katz raus!'"

"And onced the great God in them high heavens, onced He spoke and He said, 'Somebody take that there cat out!'"

11. *D' Schrotflint'* / **Th' Shotgun**

Pfarrer: Hey, Eckerle, hast du a Schrotflint'?
Eckerle: Ja, was willst damit tue?
Pfarrer: Well, bring se amol mit. Die Taube verscheisse' mei' heilige Joseph!

Father: Hey, Eckerle, you got a shotgun?
Eckerle: Yeah, what you wanna do with it?
Father: The doves 's a-shittin' all over my St. Joseph!

12. *Pfarrer Basil bei'n Tod von a frihe Liebe* / **At the Death of a Woman Father Basil once Loved**

Pfarrer: "Ich kann gar net verstehe', wie so a scheene Weibsbild Jahre z'rick so scheen war und jetzt so alt guckt."

Father: "I really can't understand how such a beauty of a woman could look so charming years ago and now look so old."

13. Father Basil's Birthday at St. Meinrad

Basil went to St. Meinrad (Abbey) for his birthday. They baked him a cake. He was full of devilment. So he goes up the steps. On the second floor one of the brothers came. He was going to fix him. He was going to throw the cake on him. It just happened to be the wrong man. It was the abbot.—"I nearly lost my place."

14. *Zur Bank oder net* / To the Bank or not

Fr. Basil hat a junger Hilfspfarrer g'habt, der war so a Maedchen fir alles.
Er hat gegrabe drausse un er hett misse sich umziehe fir auf de Bank gehe.
Fr. Basil: Komm mal rein! Du gehst zu die Bank. Ich hab Geld fir 'neintue.
Hilfspfarrer: Ich kann net gehe.
Fr. Basil: Oh, yes! Du gehst!
Hilfspfarrer: Glaubst du, I'm a damned fool?
Fr. Basil: Yes, I do!

Fr. Basil had a young assistant priest who was a handyman. He was digging outside and would've had to change his clothes to go to the bank.
Fr.Basil: Come in here! You're going to the bank. I have money to deposit.
Assistant: I can't go.
Fr. Basil: Oh, yes! You're going!
Assistant: Do you think I'm a damned fool?
Fr. Basil: Yes, I do!

15. Comment on a Nice Bridegroom

Carl Mehringer's aunt Lizzie, she lived in Ireland—Dubois County, that is. She went to mass every morning in Jasper. She went kind o' slow. She talked to Fr. Basil every morning after the 6 o'clock mass. The morning of Carl's wedding, Father said:
"Ja, ja, Lizzie. Heit gibt's Hochzeit. Jetzt kriegt da Karl erst (=doch) noch eine. A gute Kerl, aber a gross' Maul!"
"Yes, yes, Lizzie. Today's the wedding. Now Carl s'got himself a woman after all. A nice feller, but a big mouth!"

16. Not as Bad as "Hasenpfeffer"

When Claude Eckert and Martina Wehr wanted to get married (in 1940), they went to see Fr. Basil at St. Joseph's in Jasper. Fr. Basil asked Martina, "*Wer bist du?*" ("Who are you?"). Martina—hearing the likes of her maiden name—"Wehr"—promptly answered, "*Ja, a Wehr bin ich.*" ("Yes. I am a Wehr"). Fr. Basil, with a giggle, said, "*Das isch net so schlimm wie Hasenpfeffer.*" ("That ain't as bad as Hasenpfeffer").

17. Daylight Savings Time—in Jasper???

One day some workers in Jasper went to see Father Basil. They wanted him to introduce daylight savings time in town. Now why didn't they go 'n see the mayor? Let me tell you sump'n, it wasn't the mayor who was calling the shots in Jasper, it was Father Basil.

He didn't like the idea of fooling with time, so he told them "N-O". The men were awfully disappointed. But as always, they respected his authority. When they walked down the steps from Father Basil's house, heads hanging low, Father felt kind a sorry for them and shouted, "Fellers, don't you now son-of-a-bitch me for dat! You'll get your summer time some day!"

VII.

FRUGALITY, MONEY AND GOLD

"Buying a Farm the Amish Way" (VII.5.)

1. Butter *and* Jelly?

When our mother died, father had to give up farming and work in a factory. He stayed with his brother, while my brother and I came to live with grandpa, grandma and our maiden aunt. One day, grandpa's brother came to visit. At meal time I asked for jelly on my bread—I already had butter on it. My great uncle said, "Do you own *two* houses?"

2. Ever Heard of a "Cherry-Picking Nose"?

It was one of those hazy summer days at "Mugs" Waechter's farm outside Oldenburg. We walked through the garden and looked at the fruit trees. What a shame, the worms had decided to get all of the plums. Mugs said, "Well, that's the farmer's gamble, but boy, when they're good they sure make a dandy pie. And I tell you what, there's no better pie than plum pie but apple pie!" By that time Genevieve, his wife, called us in for cherry pie and coffee. "Cherry pie," Mugs smacked his lips, "that reminds me of my father, he had a cherry-picking nose. You may never have heard of a thing like that. With his nose he could hang on a limb and pick with *both* hands."

If you'd know Mugs and extend that Waechter nose of his just a wee bit, you'd swear that Mugs was telling the truth!

3. The Christmas Card

Since the Great Depression a family in Hammond, Indiana, has exchanged a Christmas card with a family in Illinois. That's right, a card. The same card.

Ida Roennau Smith bought the card more than fifty years ago from a Hammond stationer, more or less as a joke. It was in the middle of the Depression, and people were trying to save money, including Mrs. Smith. She was amused that an enterprising card company was pushing greeting cards that could be used more than once. The card, which has a picture of a penny-pinching Scottish terrier and a Scot dressed in a kilt, uses the concept of a "strip ticket," or multi-ticket railroad pass. The ticket says "One Round Trip to a Merry Christmas." It was designed to be sent from 1935 to 1940, but Oscar Weil of Calumet City, Ill., says the families "got carried away." Each year they wrote little notes on the card. In 1936 the Weils threatened to buy a new card. But 40 years later, the card was still floating around. "Hi. Hang on to this. We'll send it to the Guiness Book of Records," Mrs. Smith wrote in 1976.

Weil and Mrs. Smith grew up together in Hammond. Their parents had known each other in Germany and had settled in the same Hammond neighborhood after immigrating to the United States. They married other people, and the Weils moved to Illinois. "In the first years, the four of us were together all the time, but you get married and you lose contact with one another," Mrs. Smith said. Mrs. Smith's husband, Ernest, died four years ago. Weil's wife, Pauline, died last year. But the tradition continues, and this year (1986) was no exception.

> "Sending greetings each year
> (And I'm gonna be terse),
> Is tough on the feet
> And hard on the purse;
> So here's a "Strip Ticket,"
> Please use it each year.
> It's good for continuous
> Joy and good cheer."

4. Good with Money

It used to be said by old German settlers around Columbus, Bartholomew County, that when a new baby was born you could tell how he would handle his money by looking at his ears. If they lay close to his head, he would manage it well and not part with it too easily. If they stuck out, it would be the opposite. My grandmother told me this as a joke when my son was born. But she seemed pleased that his ears were close to his head.

5. Buying a Farm the Amish Way

My aunt Nita worked at the bank in Goshen, Elkhart County. One day the president of the bank called upon her to witness while an Amish farmer and his wife counted out the money to purchase a $40,000 farm.

When she walked into the president's office, she saw the Amish couple standing beside a large gray metal milk can, which contained the money. It was in change and small bills earned from butter and egg sales. So they spent the whole afternoon counting the "butter and egg money."

When they had finished counting, however, they had only $30.000, not $40.000. The Amish farmer turned to his wife and said, "Ma, I *told* you we brought the wrong milk can."

6. How Great-Grandpa Made a Loan

Born in Maryland, my paternal great-grandfather, Daniel W. Branstetter, was one of those Dutchmen who moved West, first to Wooster, Ohio, then to Brown County, Indiana. Although he couldn't read or write, according to census records, he could manage money. He had a chest of coins which he sometimes let children touch and from which he made them presents on special occasions. And when my maternal grandmother and her fiance needed money to start housekeeping, someone suggested good old Daniel. They explained their problem to him. He didn't say much but took them to his very large barn. Then, being a very tall and large man, he ran his hand up a stringer and brought cash down to loan them.

7.-11. Editor J. C. Leffel: Plenty to Worry about (1879/1880)

7. Beware, the Easy Life!

The older generation of immigrants from the old country watch with misgivings the absence of industry in their sons and daughters born on American soil. The lack of hardship and fight for survival, along with the easy money, the ability to travel, and generally a softer life due to many new inventions, is of great concern to those who remember the virtues of hard work, plain living, and honest dealings with friends and neighbors.

8. Beware, the Eight-Hour Work Day Cometh!

We have noted for some time that the virtue of hard work is disappearing. Now we hear of a new social proposal. A short eight-hour work day. Soon people will want pay for no work at all.

9. Girls, Stick to Grandmother's Ways!

Some of the farm ladies (in Posey County) have been sewing lovely garments from corn sacks. The thriftiness and frugality of these women are fine examples for our young people to follow. Yet we find the young ones straying far off the old path. Young girls have been observed of late tossing love letters and frivolous notes to strangers riding the railroads through the city. The mothers of tomorrow desperately need to take another look at their honorable grandmothers.

10. The End of Times Coming (Soon)!

Businessmen can't make enough money, farmers can't hire help, parents can't control their children, young people want to play rather than work. Now preachers in many area churches are pointing to the year 1881 as the end of times!

11. Hard Times? Keep Plowing!

Hard times and rising prices are on everyone's mind. Business people complain about falling sales. (We'd like to tell them this is partly because they don't advertise in the *Wochenblatt*.)

Last week, while plowing his fields, Fritz Schweikhart of Parkers Settlement was thinking about the increasing difficulties of making a living on a farm. He was pondering and planning how to make ends meet and hoping for a good crop to keep his family fed and sheltered. Suddenly his plow hit a can containing twenty half dollars and twenty $20 gold pieces. Fritz was ahead of the hard times by $410.

12. Gold in the Ground

In 1894, Mrs. W., a self-styled "Great Faith Healer" from Evansville established a temporary office in Huntingburg. Though, in general, people laughed at her advertisement in the local papers, she soon had a number of *suckers* on her line; among these was farmer H., who on a meager farm some distance from the town of Ferdinand eked out a scant living. He did not rate high for mentality, and he was known to be superstitious and a believer in witchcraft; yet he had saved up a little sum of money. After a while the *seeress* informed him that there was gold underneath his farm and that she had the ability of locating the exact spot and the power of bringing it to the surface by means of prayer. She would make the tests free of charge; but, naturally, if after she had located the gold, he wanted her to bring it to the surface, she would expect something for her time and trouble. The test would be quite simple, though sure of result; an infant was to be placed on the ground; wherever the infant would cry, there the gold would not be; but where the infant would not cry, there the gold would be. Farmer H. consented; he could lose nothing by her making the tests. She placed the infant here, she placed him there; the infant cried—a pin or pinching would take care of that. Finally a place was found where the infant would not cry. Here the woman knelt down and with much ado gazed intently upon the earth. Yes, gold was there, much gold; but it was down very, very deep, and it would take a number of prayer performances on her part to bring it to the surface. Each performance would cost so and so much. He was willing, she might try. She began, and after the first trial she assured him that she had raised the gold considerably and that eventually she would certainly bring it to the surface. As the performances proceeded—and she received a fair reward for each one—she saw that the gold was even more than she at first had thought. Meanwhile farmer H., confident of his resources, began to plan how he would use them: he was going to build a new house, the house of his dreams, and new barns and stables, and in the stables there were going to be fine horses. He went to Matthias Olinger, who at that time dealt in lumber, and ordered the lumber that would be needed; everything would have to be first class. But Matthias Olinger, knowing the man's resources and the superstitious means with which he hoped to increase them, refused to sell him the lumber. Thereupon a firm in Chicago furnished the lumber, and doors and window frames, and so forth, with oak predominating, and farmer H. built a beautiful two-story house. It is true, his money was all spent, he even had induced some friends to go security for him; but all that was nothing to worry about, because the gold was almost to the top. Now the lumber firm demanded payment; but unfortunately the woman did not show up for the final performance with which she was to have the gold out of the ground, in fact she could not be located anywhere, and digging availed nothing. The whole farm was not enough to pay for the lumber and for the work erecting the house; this stood there quite a while, a monument to a monumental folly. Superstition had cost farmer H. all he possessed. He moved away from Ferdinand, a sad, but a wiser man. The whole property came into the possession of John Wibbels, who, in 1900, sold the house to John Hochgesang. Hochgesang wrecked it to obtain material wherewith to build for himself and his young bride a home in St. Anthony.

VIII.

CONTRACTS, DEALS AND BETS

". . . then Lawrence surely wouldn't hear what was in the letter." (VIII.5.)

1. Hans und Fritz

Hans and Fritz were two Deutschers who lived side by side,
Remote from the world, its deceit and its pride.
With their pretzels and beer the spare moments were spent,
And the fruits of their labor were peace and content.

Hans purchased a horse of a neighbor one day,
And lacking a part of the Geld—as they say—
Made a call upon Fritz to solicit a loan,
To help him to pay for his beautiful roan.

Fritz kindly consented the money to lend,
And gave the required amount to his friend;
Remarking—his own simple language to quote—
"Perhaps it vas better ve make us a note."

The note was drawn up in primitive way—
"I, Hans, gets from Fritz feefty dollars to-day"—
When the question arose, the note being made,
"Vich von holds dat baper until it was baid?"

"You geeps dot," says Fritz, "und den you vill know
You owes me dot money." Says Hans: "Dot ish so:
Dot makes me remember I have dot to bay,
And I brings you der note und der money some day."

A month had expired when Hans, as agreed,
Paid back the amount, and from debt he was freed.
Says Fritz: "Now dot settles us." Hans replied: "Yaw;
Now who dakes dot baper according to law?"

"I geeps dot, now, ain't it?" says Fritz, "den you see
I always remember you baid dot to me."
Says Hans: "Dot ish so, it vos now shust so blain
Dot I knows vot to do ven I porrows again."

2. The Contract between Henry and Clem Studebaker

What is believed to be the *shortest contract* ever written and followed in Indiana was that of the Studebaker brothers, drawn up in 1863 for their wagon-making firm at South Bend. It read:

"I, Henry Studebaker, agree to sell all the wagons my brother Clem can make."

(Signed) Henry Studebaker

"I agree to make all he can sell."

(Signed) Clem Studebaker

3. Strike Settlement at Ferdinand, Dubois County

The men had been working on the church for 28 cents per week, and they wouldn't go on like that, they said. When the priest came and didn't find them working on account o' them being on strike, he said, "We'll fix that real quick." And he sent a boy down the tavern—there was fourteen of 'em that time—to get a couple o' gallon o' beer. Man, did they come back on the job real quick. "Now, you want more money, right?" said the priest, "that's fine with me. I'll pay you 28 cents from now on." And they all agreed that this was a good deal.

4. Who Washes the Mush Pot?

A story I often heard Grandma tell is of an old couple who didn't know what to have for supper. The old man said, "Let's have mush." She said, "The mush pot is too hard to wash," but they agreed to have mush and the first one to speak after it was eaten was to wash the mush pot. They also agreed that to keep from speaking they would stay in bed. A neighbor came in to see them. He found them in bed and they wouldn't talk to him. He called more neighbors in. Neither would say a word. So they called the priest. They wouldn't talk to him either. The priest said, "Well, you people will just have to take care of them." One woman asked, "Who will pay us?" The priest started looking around to see what was in the house. He said, "Here is a good-looking coat." The old lady shouted, "That's my coat!" The old man said, "Get up and wash the mush pot."

5. An Illiterate Feller in Love

An illiterate feller in Fulda, Dubois County, fell in love and received a letter from his girl friend. Since he could not read he was in a real pinch. He needed help. So he approached Lawrence, who also lived in Fulda. Uncle Lawrence was a big tease. After some bickering they agreed that Lawrence would get 1 glass of beer, valued at 5 cents, if he would read the letter to him. But suddenly the feller began hesitatin', 'cause he didn't want Lawrence to know what the girl had written. Being a practical man, Lawrence assured him that this was no problem at all. For another condsideration of 1 glass of beer the feller could hold his hands over Lawrence's ears while he was doing the reading—then Lawrence surely wouldn't hear what was in the letter.

6. I'll Bet My Horse

During Lent we would all kneel and pray the rosary every evening. Grandma had a story about distractions in prayer that is worth retelling. Two men met at a bridge. One man was walking, the other on his horse. After some conversation the horseman said, "I bet you can't walk across that bridge saying the 'Our Father' without distractions." The man on foot said, "What will you bet?" The horse rider said, "I'll bet my horse." The man started walking and praying. When he got halfway across the bridge he looked back and asked, "Do I get the saddle, too?"

7. Wendell Willkie's Wager at Fort Sill, OK (1918)

One dramatic detail of his stay at Fort Sill—a voluntary parachute jump, which he liked to recall later, although at the time he apparently said nothing to his friends. According to the version that he gave to a later friend, A. C. Blinn, Willkie had made some casual remark about not being afraid to jump from a balloon, and "quite an argument developed resulting in a $50 wager that I didn't have the nerve to do it." So they went to the commanding officer and told him the story. "I expected him to say 'Get the hell out of the place and mind your own business. . .' But instead of that, he said, 'Why sure, it's all right with me. I have some French parachutes I would like to try out. Do you want to use one of those or do you want one of ours?' 'Well,' I answered, 'I will take one of ours.'

They put the parachute on me and told me how to pull the rip-cord. . . . The instructor was a very nice chap; as the balloon was slowly going up he talked to me most casually, asking me where I was from, what I was going to do after the war, whether or not I was married, etc., etc. Finally we got up to about 1,500 or 2,000 feet; he looked at the instruments and said, 'Well, if I were going to jump I would do it now,' so there wasn't anything for me to do but go over the side of the basket, which I did, pulled the rip-cord as I had been instructed, landed safely and collected $50."

At this point Blinn could not help asking, "Wendell, why in the world would you do such a crazy thing? I will never forget his answer. He said, 'If you are going into war you can't be a coward.'"

IX.

KIDS

". . . and gave him a good whipping with his stick . . ." (IX.11.)

1. Three Little Boys and the Mystery of Life

Three little boys were discussing the mystery of life as to were they came from.

The first one said, "Mr. Stork brought me."

The second one said, "My mama and my dad got me at the hospital."

Whereupon the third one said, "My mama and my dad were poor, I was homemade."

2. Emma, the Thirteenth Child

My sister next to me was five years old when I was born. I used to kid Mom about I was sure I was adopted, because after twelve kids who needs another one?

3. Doing Dishes

One day after Sunday dinner we girls didn't want to do the dishes right away. But father didn't approve. So we tried again, *"Aber wir haben noch unsere guten Kleider an"* (But we're still in our Sunday clothes). Father wouldn't fall for that either. He said, *"Ich hab nicht g'sagt, dass ihr das G'schirr mit den guten Kleidern waschen sollt"* (I didn't say you should wash the dishes with your Sunday clothes).

4. The Little Beer Carrier

I seen a lots of taverns when I was a boy (in Oldenburg). . . Every night I had to go to Frank Heppner's saloon—and get a can of beer with a nickel. The man filled up the can and I would crawl up to the bar stool and get to the pretzel jar and fill my pocket full of pretzels, and then I would go home. Half way between there and home, I would take a big swig of that beer. Got home, my Dad would say, "Gee whiz." I said, "I kinda tripped a little bit and some spilled out. That was every night, Saturday and Sunday.

5. "Button up Your Bottom!"

We used to sneak over to the Fink's house and eat the eggs off their breakfast table. In those days boys wore slat pants that buttoned up on the bottom. I slid under the fence and broke the buttons off. And old man Fink yelled: *"Robbie—geh mal heim und mach dei Hoselaude zu!"* (Robbie— why don't you hurry home and button up your bottom!).

6. "Mush! Mush! Mush!"

In our neighborhood there was a boy whose mother sent him on horseback to the neighbors to get some corn meal so that she could make some mush.

The boy started out on his horse. He was afraid that he'd forget what he was going after, so he rode along saying to himself, "Mush, mush, mush, mush, mush, mush, mush."

After a while his attention was distracted and he could no longer remember what he'd been saying. There was no use to go on until he could think of the magic word. He stopped his horse and began riding around in a circle. Since it had rained the ground soon became a slush.

After a time a farmer rode up on his horse. He looked things over and said, "What you doin', makin' mush?" "That's it," said the boy and rode happily on his way saying, "Mush! Mush! Mush!"

7. The "Dutch" and the "French" Boys in Old Fort Wayne

The only access to the new Bloomingdale German area of old Fort Wayne was by the single Wells Street bridge across St. Mary's River. Any non-German boys trying to cross the bridge looking for girls were summarily beaten up by the Bloomingdale boys and sent back—as were the German boys trying to "explore" into Frenchtown on the other side.

8. *Johann der Langsame* / John the Slowpoke

Johann Buechler in St. Anthony (Dubois County) war a wenig arg langsam und sei Vadder hat sich viel gaergert ieber ihm. Einmol ist es ihm zuviel worde und er hat zu ihm gsagt: "Du, wenn d' net a bissl schneller machst, ich mecht dich grad in Arsch kicke, dass du nach Ferdinand fliegst!" Da hat der Johann gsagt: "OK,

Papa, das waer mir grad recht, 's is nemlich a Tanz da drieba un na muss i net nieba laufa!"

John Buechler in St. Anthony was kind'a awfully slow and his father was pretty angry with him. Once he just blew his top and told John, "Listen, you, if you ain't get goin' a bit faster I'll kick your ass that you'll fly right over to Ferd'nand!" John didn't mind that at all and said, "OK, Papa, that'd be jus' fine with me. You know there's a dance over there and that'd save me the walkin'."

9. Henrietta Willkie Looking for Her Children

"One Sunday afternoon, at home, everything suddenly seemed too quiet. . . . Diligent search yielded no children but she thought she heard a noise in the attic floor and there were Bob, Julia, Fred, and Wen(dell) playing cards, and about that time Julia said, 'Well, I guess that's my trick,' and Wen replied, 'No it isn't, I'll just take that with my little Jesus.' They had made a deck of playing cards by using the cards they had gotten at Sunday School and of course, Jesus was the joker, he took everything."

10. Thank God for a Good Stepmother (1867)

Anne Dahl had lost her husband and son in a drowning accident. She had been very sickly and a doctor told her she wouldn't live long, maybe not another year. She didn't know what to do with her two girls. She didn't want to send them back to Germany. She had heard from her brother-in-law that Henry Tastove of Mariah Hill was looking for his third wife. She thought that by marrying him the girls would be taken care of. She had her brother-in-law send Henry to Lousville, and they were married there.

While Henry was in Louisville, Catherine, his oldest daughter who was 14 or 15 years old kept house for him. She went to the store to get groceries and while there saw some pretty material, and the storekeeper insisted she buy some. She told him she only had money for groceries. He said, "Surely, your father has hams in the smokehouse and wouldn't miss one." She did what he asked.

When Henry came home with his new wife and went to the smokehouse he counted the hams and found one missing. Catherine told him what she had done and, as she walked past him, Henry took a scissors and cut off one of her long braids. She cried pitifully. Anna, now her stepmother, said to Henry, "What you just did is much worse than what

Catherine has done. The ham can be replaced, but it'll take a long time to grow her braid back." She went to the bedroom to console the girl. She told Catherine the next best thing to do was to cut the other braid, too. This they did, and it sealed the friendship between stepmother and stepdaughter, and they remained on good terms with each other.

11. You Better Believe in Belsnickel!

Belsnickel came—at times with Christkindl played by a gentle woman. When some of the teenage boys denied the existence of Belsnickel, the usually sturdy helper of St. Nikolaus grabbed the doubting Thomas and gave him a good whipping with his stick—which was great entertainment for the older folks.

12. James Whitcomb Riley's "Dot Leedle Boy"

Ot's a leedle Ghristmas story
Dot I told der leedle folks—
Und I vant you stop dot laughin'
Und grackin' funny jokes!—
So help me Peter Moses!
Ot's no time for monkeyshine',
Ober I vas told you somedings
Of dot leedle boy of mine!

Ot vas von cold Vinter vedder,
Ven der snow vas all about—
Dot you have to chop der hatchet
Eef you got der saur kraut!
Und der cheekens on der hind-leg
Vas standin' in der shine
Der sun shmile out dot morning
On dot leedle boy of mine.

He vas joost a leedle baby
Not bigger as a doll
Dot time I go acquaintet—
Ach! you ought to heard 'im squall!—
I grackys! dot's der moosic
Ot make me feel so fine

Ven first I vas been marriet—
Oh, dot leedle boy of mine!

He look yoost like his fader!—
So, ven der vimmen said
"Vot a purty leedle baby!"
Katrina shake der head. . . .
I dink she must a-notice
Dot der baby vas a-gryin',
Und she cover up der blankets
Of dot leedle boy of mine.

Vel, ven he vas got bigger,
Dat he grawl und bump his nose,
Und make der table over,
Und molasses on his glothes—
Dot make 'im all der sveeter,—
So I say to my Katrine
"Better you vas quit a-shpankin'
Dot leedle boy of mine!"

I vish you could a-seen id—
Ven he glimb up on der chair
Und shmash der lookin'glasses
Ven he try to comb his hair
Mit a hammer!—Und Katrina
Say "Dot's an ugly sign!"
But I laugh und vink my fingers
At dot leedle boy of mine.

But vonce, dot Vinter morning,
He shlip out in der snow
Mitout no stockin's on 'im.—
He say he "vant to go
Und fly some mit der birdies!"
Und ve give 'im medi-cine
Ven he catch der "parrygoric"—
Dot leedle boy of mine!

Und so I set und nurse 'im,
Vile der Ghristmas vas come roun',
Und I told 'im 'bout "Kriss Kringle,"
How he come der chimbly down:

Und I ask 'im eef he love 'im
Eef he bring 'im someding fine?
"Nicht besser as mein fader,"
Say dot leedle boy of mine.—

Und he put his arms aroun' me
Und hug so close und tight,
I hear der gclock a-tickin'
All der balance of der night!. . .
Someding make me feel so funny
Ven I say to my Katrine
"Let us go und fill der stockin's
Of dot leedle boy of mine!

Vell.—Ve buyed a leedle horses
Dot you pull 'im mit a shtring,
Und a little fancy jay-bird—
Eef you vant to hear 'im sing
You took 'im by der top-knot
Und yoost blow in behine—
Und dot make much *spectakel*—
For dot leedle boy of mine!

Und gandies, nuts und raizens—
Und I buy a leedle drum
Dot I vant to hear 'im rattle
Ven der Ghristmas morning come!
Und a leedle shmall tin rooster
Dot vould crow so loud und fine
Ven he sqveeze 'im in der morning,
Dot leedle boy of mine!

Und—vile ve vas a-fixin'—
Dot leedle boy vake out!
I t'ought he been a-dreamin'
"Kriss Kringle" vas about,—
For he say—*"Dot's him!—I see 'im
Mit der shtars dot make der shine!*
Und he yoost keep on a-gryin'—
Dot leedle boy of mine,—

Und gottin' vorse und vorser—
Und tumble on der bed!

So—ven der doctor seen id,
He kindo' shake his head,
Und feel his pulse—und visper
"Der boy is a-dyin'."
You dink I could *believe* id?—
Dot leedle boy of mine?

I told you, friends—dot's someding,
Der last time dot he speak
Und say *"Goot-bye, Kriss Kringle!"*—
Dot make me feel so veak
I yoost kneel down und drimble,
Und bur-sed out a-gryin'
"Mein Gott, mein Gott im Himmel!—
Dot leedle boy of mine!"

* * * * * *

Der sun do n't shine *dot* Ghristmas!
. . . Eef dot leedle boy vould *liff'd*—
No deefer-en'! for *Heaven* vas
His leedle Ghristmas-gift!. . .
Und der *rooster*, und der *gandy*,
Und me—und my Katrine—
Und der jay-bird—is a-vaiting
For dot leedle boy of mine.

83

X.

SCHOOL DAYS

"Who makes the sun shine?" (X.7.)

1.-4. The Boys at the German-English Independent School in Indianapolis (1859-1882)

1. How Little Clem Vonnegut and the Boys Met Abe Lincoln

The train bearing the Lincoln party to Washington in February, 1861, stopped at Missouri and Washington Streets. Lincoln and his companions were placed on carriages and driven eastward to the capitol. The streets were cleared from curb to curb and the sidewalks were packed with enthusiastic people who cheered the honored visitor to the echo. We school children were lined up on the curb, the grown people behind.

Our school was on the south side of Washington Street, just opposite the capitol entrance. Our teacher, Mr. Schumm, warned us particularly not to leave our position until he should command us to march back. The train had been slow in arriving, and the crowd became anxious and restless. As the Lincoln carriage approached the crowd forged forward, and when Lincoln's carriage was stopped just opposite our class by a jam of people that broke into the street at the head of the column, we children were suddenly rushed off the curb. Everybody was cheering and, with a hurrah for Lincoln, I (Clemens Vonnegut) ran and leaped into his carriage. Several of my companions followed and got a handclap from Lincoln and a quick shove out on the other side of the carriage.

I remember that all of the party laughed heartily over the incident. It came and went like a flash; the guards very quickly stopped the mob. Well, we youngsters were elated over our feat and I recall that we talked rather loudly about ourselves on the playground about it.

2. Settling with Jake

I (Charles L. Dietz) remember Prof. Schumm, especially from the fact that he was vigorous, both in teaching of discipline and his enforcing same. . . I also recall a boy by the name of Jacob Streicher. Jake was seated beside me in school, and I took a strenuous dislike to him from the fact that he would bring apples to school, and then would retire to some secluded corner and eat the whole apple, not even contributing a bite, or even a core. I saw him once take a big bite out of an apple and put it back in his pocket, so as to avoid 'passing it 'round.' That settled it with Jake! I made up my mind to get my evens. . . In the schoolroom there was a map of the world hanging on the wall, and when we had geography lessons the teacher would hand us a billiard cue, or something similar, and ask us to point out a certain city in South America. Now, in order to reach North America, or some of the northern points of the world, it would be necessary for us to stand on the top of the desk or on a table in order to point them out. Once Jake was requested to point out certain places on the map; the teacher told him to point to a certain city in South America. I saw my chance and stuck a pin into Jake's leg; the billiard cue jumped from the extreme southern part of the world to the extreme northern. The teacher called Jake to the desk, and Jake got it and he got it good.

Another time when Jake became demonstrative, because he sat down on the point of a pin that I had bent so as to fit him, I was conscience-stricken, and arose in my seat and snapped my fingers at the teacher. Schumm had the whip raised ready for Jake, but paused long enough to hear what I had to say. This is what I said: "Mr. Schumm, I feel sorry for Jake. Won't you allow me to take his whipping instead?" Then the unexpected happened. Instead of Schumm appreciating my heroic act, as I expected, he invited me to the rostrum and gave me about the worst licking I ever had in my life, and after he had finished me, he also gave one almost as good to Jake. When school was out that day Jake and I met, exchanged looks of sympathy, and forever afterwards we were good friends.

3. Big Bad John (better known as "JP" Frenzel)

Do you remember the gymnasium in the school yard, which consisted of a horizontal bar, ladders, etc. I remember the horizontal bar particularly. On one occasion John P. Frenzel, who was considered quite a 'cutup', thought he would get even with some of the boys against whom he had some grievances—particularly because they had beaten him to the horizontal bar. He smeared the bar with something of an indescribable smell, and at recess I made an unusual sprint to get there before John. I got there—I also got the smear—and Schumm got John.

4. The Boy Who Stoned Teacher Mueller

A story akin to romance is the following: Along about 1867 our good teacher, Wilhelm Mueller, punished one of the boys in his usual manner by pulling and slightly twisting his ears. In this instance the boy was of the unruly sort, the kind usually held up by parents to their children, as the horrible example.

At the recess hour this particular boy went out on the street with other children, the punishment meted out to him by Mr. Mueller uppermost in his mind. As was the custom, Mr. Mueller stood at the open window looking out on the street from the second floor, when suddenly the boy in question threw a boulder and hit the teacher. The boy disappeared, never to return to the school. He had finished his education as far as Indianapolis and our old school was concerned.

The boy wandered about for a while and finally started out into the wide world. He was a born mechanic, developing into a veritable genius for inventions. He was industrious and, after visiting every part of the globe on behalf of his employers, returned to his native city, Indianapolis, to enjoy the fruits of his labors. He had invented important parts of a very necessary commodity, became the patentee, and thereby became the recipient of a handsome income.

The boy is now a man of fifty-seven years, as studious a mechanic as ever, notwithstanding his independent income, and so modest, he would resent the publishing of his name; so I will withhold the latter, but I will say that not one of Mr. Mueller's many pupils bears a kindlier feeling for him than the boy who resented punishment at his hand so many years ago.

5. First Day at School

Well, the first day I went to school, Sister said, "What is your mother's name?" And I said, "Ma'am." She said, "What's your father's name?" I said, "Pap." And, of course, everybody laughed. I was dumb enough, I didn't know they had another name but that. The gal that kind a took me under her wing, she told Sister what my father's name was and what my mother's name was. I didn't know it until then: Mary and Toni.

6. Kindergarten

I went to Kindergarten in Peru, Indiana. One day my teacher was talking with my mother and after a while asked her if I was German. My mother said that I was. The teacher replied, "I just knew it." Mother wondered how she could tell. The teacher said, "A German child needs to be told only once."

7. Who Makes the Sun Shine?

One day, the nun teaching the second graders in Ferdinand asked the children, "Who makes the sun shine?" The class just sat there, you know. But Robert Leinenbach, he raised his hand and said, "Sister, I don't know who makes the sun shine, but I know my uncle Joe, he makes the moon shine."

8.-10. Young Talents in Oldenburg

8. An Unrecognized Hoosier German Poet

When you needed a poem in Oldenburg for any occasion, why, Ed Hoelker would make one in no time. He was only a little feller when he giggled this one for Nora, a girl in school:

Nora Kopf	Nora Kopf
sitzt auf 'em Stock,	sittin' on a stick,
Stock kracht,	crack goes the stick,
Nora lacht,	Nora laughs,
Nora, Nori, Schnupftabak.	Nora, Nori, snuff.

9. How to Get to Heaven

In 1903 Father David checked the Oldenburg schoolboys on their Catechism. And when he asked the crucial question: *"Was muessen wir tun, um in den Himmel zu kommen?"* (What must we do to get to heaven?), Ed Hoelker, quick as he was and practically-minded, why, Ed replied: *"Wir muessen zuerst sterben"* (We must first die).

10. "All Musicians Are Bums!"

Grandmother Anna Langferman had strong convictions: *"Alle Musikanten sind Lumpen!"* she said, when her son expressed that he would want to make music his lifelihood. But a feller can't let his talent go by the wayside, either. So later in life he played for dances and weddings all over the place.

11. Two Fingers

John Gottschalk, age six, was the champion of the entire gang (at the Kewanna school). He had the habit of holding up two fingers to signify that he had to go to the restroom, and when the teacher consented, he would leave the room and that was the last we would see of John for the rest of the day. One day he held up two fingers and the teacher shook her head. *That* time John *had* to go. John had little "spindly" legs which protuded from an oversize pair of his dad's "hand me down" pants. He glared at the teacher for about five minutes, then sliding to the edge of his seat, he pulled one pants leg over far enough and did his duty right in the aisle. After that when John held up two fingers, she let him go, and she didn't care if he never came back.

12. My Worst Day at School

One day, I was still a little girl, I went to school and had to go to the bathroom. Well, I mean it wasn't exactly a bathroom, it was an outhouse that had seven diff'rent sizes of seats for all ages. While I was in my little chamber, one of the older girls locked me in from the outside and she wouldn't let me out, no matter how much I pleaded with her, and I was so afraid being locked in there and missing class, 'cause our teacher, he was very strict. Well, they finally came to my rescue. But I tell you, I've never forgiven that girl—and I dislike that woman to this day.

13. "Tony" Romweber Wants Bishop's Blessing

To truly appreciate this story one must try to understand what Oldenburg was like in the late 19th century. Oldenburg, like Ivory Soap, was 99.44% pure—German and Catholic. German was spoken at home, on the street, in business, and taught a half a day at school.

The Convent was on one side of Main Street, the Monastery on the other. Brown robed friars staffed our church and were a common sight about the town. Black habited nuns taught us in school, and at home we were taught early to have great respect for them. Our school was situated sort of in between these two walled institutions.

The bishop of our diocese was periodically in town for ordination or investiture of the nuns. Now it was the practice then when meeting the bishop to show our respect for his high office, to drop to one knee, kiss his episcopal ring, and ask his blessing. This was drilled into us by the sisters who taught us. As the brick walk between the Monastery and the Convent went through the school yard, if his excellency chanced to walk by we children would flock over to get his blessing.

Now behind the school and standing astride the girls' side of the playground on the east and the boys' side on the west was this long gray painted privy. This was in our speech *das beckhaus* or, if one used the dialect, *"de beckhus"*. This now is the scene of our story.

The bishop had on this morning spent several long hours receiving the vows of a large class of candidates, and as he and his assistants were passing through the school yard he felt the need to answer an urgent call of nature. He dismissed his retinue, went over to the gray building and selected a stall.

Now at this same time the boy Tony had also the urge and, being dismissed from his classroom, hurried out and by coincidence picked the very same stall. As he pushed open the door his eyes grew wide, for there sat his excellency, in cassock, cape, and biretta. True to his training, Tony plopped down to his knees and asked a blessing. The bishop, equally surprised, waved his hands around to shoo him out.

Tony could hardly wait until noontime came and the Angelus was prayed to run pell mell back home. There he burst open the kitchen door, and using his dialect he cried, *"Momma, Mama, wot meenst de? De Biskup stuent in beckhus un heff mi den Saeigen geiwen!"* ("Mama, Mama, what do you think? The bishop was sitting in the beck house and gave me his blessing!").

His mother then tried to assure him that the bishop was just trying to get him to go away. But no amount of explanation could convince the boy Tony that he had then and there received the good bishop's blessing.

14. Deer Steaks Served in School Cafeteria

A first grade teacher was teaching her class the various kinds of meat dishes they had served in the cafeteria. They had already had ham, chicken, fish, etc., when one day they had deer steaks. The teacher asked who would know what meat this is. No one knew. The teacher said, "I'll give you a clue. It's something your mommy calls your daddy quite often. Quickly, one little boy raised his hand, excitedly saying, "I know. Don't eat it. It's Jack Ass!"

15. J. C. Leffel Raises Questions about Schools (1879)

There are several problems in our schools. The condition of our youth causes much headache among the older folk. Until a solution is found, we ask these questions: Is this only a sign of the modern times in which we live? Are our lady teachers too young to command respect? Are the parents too lenient? Are our local youths rowdier than those in other localities?

XI.

WEDLOCK, WOMEN'S POWER AND STUFF

1. Shy Couple United in Huntington (1893)

George Strobel is the son of a prominent German from Huntington. He loved the both virtuous and beautiful Sarah Schmidt, daughter of a rich German grocer. Both were the epitome of shyness. Thus Louis Heller had to be employed as match-maker. Stoutheartedly he went to work, bringing a justice of the peace with him from the very start. After two hours George and Sarah were man and wife, while Heller as match-maker earned himself a salary of $500. This successful occurence brought about general good cheer.

2. The Jasper Paper Called It "Prolific" (1875)

We received a call this week from Mr. Bernhard Henke, one of our oldest German citizens. He will be 74 years old next month and his wife has just blessed him with another heir. He has been married 4 times, and is the father of 25 children—20 girls and 5 boys, 14 of whom are now living. This last heir is the 11th with his present wife, and he is just as proud of it, as he was of his first, and he expects to be of the next one.

3. Getting Married at Ninety

Herman, age 65, was all dressed up as he met George, an old acquaintance, downtown. George asked, "Why are you so dressed up today?" Said he, "Oh, my dad is getting married and I am in the wedding party." George said, "Oh, great! Just how old is your dad?" "He's pushing ninety," said Herman. "Gosh, at ninety," said George, "I don't think I'd want to get married again." Herman, with his voice lowered, conceded, "Dad didn't want to either."

4.-14. How Women Manhandled Men in Posey County and a Case of "I'll Never Come Back!" (1878/1880)

4. The Evansville Widower

Word came to an Evansville widower that a wealthy eligible widow dwells in our midst. He came to Mount Vernon to pay the fair lady a visit, but was promptly sent on his way with the aid of a broomstick. He stated later that he will pursue this matter no further.

5. The Beggar

A beggar, playing a little tune, sat down to rest on widow Aldrich's front porch. Since she is neither a lover of music nor of beggars, and is known for her temper and great strength, the poor man received such a thrashing with her broom that he was obligated to find a physician to bind up his wounds.

6. The Proprietor

This editor (J. C. Leffel) did witness a scene the other day in one of our local stores in which the proprietor was literally beaten up by his wife. He finally managed to dodge the blows by escaping out the back door, while the stunned customers thought it best to leave quickly by the front entrance. Ladies???

7. The Wharf Laborer

A wharf laborer, who roomed with a local widow, was slow in paying for his board and tried to cheat the lady for two weeks of rent. A thrashing with her broomstick convinced him to move to safer quarters.

8. The "Evil of Mankind"

The "evil of mankind" has long been the topic of philosophers and sages. A wife in the northern part of Posey County literally believed that the evil of mankind was living in her house—and she proceeded to do something about it.

While her husband was sleeping off the effects of too much whiskey which caused him to have an unusually violent temper tantrum, she sliced off his ear with a butcher knife. The doctor said he will live and the wound will heal. The specimen of "evil mankind" promised no more whiskey.

9. Onions and Snoring

A Posey County lady, who for obvious reasons desires to remain anonymous, has looked for a long time to combat her husband's habits of eating onions and snoring. She believes to have found the answer when she began eating large amounts of Limburger cheese. At any rate, she now claims they "are even."

10. "I'll Never Come Back!"

Thomas Thomasson "lost" his wife last week after a stormy domestic quarrel. Neighbors saw him throwing her dishes out of the house and observed how he cut her clothing into shreds. The husband's jealous tendencies have long been known by friends of the couple. Mrs. Thomasson decided to end her marriage to the Hominy Mill worker, boarded the L & N night train and shouted to her husband, "I'll never come back!" He answered loudly as the train pulled out, "I hope you don't!"

11. "The Entertainment of the Week"

Saturday morning two young women, who had traded angry words for some time on Main Street, finally resorted to physical combat in front of Rosengart's store. They hit and kicked and flailed about, they screeched and scratched and spat, they pulled hair, and finally they tore the clothing off of each other. No one tried to stop them and the spectacle attracted a number of, mostly male, onlookers.

12. Seven Policemen vs. One Woman

It is often a painful experience for a landlord to have to evict a renter for nonpayment of long overdue rent. Such was the case last week on Second Street which required all seven policemen to pry one obstinate woman from her home. Before the last possessions were finally taken out of the house she quickly managed to break three windows, unhinge two doors, and kick a hole into a wall.

13. The Groundhog Was Right

The groundhog was indeed right; winter has visited us once more. The editor of the *Mount Vernon Wochenblatt* (John C. Leffel) remarked to his neighbor yesterday: "Here we are in March and it is so cold that my wife's teeth chattered all day long." The neighbor answered: "You are a lucky man; my wife chatters all year long, cold or not."

14. A "Fast of Silence"

A lady of our acquaintance proposed to undertake a "fast of silence" for forty days. This she commenced at 9 a.m. Monday. At 9:30 her pulse became very weak and by 11 a.m. her heart beat was so faint that a physician had to be called. He seemed unable to help her in any way and, as her condition worsened rapidly, her friends and family urged her to give up her plans of silence. They then began to relate to her the very latest gossip of the juiciest kind. Our lady friend, with wide eyes and mouth gaping, bolted from her chair, ran out of the house and into the kitchen of her nearest neighbor and didn't stop talking till 6 p.m. Yes—all health was restored and no—we will not tell her name.

15. A Ferdinand Divorce, a Death, and "Doctor" Baer

William Poschen. . . was quite wealthy for his times and in many regards a good man; but due to domestic troubles he gradually experienced a thirst stronger than water could quench. For this and sundry other reasons Poschen and his wife Katharina had many unpleasant domestic differences. They finally agreed to separate. There was still another point they agreed upon, namely to divide all their possessions evenly between them. William took his wife into the store and there he put two dishes upon the counter: one for his wife, one for himself. Thereupon he brought forth the money box and put one piece of silver into the one dish and another piece of silver of the same value into the other, and so forth until the box was empty. The one dish he gave to his wife, the other he kept for himself. The goods in the store were divided similarly. Finally there was left one plate. Lest either party ever complain that the other had received more, Katharine with a Solomonian gift of settling the perplexing problem broke the plate into halves and apportioned accordingly. After that William Poschen left Ferdinand and lived at Santa Claus, Spencer County.

Some time later Poschen became very ill. Feeling that he was about to be gathered to the pioneers, he sent for "Doctor" Baer, of Ferdinand. "Doctor" Baer was a harness-maker by trade and a self-made doctor by profession, dealing not only in straps and buckles but also in various patent medicines. Moreover, he had associated a good deal with Doctor Bindewald, so that, when the latter left Ferdinand, Baer figured that he knew how to prescribe epsom salts, quinine, and the various "teas"; as to whiskey the people themselves generally knew its medicinal qualities both before, during, and after any ailment. He was not known for intelligence, and, as a physician, he was of the type that reasoned that what would take effect on a horse would surely help a man. But in the case of Poschen it seems that the horse would not have recovered. Before Poschen died, on February 27, 1867, he somewhat incoherently spoke of money buried in Ferdinand; but it was not possible to obtain from him a designation of the place. When he had agreed with his wife to divide the money, he perhaps did so with a *metal* reservation; this may not have worried him. Poschen's body was brought to Ferdinand and buried in the cemetery, next to the southern edge of the center walk, and the marble obelisk, still standing, was erected over his grave. Meanwhile the store had been rented by Albert Th. Sondermann and Frances, his wife; Katharina Poschen had moved to Louisville.

For some time "Doctor" Baer carried his secret with him; in his imagination the size of the buried treasure grew in proportion to the length of thought of it, and the more it grew the more he deplored his inability to locate it. Finally he decided upon an uncanny way of forcing the secret from the dead Poschen. His ignorance of religion having kept pace with his ignorance of medicine, this modern Doctor Faust procured a copy of the *Sechstes und Siebentes Buch Mosis*; this he studied deeply, for by means of the necromantic process described therein he would compel the dead man to appear and to speak. So sure was he of the result, that he even revealed to someone the very night in which he would carry out his ghastly task. The "Doctor," his nerves keyed up to the unholy task, toward midnight entered the enclosure of the dead and went up the center walk toward the Poschen grave. Was it his imagination that made all the white tombstones grow bigger and move about excitedly as if in protest over the sacrilegious attempt upon a blessed grave? As the necromancer began the citation of the dead man, one wraith-like white figure suddenly stood to the one side of the tombstone and another figure to the other side. The apparition of two ghosts disconcerted him; he had expected but one. Then, too, instead of standing obediently for questioning, the two with outstretched arms moved toward the audacious wretch who called them forth at the ghost hour of the night. Panic-stricken, Baer ran from the horrible sight. In his fright missing the cemetery gate, yet intent upon the quickest way out, he thrust himself through the black locust hedge that inclosed the cemetery, ran across the church yard in back of the sanctuary, made straight for the priest's house, threw himself with full force against the locked two-winged entrance door, crashed through it, and called for Father Chrysostom. Awakened by the crash and the cry of distress, Father Chrysostom came downstairs. The terrified Baer, with clothes and body torn and bleeding from the steel-like thorns of the hedge, panted out his bold meddling with the spirit world, much like Goethe's *Zauberlehrling* (Sourcerer's Apprentice):

"Herr, die Not ist gross!	Oh, the foul deed's toll!
Die ich rief, die Geister,	Spirits, that I summoned.
Werd ich nun nicht los.	I cannot control.

Father Chrysostom merely answered: "You let the ghosts alone and the ghosts will let you alone. Now come and wash yourself."

Meanwhile the two ghosts, who had followed Baer to the hedge, sent after him a fiendish laugh—then folded their bed sheets and went to their homes in town. The man to whom Baer had spoken of his intentions in the graveyard had taken a friend into his confidence, and the two had hid behind the tombstone.

Next morning Father Chrysostom sent for Peter Gerber, a carpenter, to repair the door and lock. Gerber went to the old Poschen store for a lock. Frances Sondermann was working in the garden, and Gerber stopped to talk to her. As he leisurely rested his hand on a fence post which was loose in the ground, he noticed that the post struck something hard whenever he yanked it over to one side. "Frances, I believe there is something down there. Frances brought her spade and Peter Gerber dug down. Before long he unearthed a pot containing a large number of gold coins. Since Gerber and the Sondermanns did not think themselves entitled to the money, they informed *Frau* Katharina Poschen. It is not known whether *Frau* Poschen considered the one half of the amount as hers by reason of the division between herself and her former husband, but it is known that the Sondermanns and Peter Gerber, as finders, were given a portion of the money. Further, at that time Father Chrysostom, building the tower, was in sore need of money. One Saturday, at pay-off time, he told the workmen that he had no money to pay them, but that they should come again next week; he hoped that Providence would provide by that time. On the Saturday of the next week he told them that "a good woman" had brought him nearly $300. In all likelihood the sum—to be exact, $275—was the remaining half which *Frau* Poschen thought best to devote to a pious cause and which Father Chrysostom recorded as her contribution to the church tower.

Baer, who as a physician had not been taken seriously at Ferdinand and who had been the butt of many a joke, soon after this distressing experience left Ferdinand.

16. Bastardy (1868)

An interesting case of bastardy was heard before Esq. Brelage on last Wednesday. One Louise Miller swore that she had "loved not wisely but too well," a gay and festive chap by the name of Michael Striegel, and she brought the product of their illicit love in her arms—hunting a legal father. The young man was recognized in a bond of $200, to answer for having ruined the virtue and fair name of Louise.

XII.

STRANGE THINGS AND SIGNALS

"It's the Second Coming of Christ! It's the end of the world!" (XII.4.)

1. Magical Growing Barn in Morgantown (1898)

F. W. Fesler from Morgantown owns a growing barn. The man built the structure in 1891, using willow posts which he himself had cut to size. A year later he noticed that the posts had grown roots and that they were growing skyward, naturally taking the rest of the barn with them. Last spring he had to add a new floor, and now the building has two stories. If the posts continue to grow at this rate, Fesler will soon be able to claim proud ownership of a three-story barn.

2. The Snake Eggs

Grandma's grandpa was a blacksmith in the village of St. Peters. Since they lived on a farm, the meadows and woods around it were just great for the kids to roam and look for blackberries, hickory nuts and what have you. One time grandma—she was of course still little Gertrude—found some wonderful, soft eggs. She gathered them in her apron and took them to her grandpa. *"Schlangeneier!"* he exclaimed with a terrified look in his face. He knew that the mama snake would soon follow into the house. So he grabbed the snake eggs and quickly took them back to the woods. And the snake never showed up.

3. The Blacksmith Got Rabies

This blacksmith was a very strong man, and he was always everyone's friend. One day a rabid dog came in the shop and bit him. He knew he would go mad. This made him worry about the harm he might cause once his strength would be uncontrolled. So he quickly put some steel in the fire, made a couple of shackles, and chained himself to the anvil. Now he was sure that he wouldn't hurt anyone.

4. The End of the World

Grandma told me that this happened when she was still a child. There were three little girls who went for a stroll outside St. Peters, down near Brookville, on one of those winding, narrow and graveled roads. And as the threesome were happily walking along, they saw something strange in the sky, something they'd never seen before. They stopped and were awfully terrified. After a while the older girl found the answer, "See the two figures! It's the Holy Mother and Baby Jesus! It's the Second Coming of Christ! It's the end of the world! Let's kneel down and pray!" So right where they were, in the middle of that graveled road, they genuflected and prayed and never minded the sharp edges of the gravel cutting deep into their knees.

After a while—nothing had happened—they breathlessly ran to Grandparents Wissel. When they got there, knees all bloody, and told what they had seen, the big folks smiled and told them they had read in the paper that there was going to be a hot air ballon up with two people in the gondola.

5. Light Flashes from the Cemetery

At the Wampler family cemetery on Union Valley Road near Ellettsville some weird thing occurred that had the whole neighborhood scared. It seemed there was a certain time of the month that flashing, moving lights were seen at the burial place. People were becoming real fearful. Not so Grandfather James Wampler. He said, "That's all nonsense." But when the lights kept on coming at that certain time of the month, he decided to do something about it. So one night he placed himself at the cemetery to see what really happened. Sure enough, there it was again, that flashing light right off the stone wall. A fearless man he was, Grandfather Wampler, but this called for extra caution. So he moved very slowly toward the light. And when he got close to it, the mystery revealed itself to the brave man: On the stone wall there was a piece of colored glass from a broken bottle that reflected the light of the moon, but only at a certain angle.

6. Warts

Oh, I was so mad when I got one wart after another. Some people said you get 'em from holding toads and frogs in your hands, and that surely would have applied to me. I tried scratching them away till the blood came running, but to no avail.

One day, our neighbor told me that she could make them disappear if I'd only do what she says, but I'd have to come over to her house. That was good news. The next day after school I ran over to Frau Dinkel. She took a potato, put it on a clean white cloth and cut it in half. Then she rubbed my left hand with one of the halves murmering some German incantation that I couldn't quite make out. Once she had finished my left hand she threw the potato half she had used over the barn. Now came the same procedure for my right hand, and when she was done she hurled the second half of the potato over the barn.

"Well, my child," Frau Dinkel said, "your warts will be gone when the potato halves will have rotted. But, if you tell anybody what we did, it won't work."

A couple of months later I woke up one morning and my warts were all gone. Oh, was I happy. I ran over to Frau Dinkel's and showed her my hands. "Good, gone, all gone," she said, "the potato has rotted away, and you have kept our secret."

7. The Spinning Easter Sun

One thing my mother did every Easter morning, she would get up before sunrise. She swore by this. She'd stand out in the yard facing the east, and as the sun came up, she said it would spin, the sun would spin, it would go around and around, then it would go back the other way. She would stand out there in the yard and see it happen. She always told us this. She had to get up early in the morning and see the sun spin. I didn't believe the sun would spin. So one day she got me up and I watched it. I don't know if it was our imagination, but it sure looked like the sun was spinning.

8. The Skinned Horse

There was a family who had a horse that meant a great deal to them. One day they went out and found that the horse had died. After talking things over, they decided to skin the horse so they could at least save the hide. So, they skinned the horse and placed the hide in the smoke house.

The next morning when they went out—there stood the horse. It wasn't dead after all. Now, what would they do? The only thing was to sew the skin back on the horse. When they got ready to sew the skin back on the horse, they found that rats had eaten holes in the skin. This wouldn't do. So, they killed a sheep and patched the holes with sheep skin.

The horse lived for several years with its hide sewed back on. It grew enough wool on the sheepskin patches each year for the women to knit several pairs of stockings.

9. Signals in the Night

We lived out in the country, on a farm, and we were very close with the Millers. Every time one of theirs died, an unusual thing happened at our house.

This time it had snowed and nobody was out. Suddenly, a knock at the door. My brothers opened it. There was nobody. After a while it knocked again, loud and clear, three times. Again, my brothers opened the door and looked out, but they could see no trace in the snow. I got pretty scared and told mother, "We are not finishing the dishes tonight!?" "Oh, yes we are," mother said. The eerie feeling didn't go away. And, oh my God, before too long there was that same knock again. Now the brothers really went after it and checked all around the house inside and out. They came up with absolutely nothing.

Mother decided that something was indeed wrong. "Let us pray a Rosary," she said.

Next morning, the telephone rang. Frau Miller, we always called her Mutter Miller, had died during the night.

And then there was that summer night. We were all in the dining room. All of a sudden the dog started howling. He'd never done that before. We took him on the porch. That didn't help. We chased him away from the house. He wouldn't quit. We tied him to the barn. No luck, either. He just kept on howling all night long.

Next morning, Joe Miller died.

10. When the Painting Fell off the Wall

My great-aunt Bertha Martens lived in Indianapolis. They also had with them her father-in-law, and there was a big portrait of him hanging at the bottom of the stairway. One night, she walked down the stairs, and when she reached the landing, that painting fell off the wall and broke. The next night, at the same time, her father-in-law fell down the stairs and broke his neck. They picked him up right at the spot where the painting had crushed down.

11. Father Unverzagt's Ghost

The following is related by trust-worthy persons: Two men of St. Maurice parish (Decatur County) were staying with and waiting on a very sick neighbor. While they were chatting in an adjoining room about three o'clock a.m., they saw Father Unverzagt—who was supposedly at the Alexian Hospital in St. Louis—standing at the door facing them dressed in his cassock and black traveling cap which he usually wore about the house. That morning one of the men had business to attend to in Greensburg and, by the way, called on the priest there to tell him of what they had seen. That same morning a few hours before, the priest had received a telephone call from St. Louis, that Father Unverzagt had died at three o'clock a. m., and enquiring about the funeral arrangement.

12. ESP in Paris

You may not believe in ESP. But I do. Because it happened to me. In Paris.

After my unforgettable year as an exchange student in America, I took the S.S. *United States* from New York to LeHavre. A beautiful ship it was and so powerful that it crossed the ocean in three days. It was her second voyage to Europe, in the summer of 1952.

What a nice coincidence: my friend Paul Kaiser—we had known each other from Kindergarten days in Stuttgart—was on the same sailing and also headed for home. Given the simple geographical fact that we had to travel by way of Paris, which neither of us had ever "experienced" before, we were immediately agreed that we would spend three days in the dream city (of all bachelors).

The last night aboard ship we had a grand time until the wee hours of the morning when the last pianist quit playing—and the girls were back in the safekeeping of their mothers. The boat train took us to Paris. We found an inexpensive hotel right across the station from which we eventually would catch our train to Stuttgart.

Around noon, we had hardly arrived in our room, I suddenly felt dead tired that I told Paul I had to lie down and take a nap. "That's ok," said Paul, "I'll do a little exploring in the meantime." I took off my shoes, stretched out on my back, and was gone. The next thing I remember is that Paul shook me and woke me up: "Come on, do you want to sleep forever? We're in Paris, man, the town is fabulous!" "What time is it?" I wanted to know. "Twelve o' clock noon," said Paul. "Well, so I slept about ten minutes," I said. "Add 24 hours," said Paul, "sorry, I had to wake you, but I really was beginning to worry that something was wrong with you." I had never slept that long in my life. Paul started to tell about his explorations and where he would like to take me. But when I got up and stuck my head in cold water, the idea of "experiencing Paris" vanished totally. Paul first thought I was kidding when I told him that I would catch the next train to Stuttgart. When I said that I was serious, he thought I was out of my mind; he simply could not understand my change of plans. Neither could I. All I knew was that I had to go home as fast as possible. I gave him two bucks to pay for my share of the room, grabbed my suitcase and dashed over to the train station. The Orient Express was just ready to leave. Excellent. I could always buy a ticket on the train.

If you would ask me what I saw as the train headed toward Strassburg and then through the Black Forest, I couldn't tell you. All I remember is that at one point a friendly Austrian conductor opened the door to the compartment, which I had all by myself, and wished me *Gute Reise* (Have a good trip). He didn't ask me for my ticket, and I didn't think about it either.

As the Orient Express approached the Stuttgart-West station, which was not a stop for fast trains, it suddenly slowed down and came to a complete halt. I could almost see my parents house. In a flash I knew what to do. And in less than five seconds, I am sure, I was out of the train, running across the tracks and on to the street. No streetcar was in sight. But there came a car. It stopped immediately. "Can you take me to Bebelstrasse, it's an emergency." "Of course," was the answer, and within a few minutes we were at the house. I ran up the stairs. My father opened the door and he had tears in his eyes. "What's wrong, Papa?" "Go see Mama, she is in bed." I rushed to the parents' bedroom. There she was, sleeping peacefully. "Mama, you hear me? I am back!" Her eyes opened briefly, and she raised her hands toward me and said with a little smile: "Eberhard, you're back. Now everything is fine." These were the last words she spoke in her life. She fell back into her coma for another four weeks until the Lord called an end to her silent struggle with cancer.

When I met Paul again and told him the story, he said: "It may not be appropriate to say it, but I say it anyway: It was good that you went nuts in Paris."

XIII.

WITCHES AND THE DEVIL

". . . the man who was winning had horses hooves instead of feet . . ." (XIII.18.)

1.-12. The Miniature Lady and other Witches in Ferdinand

1. Apples

As small children, we in our family were severely warned not ever to eat anything that anyone gave us to eat, but always to bring it home. One day while visiting an aunt, her neighbor lady came by and, seeing me, came through the gate to me and gave me four little, red apples. She began a conversation with my aunt, then—noting that I was still standing there holding my apples—urged me to go on and eat them. When I said that I had to bring everything home and share with my brothers, she said I could have more if I would go with her to her home and pick them up. Again I declined saying I must hurry home because my mother would be timing me and would suspect I was loitering along the way. Thanks anyway.

This woman was what I always called a "miniature" lady, always dressed in a long, black satin dress with a stiff high neck and long sleeves and a black hat that had been style about twenty years before that. She also wore high buttoned shoes and looked so different that I wasn't about to go home alone with her. Her small piercing eyes were frightening to all small children.

When I came home and gave mother the apples, and told her where I got them, she took them to my dad who was reading in the kitchen. She pointed to the apples, mentioned the lady's name and pointing to the stove and asked, "Shall I?" Dad nodded, so mother opened the stove lid and threw them in. There was a sudden piercing scream from the apples as their skins burst. (I can still hear the sound.) Mom and Dad exchanged knowing looks and smiled. I did not go back to get any more apples.

2. Dad Didn't Say "Yes"

Some other time this same lady came to our house with a basket on her arm. She said she wanted to share her goods with the poor and that we were worthy of that name. She walked to the table and placed on it a small box of Rolled Oats, about a dime's worth of sugar in a sack and two oranges. Then she turned to Dad and told him she had a few suits of her husband's, underwear and other of his clothes and wondered if Dad could wear them. Remembering the man, Dad replied that her husband was much taller and larger than Dad was, therefore they might not fit him. However, he told her that Mother was handy at sewing, she could make underwear for the little boys. I noticed Dad had avoided using the word "yes" which one should never use in the presence of a witch, for by it he would "give over his will to her."

The following Sunday—or soon after—the parish priest told of a poor man who was offered clothing by a kind person, refused to accept it and instead called the person a witch. The priest berated him for treating such a good woman in such a shabby way. Dad might have called her a witch in his mind, but he had not actually called her that name. Practically, all the town's people were suspicious of her, for she was often seen bringing two oranges to the home where one was sick.

3. Stomach Fever Making the Round

Shortly after that there was a peculiar epidemic of some kind of stomach ailment which the doctor couldn't seem to cure. He called it "Magen-Fieber" (=stomach fever). When asked what caused it, he answered, "You have too many old women running around here."

One case of this fever was another aunt of mine who lived in the same neighborhood as the "Lady in Black." She had six children and couldn't very well be spared, but she felt so bad that she went to bed. Her husband, who took time off from his job, decided to perform a ritual called "Brauchen" which was supposed to break the witches' spell. This ritual consisted of tying a silk thread around a raw egg and place the egg into the "ash box" in the kitchen range among the hot ashes and cinders and closing the box. If after a few minutes the thread had not burned, then that was a sure sign of witchery. He was to pronounce some words while performing the ritual. I once asked my mother what these words were. She answered it was a prayer to the Holy Trinity begging protection from the works of evil. She then recited the prayer for me, but I didn't learn it, it was in German. A few moments after performing the ritual my uncle was in deep trouble. There was a sudden explosive "bang"—the ash box door flew open, the ash box flew out, a great flame of fire set the curtains at the windows ablaze and Uncle had all he could do to put out the fire. At the same time, my aunt felt a sharp flash of severe pain and then was completely relieved. She got up and came into the kitchen and asked her husband, "Was mahsch du?" (=Whatcho doin'?). All he could answer was, "Ach, sei still!" (=Oh, be quiet!). The egg had burst, but the thread had not burned.

116

4. Mother Turned to St. Anthony for Help

One religious minded woman in my mother's neighborhood corrected my mother's thinking by telling Mom the best cure for stomach fever was to go to the shrine of St. Anthony, light a candle, and pray an "Our Father," "Hail Mary," and "Glory be to the Father" five times for the intercession of St. Anthony against the powers of the devil. After she heard that, Mom nominated me to do the praying. When my teacher told us we should always make a visit to Jesus in the Blessed Sacrament before we pray before any statue, I added this visit to the Blessed Sacrament, prayed an Act of Contrition to clear the "track", then I consulted St. Anthony.

When I was in the fourth grade, my dad came down with a stomach problem. Dad had never been sick, so Mom gave me a nickel—at that time a nickel was the offering for a candle. She told me to go to the church at recess time (10:00) and light a candle for Dad. That morning we had to stay in at recess because we didn't know our lesson. I didn't get to carry out Mom's orders until 11:45. Then I hurried to church. Mom had a strong faith in my prayers. She had asked Dad at 10:00 o'clock if he could eat. He hadn't had breakfast yet. But no, he couldn't eat. For the next hour she asked again and again, and at 11:45 Dad came to the kitchen and said, "Now, I can eat!" After that, St. Anthony was our doctor.

5. Witchcraft and Bad Books—Notably One

A Benedictine Father was visiting a sick child in our house. He asked Mom what was wrong with the child. Mom answered, "Wahrscheinlich Hexerei!" (=Probably witchcraft!). "Ach nein, es gibt keine Hexerei" (=Oh no, there is no such thing as witchcraft), answered he. Then Mom said, "Es gibt aber boese Leut', was schlechte Buecher lesen!" (=But there are evil persons that read bad books). "Ja, ja," said the priest, "Das ist die Wahrheit" (=That is the truth).

The bad books Mom was referring to was *one* particular book called "The Sixth and Seventh Books of Moses." I have seen the book advertised in a catalog selling strange signs, symbols, etc., of an occult nature. Mom warned us never to read the book —should we ever see it. It has strange drawing power for the inquisitive. I have never seen one.

117

6. Over Thorns and over Bushes

One evening in preparing for a "Versammlung" (= meeting) of witches, a woman read from "The Book" a few words and then was gone on her broom. The words were: "Ueber Dornen und ueber Strauch" (= over thorns and over bushes). The husband, being curious, tried to repeat her words, but they came out: "Durch Dornen und durch Strauch" (=through thorns and through bushes). He found her, but she hardly recognized him. He was a sight.

7. The Spooked Horse

Now this story I heard a young man tell to my parents over sixty years ago. The young man was on his way to see his girl friend. He was riding a horse along a dark country road, when his horse suddenly was spooked. The horse snorted, reared up and started up the embankment, before he finally came under the young man's control. At that moment, a billy goat came galloping by with a woman as a rider. Naturally, the story came out, witches ride goats on their way to their meetings.

8. Step Crossing

In addition to "Brauchen" there was another way we could use to break away from "Hexerei," and that was step crossing the foot prints of the "Hex'" (=witch). This is done by stepping into her right foot print with your left foot and into her left foot print with your right foot, thus making a cross over her tracks.

Mom tried it to an old lady who was on her way to church. Mom was still small but knew about the trick. She tried it three times, and each time the lady stood still and couldn't move. The third time, the lady waited for Mom and told her, "You walk ahead o' me now and hurry on, or you'll be late for school!"

9. Another Step Crossing

When my brother was a teenager, he discovered another "Hex'" we hadn't suspected. He had been to early Mass one Sunday in the summertime and was headed for home with a cousin who lived in the same neighborhood as the first "Lady in Black" did. The two boys were standing on a country road, when a woman we all knew, in fact she was a not too distant relative, came by. She passed the two boys, then walked along the dusty road—leaving deep tracks. My brother, who remembered the trick with tracks and was easily tempted, began step-crossing her tracks after she was some distance away. She immediately stood still, then she turned around. By the time she could see him, my brother had walked aside some distance and was throwing stones at a telephone post in another direction. Since my brother was no longer crossing her tracks, she was released and so she went on. Again my brother did the same thing and then once more. After the third time the woman ran from the road into a field and then she ran on toward her home. My brother was convinced.

10. Three Babies with a Weak Neck

Another uncle and aunt of mine had the misfortune of having three babies in succession who had another strange syndrome. These babies never became strong enough to hold up their heads and died shortly after birth. Those were the days before Ferdinand had a funeral parlor. The dead were "laid out" for viewing in the home. My mother was present at the home some time before the funeral, when one of the neighbor ladies came in. She was also always dressed in a long black dress and a small black hat. After viewing the baby and "making over it" she turned and, noticing the drapes at the window, she took the material between thumb and forefinger and, rubbing it, asked, "What kind of material is this?" as if she didn't know. Someone answered. Then she turned and entered another room to talk to my aunt. There on the table lay a piece of material my aunt had gotten to make a new dress. The lady in black again went through the ritual of rubbing the material and asking what kind of material it was. By this time, a "light" went on in my uncle's mind and he knowingly winked at his wife. What they did after that, I never found out, but the next baby was perfectly healthy.

11. Hold Tight and Cut in Two

Our neighbor told us of another case where a "witch" was captured. A farmer in the vicinity was having bad luck with sick animals. One of his friends, who was "in the know," told him he could do something about it if he was willing to do the thing he could tell him. The farmer was willing, so his friend told him to enter the stable quietly, i n t h e d a r k, right after midnight, and go to his sick horse and feel all over the horse's back and sides. If his hand came upon something, even if it was just a bit of hay or straw, he should grasp it tightly, he repeated, "be sure to hold it tight, then cut it in two with a sharp knife." The farmer did as his friend suggested. A short time afterward the two met. The friend, after looking strangly at the farmer, asked, "What happened to you?" The farmer replied, "I did as you said, but I forgot to hold tight." The farmer looked as if he had been in a cat fight—all scratched up.

12. How Mom Tried to Protect Us from Witches and Evil

There were cases whispered about, lots of them. Mom told us that a "witch" can get a "hold" of you in two ways. First, if you eat what she gives you to eat, you will be in her fingers. Secondly, if you consent to anything she asks you to do or use the word "yes"—which is a word of consent. So we were very careful to observe these rules.

Powerful additional protection came from the St. Benedict medal. Mother had one fastened over every window and door to keep all evil spirits out. She also had one pinned to each of her children.

13. The Butter Witch

Just east of the little town of Giro (Buena Vista, Gibson County) was once a German settlement that strongly believed in witchcraft. When anything went wrong in the daily routine of the housewife, she was certain that a neighbor was angry and getting revenge by "bewitching" the particular task.

Mrs. Brown had been laboring over her large wooden churn for hours, and yet no butter. Turning to her husband, dozing by the fireside, she quickly exclaimed, "Someone has a foot in my cream, so I'll find out who the witch is this time!" So Mrs. Brown hurriedly heated an iron and dropped it into the contents of the churn, thus burning out the foot that was in her cream. It was only a matter of seconds that she had a generous supply of nice yellow butter.

The next day, Mrs. Brown was making some calls in the neighborhood and stopped for a chat with Mrs. Jones. There sat Mrs. Jones in great pain with a badly burned foot. So Mrs. Brown turned homeward, happy and satisfied, for she had found the witch that had had her foot in the butter.

14.-16. The Witch of St. Peters and the Devil, too

14. Cats

In the tiny little village of St. Peters, south of Brookville, there lived this very old and peculiar woman. She was so strange in her ways that the folks around there thought she might really be a witch. One of the things that seemed to confirm it was the fact that she had the whole house full of cats. After a while even her husband couldn't take it any longer, especially since they were crawling all over him in bed at night. So he built him a wooden wall in the middle of the bed. And whenever a cat showed up on his side he threw it over that wall to his wife. Nobody heard that she got mad at him for that. Well, 'cause witches don't mind having cats thrown at them.

15. Hair

One day in 1905, grandma's cousin Catherine walked by the witch's house and the witch was there and startled her. She took Catherine's hand and went over her arm and shoulder and to her head and her hair. *"Du hast schoenes Haar,"* the witch said. The next morning when Catharine combed her hair, that whole side which the witch had stroked fell out. The poor girl's mother then combed her so that the bald side would be covered also. The following morning when Catharine combed her hair again, the rest fell out, too. So she had to wear a wig all her life.

16. The Priest and the Devil

Grandma in St. Peter's knew this priest well. He was a virtuous and pious man, and he was so successful living up to his responsibility, namely saving the souls of his parishioners. He spent hour after hour in the confession box bringing the Lord's forgiveness to the sinners and giving them their assignments for doing penance. Grandmother said that the church was always filled with people who respected and loved him dearly.

Now who do you think would despise a man like that? Nobody in the world, except one—the devil. Because this priest really kept the souls entrusted to him out of the devil's clutches. One night it happened that the devil came to pay him back. It must have been awful for the good priest, for his hair turned all white, and the devil scratched him from hand to shoulder, leaving him with a scar that showed for the rest of his life.

17. The House the Devil Built

Over by Schnellville in Dubois County lived a hardworking farmer and his wife who was never satisfied. She always nagged her husband to do better, but the crops would fail, and the livestock would die in one bad turn of events after another. All she really wanted, she would tell him, was a house as nice as her neighbor's, and he was a poor excuse of a husband if he could not provide this.

One day, after a particularly harsh tongue lashing, the man sat dejected out by the barn. Who should walk up, and begin a conversation, but the devil himself. He offered to help the man get his house, the finest house in the neighborhood—in return, of course, for his soul. Hell can't be worse than her nagging, thought the man, so he struck the bargain.

From this time on, everything started to go well. The farmer had a bumper crop, and the money started rolling in. He started work on his house, the finest house in the neighborhood. One day, when it was nearly finished, all but for one piece of the roof, who should return, but the devil—to claim the man's soul. Only now, the man wasn't quite so sure about what he had done. So he thought on it, and figured that since he already had most of the house finished, he could do the rest without the devil's help, and he reneged on the bargain with many a sign of the cross. The devil shook his head and walked away.

The man roofed the house as fast as he could, and he and his wife moved in. That same night a terrible storm came up and tore the roof completely off. After that, no matter how many times the man put a roof on the house, something always happened to it. It never had a roof, and could never be lived in.

P. S. Grandpa John Gress always insisted that this was a true story. The house stood over by Schnellville, a lesson for all to see. Only he never took us to see it, though he always said he would someday.

18. Playing Cards with a Stranger

Around the turn of the century, when Grandpa John Gress got to be a teenager, he wanted to see the world. So he traded his native Celestine for the road and the freight trains and the life of an itinerant farm hand. Once, while working on a farm in Illinois, a group of hired hands played cards at night after the work was done. That night, a stranger came to join their game. The stranger was winning big. During the tense moments of the game, young John dropped a card. When he leaned down to pick it up, he noticed that the man who was winning had horses hooves instead of feet. John hastily folded his hand and ended his gambling days.

XIV.

MISHAPS, ACCIDENTS AND TRAGEDIES

"The Lady and the Skinny Dippers" (XIV.2.)

1. The Blackberry Cobbler

Grandma Ruhe was a very large German woman and she wore a size 9 man's shoe. One day the men in the neighborhood got together to thresh at the Ruhe Farm. The wives, of course, did all of the cooking for the day—and there were many hungry men to feed.

Early in the morning, Grandma Ruhe went out to pick blackberries for a cobbler. Much work went into this cobbler with washing the berries, rolling out the dough and baking in a wood stove. She then carried the cobbler out to the porch to cool. She set it down on an old bench. But—ouch!—she stepped on the dog's tail with her size 9 man's shoe. The old farm dog, being so rudely awakened from his nap under the bench, immediately jumped up and turned the bench over and spilled the large cobbler upside down on the porch floor. Grandma hollered, *"Mein Gott, du verdammter Hund!"* (My God, you damn dog!) and with her large shoe and one movement swept the dog completely off the porch and into the air—at least 20 foot! She promptly swept the cobbler back into the pan and served it later for dinner to the threshers!—*Guten Appetit!*

2. The Lady and the Skinny Dippers (1879)

Down in Posey County. . . several boys were bathing in the creek as Mrs. Dickson of Marrs Township drove her team across the bridge. The noise in the water below so excited the horses that they shied and threw her from the seat and she found herself in the water with several nude young men.

3. "Stonewall" Watermann of St. Phillip, Posey County (1880)

Herr Watermann, St. Phillip, was unable to slow his team of horses which were running away. Near despair, he was able to steer them straight into the wall of the St. Phillip church yard. Although he was thrown across the wall and remained unconscious for two days, he now boasts proudly of stopping the "wild beasts."

4. Gunpowder

Uncle John Joshua Wampler was working in a factory that made gunpowder. They had big silos full of it. One day he went into a shed to shovel gunpowder. He walked in there with a lighted cigarette. He mustn't have been quite with it that day, because he even dropped it on that stuff. Of course, it immediately went up in flames, a whole bushel or more. And he said it took him quite a while to stomp it out with his foot.

5. More about Smoking and Shooting (1880)

Watch your pockets! Henry Maus emptied his pipe and, as customary, put it into his coat pocket. Still hot, the pipe made contact with a few bullets which were in the bottom of the pocket. The resulting explosion tore the coat and vest off Mr. Maus and left a flesh wound in his hip.

John Harp was in a hurry last week; instead of walking the road he thought to save time by scaling a fence. This action, somehow, triggered a revolver in his pants pocket. He now has to watch the world go by from his bed where he is confined with a hole in his leg.

6. Narrow Escape at the Fette Mill in New Alsace

In the basement engine room we had a grindstone on which the mill picks were sharpened. Many times as a schoolboy after school, the writer had to take his turn cranking the grindstone. At this point the reader might think: Why not run the grindstone by power and obviate all that tiresome turning of a crank? Well, previous to the writer's participation in the mill activities, an accident took place, as was often told. Older brother Nicholas decided to turn the grindstone by a pulley and belt from the main engine shaft, which was six inches in diameter, and while he was grinding, the belt came off and wrapped up on the engine shaft. Brother stepped into the flywheel pit to unwrap the belt and had it almost free, when the belt caught his hands and wrapped up again and pulled him off his feet and spun him around with the engine shaft, like a pinwheel, his feet swinging out. He knocked off the grindstone frame, which was spiked to one of the mill posts.

His older brother George just happened to pass through the engine room when that was happening. He saw it, and quickly stopped the engine. When father saw the mill stopping he rushed downstairs, and together they freed Nicholas. His shoes and stockings were off his feet, and father carried him unconscious to the house. He soon revived. Fortunately he had no broken bones, and apparently no after-effects. After that father allowed no more belt drive on the grindstone. So we had to crank it by hand.

7. An Unfortunate Mistake in Maysville (1890)

Because of his poorly thought-out actions, the German farmer George Zimmer from Maysville incurred great damages. Acting on a neighbor's advice, Zimmer coated his eight cows with mineral oil in order to free them from vermin. However, he then made a big mistake by branding one of the cows. Within seconds the cow was covered with flames, and, being in excruciating pain, it ran wildly about the fenced-in area, whereby the other cows also caught on fire and ran wildly for shelter in the stalls—which were subsequently also set ablaze and which burned down along with the haystack. The vermin surely perished, but so did the cows, and to top it all off, the farmer received serious burns from attempting to put out the fires.

8. The Sudden Death of Jacob Wertz (1876)

. . . Mr. Wertz, 64, was on his way home from Edinburg just at the time that Mr. Wm. Gutsinger's home was burning. Discovering the fire from a distance he drove in the greatest haste to the scene of conflagration and began to assist in snatching the household goods from the flames, but in a few minutes he sank down, saying: "I have done all I can." He was helped to a lounge that had been carried out of the house, on which he rested himself for a few minutes. When feeling somewhat recovered he got up and started toward the house, made a few steps and again sank down and expired immediately. . .

9. A Gruesome Accident in Posey County

A solid Posey County German lost his life in a terrible way.

. . . Herr Wilhelm Hofmann, a highly esteemed German of Parker's Settlement in this County, where his brewery is and where he served as postmaster and trustee of Robinson Township, had gone to Evansville on foot, having left his buggy at home on account of the bad weather. Around 2:30 p.m. he had finished his business and started on his way home. Somewhere on the road two of his neighbors on a gig, Herr Wilhelm Huf and Herr Heinrich Daub, happened to meet him and invited him to come along. He accepted gratefully and took his seat between the two men. When they were about 1.5 miles beyond Farre's Place, suddenly the gig's tongue broke and the seat fell forward. While Huf and Daub fell off to the left and the right, Hofmann, from his seat in the middle, landed under the hoofs of the horses. The piece that had broken off the gig's tongue was pushed right into Hofmann's throat. The horses, frightened by the breaking of the tongue and the gig's fall, ran away, dragging Hofmann with them for about twenty feet before stopping. Huf and Daub were unhurt, but Hofmann was critically hurt at his head and other parts of the body, and he was unconscious. They took him home, where he died about midnight. . .

10. The Hulman Brothers of Terre Haute

Terre Haute was a young town of 6,000 people when Francis Hulman established a wholesale grocery business here in 1850. He was the second member of his family to emigrate to America from Lingen-on-the-Ems, Germany; his brother Diedrich had earlier settled in Cincinnati. Although Francis lived and worked here briefly, he was eager for a greater challenge. The Hulman family had been in the mercantile trade for generations in Europe, and his keen business sense told him the growing community on the Wabash River would be a prime wholesale distribution point.

After a trip to Terre Haute, he wrote an excited letter to his brother Herman. Dated November 10, 1849, it detailed his plans for the new venture and urged Herman to join him "in this free and happy America; where ignorance and poverty do not reign, and well-being and enlightenment do."

At first Herman was reluctant to leave his family, but ultimately the promise of freedom and opportunity in the New World won him over. He arrived in Terre Haute in 1854, at the age of 23, and went to work in Francis Hulman's wholesale store. As sales increased steadily, Francis decided he could afford a visit to his homeland. He died when the ship burned at sea, leaving his brother to manage alone. . .

11. A Sad Day in Schnellville, Dubois County (1883)

. . . On September 10, 1883, a man by the name of Doctor J. P. Salb married Margaret Betz. . . Doctor Salb was having a well dug in his backyard. Of course, back then, these wells had to be dug completely by hand and tool. After the well was dug about twelve feet deep, the men hit rock. Then they had to use dynamite to break through. This was fairly common practice. After they'd dynamite, they'd wait until they thought it was safe to go back into the well. Then, as always, the loose dirt and rock had to be put into a bucket with a rope attached for the men above to pull it up.

Having put in a hard day, the men called it quits and decided to pick it up the next day. The first man to go back down into the well the next day was a twenty-two year old man named Aegidius Schnell. Before anyone knew what was happening, he was overcome by fumes. The men above called out, but there was no response. Aegidius was followed by Johannes Fitterer, 27, who went down into the well to find out what was wrong with his friend. Johannes was also overcome. Finally, Matt Neu, also a young man, went to help both of them, but he, too, was overcome by fumes. By this time the men who had gathered above realized what was happening. It all must have happened very fast, and I cannot imagine the horror they must have gone through as they frantically tried to help the men below.

Finally it was decided to try to burn the gas out of the well. Local people have said that even today when wells are dug, and especially after using dynamite, it is common practice to light a fire and lower it into the hole. If there is gas (methane) in the well, the fire will go out. You have to keep on trying until the gas is burned out, until the flame stays lit. Only then is it considered safe to go down.

In this case the men burned papers and carefully lowered them down into the well in order to consume the toxic fumes and also so they could get the men out.

By the time all three men were pulled out, what was feared the most was true. Two of the three were dead. Aegidius and Johannes had inhaled what later was believed to have been methane, a deadly underground gas found occasionally in this area. They accidentally created a deadly pocket of fumes when they dynamited. Without knowing it, they had in a sense dug their own grave. . . Fortunately, Matt survived. . . He most probably covered his mouth with a handkerchief, and that may have saved him. . .

Schnell and Fitterer were both buried in the Schnellville Church Cemetery. A double tombstone. . . marks their gravesite and serves as a grim reminder of that tragic day in September of 1883. . .

After the accident, the well was filled with dirt and Doctor Salb moved to Jasper. . . The house proper was burned beyond repair on April 19, 1989, when a skillet on the stove accidentally caught fire. . .

This property has had its share of tragedies related to fire and fumes. It's somewhat ironic that Schnellville's new fire station is being built on this site.

XV.

RIGHTS AND WRONGS

"*. . . the court-house and jail were surrounded by a large and noisy crowd . . .*"
(XV.4.)

1. Eli Schoppell on Jury Duty (1866)

In 1866, James Johns, railroad agent at Gosport (Owen County), was killed one dark night by Willis McMinimy. This was a cold-blooded, premeditated murder for the purpose of robbery. McMinimy was a drayman, and was trusted implicitly by the agent, Johns, who had no suspicion of him, and was thus easily killed by being beaten to death with a short bar of iron in the hands of McMinimy while they were alone at the office of the Louisville, New Albany & Chicago Railroad at Gosport, late one very dark night. Mc Minimy was arrested, tried, and convicted on purely circumstantial evidence, of a very strong character, however, and sentenced to the State Prison for life. The jury was unanimous on first ballot. On the question of guilt, every vote read "guilty." On the question of punishment, six were for hanging, six for imprisonment for life. All night the question was argued. One by one they changed until at daylight the jury stood eleven for death, and only one, Eli Schoppell, still stood firm for imprisonment. He was a German, a man of sound sense, honest and conscientious. . . In his broken American he argued as best he could, beset on all sides by the other eleven. He listened to first one and then another; argument after argument poured in upon him, until at last he grew desperate. He stood erect upon his feet; his countenance expressed the most intense feeling possible to the human face; great drops of sweat broke out and stood on his face and forehead. "Shentlemens," he broke out, "Shentlemens, I can not talk, but I can feel. We all believe this man guilty; in mine heart I feels he is guilty, but nopody sees him kill the man; maybe somepody else do it. If we sends dis man to State Prison for life and some time it is found out that somepody else kill the man, den dis man come out, he be not dead. But if we hangs this man and it some time be found out he did not kill the man, den this man be dead, and," putting his hand solemnly upon his own head, "den de blood of this man be on our hets. I—I can not do it." The effect of that speech was electrical. The intense earnestness of the German, with his imperfect speech, his strong convictions of right, and the terrible consequences of a possible mistake in their verdict was such that at once a verdict of guilty was written and the punishment fixed at imprisonment for life in the State Prison.

2. Don' Let 'Cherself Be Fool'd (1870)

A certain German by the name of Robert Schwaner, a resident of "Nowhere" or "Everywhere," visited Huntingburg last Friday evening during his whirlwind world tour by foot and took up quarters with Herr

Berger at the Union Hotel. Dead tired as our Robert was, he strengthened himself quickly under the care of the "kitchenly" queen, in that he didn't even come close to abstinence at supper, but rudely dug right in instead, as if it were a matter of taking over the world. This had its good results afterwards. Robert felt better and regained the power of speech. He felt himself so at home that he expressed the wish to buy a farm in the area because, according to his own declaration, he had a lot—a whole lot of money: the biggest trouble for him was getting change for $500 bills, the smallest that he had. Naturally, one can use such people: they are so hard to find these days. And certainly it's the duty of every well-meaning citzen, for whom the prosperity of his beloved home town is close to his heart, to welcome such people with open arms and to help them with their plans; because such people can be of more use to a city (which wants to grow with yet to be layed railroads) and to the surrounding area than can a poor pauper who wants to feast on the fat of the land.

This was then also soon to be felt in our not so very big city, and after a lot of thinking back and forth, someone recalled that Herr Friedrich Wiesmann, residing about three miles south of here, was willing to trade his farm for gold, silver, or greenbacks. Herr Christian Fuchs, part owner of the local Bretz Brewery, took it upon himself to take our Moneybags as well as Herr Landgrebe—who was to be helpful in these dealings—to the location and site. Having arrived there, they found that Herr Wiesmann lent a willing ear to the dealings. And since Robert was no miser the negotiations quickly turned into an agreement. After taking on refreshments, the three already named gentlemen along with the Wiesmann family went to Huntingburg in order to have the deed—necessary in today's so disdainful world—drawn up by the hands of the respectable E. R. Brundick, justice of the peace. The latter immediately went to work with all the power of his office, and visibly, under his industrious hands, the papers soon took on the appearance of legal documents. Meanwhile, our land speculator felt the need to "wet his whistle" and proceeded to the barroom right next door, owned by Herr Brandenstein—who constantly keeps good liquors and good beer on hand for thirsting people—and downed a brandy. After this operation was completed, he hurried out and, in his haste, forgot to pay—which, under the circumstances (since Herr Brandenstein has his liquor licence and has to pay for his bitters too), could not be considered a very nice thing to do. Only, Schwaner still had some hurried business: he left—and didn't come back again. He had forgotten that Judge Brundick had the featherpen at work for him; he forgot the land he was buying; he forgot the silk dress he had promised Frau Wiesmann; and, last but not least, he forgot the bed and breakfast fees he owed Herr Berger. And he ran through the streets and mumbled this pretty song to himself:

"Now we are forever parted,
and we'll never see each other in this life."

His song was so touching for the concerned parties that they wanted to catch this moneygrubber again in order to have at least a memento from him. A general foxhunt occurred, and with the tune and text of:

"Du, du, liegst mir im Herzen. . . "

Herr Berger was lucky enough to meet up with him in the brewery of Herr Nic Schmidt. Herr Berger received as an eternal keepsake a really nice pocketknife, and the "others" had the pleasure of revenge.

3. Your Honor (1870s)

Before the turn of the century Oldenburg had Justices of the Peace. It was many hours of travel by horse and buggy to the county seat, so minor disputes and lesser infractions of the law were more conveniently settled by the JP Court. This was periodically held in the council chambers of the Town Hall. This story occurred sometime in the 1870s.

On this warm summer evening Justice Fisse was hurrying along the brick sidewalks toward the Town Hall carrying a leather case bulging with record books and papers. It promised to be a long evening for he had a full docket. Perhaps, he thought, as he walked along, it would be a good idea to refresh himself a bit before starting, so he stopped in at the saloon close by. Joe Hoelker had a reputation for serving a good lunch at the bar.

As anticipated, the session proved to be long and tiring. At dusk extra lamps were lit. The open windows offered little relief from the warm night. But finally the last case was now in progress, a good thing, too, for by now the JP had grown tired and drowsy and could scarcely keep his eyes open.

The defendant, now summing up his case, noticed the Judge's eyes drooping and head nodding, approached the bench and shook the Judge's arm while in conclusion saying, ". . . and so now wake up, Your Honor, and decide the case."

4. Evansville Sheriff "Gus" Lemcke and the Riot (1880)

One Saturday night during the campaign of 1880 the democrats and republicans of Evansville turned out at the same hour in separate torchlight processions. At the windup a shooting scrape occurred between a Kentucky democrat and a colored man. The Kentuckian, badly wounded, was cared for by friends, while the darky, with a bullet in his head, was taken to the lockup by the city police.

By midnight a howling mob of "law-abiding American citizens" had gathered to hang "the nigger." At two o'clock in the morning the chief of police came to the jail, where, as sheriff of Vanderburg County, I had my residence, and asked that for safety's sake I take the prisoner off his hands, and as the wounded darky feared the threats of the mob, and begged for protection from a republican official and the strong walls of the county jail, I complied with the request without waiting for a command from court. After obtaining from the chief a squad of the city force to assist me during the remainder of the night, I sent for Mr. Keller, proprietor of a nearby gun store, and provided myself with a stock of guns and ammunition.

By this time the court-house and jail were surrounded by a large and noisy crowd who, in their blind frenzy, threatened to storm the jail and take the prisoner from me. I therefore deemed it advisable to remove my family to a place of safety up town, in which undertaking I was aided by friends who had left their beds to come to my aid.

When, after hours of anxious vigil, daylight came and the judges of the two courts and the mayor of the city had appeared on the scene, we, with the cooperation of many influential and peace-loving citizens, labored hard with the mob, counseling peace and submission to the law. But it was all in vain; the leaders wanted a hanging and they would have it.

With the crowd increasing and becoming more determined I now began to prepare for enforcing the law by assembling a *posse comitatus*. I swore in fifty prominent citizens, who readily responded and put themselves under my command. A number of them were members of the bar and staunch and courageous men, who stood ready to avert a calamity which would have proven a disgraceful blot on the fair fame of the city and the state.

As the day advanced reliable information reached me that there was on the road a large company of men on horseback from Mt. Vernon, Posey County, where the previous year the mob had hung five negroes on the same tree. They were cutting the wires as they advanced, and the outlook became promising for a hanging or a killing in good earnest.

While I busied myself with the strategic distribution and direction of my forces I spied a Mr. Peelar in his buggy coming around the courthouse corner behind a trotter of great speed. No sooner did he come in sight than it occurred to me that here was a possible means of escape out of the dilemma of threatened war.

Major Mattison, a brave veteran, who, when a prisoner of war in the Confederacy, had tunneled out of Libby Prison, and who had, through the night and morning hours, given staunch and valuable support as my main lieutenant, followed as I bolted through the crowd. At a wink to Peelar he drove out of hearing of the mob into another street, where I made a demand on him for his rig. Not, however, until I gave him my personal guarantee of a thousand dollars, in case of loss or damage to the outfit, did he surrender. In an adjoining alley, and out of sight of the crowd, the major at once mounted the vehicle, while with the help of the jailor I slipped the prisoner through the sheltering gloom of a narrow cross-alley to the waiting buggy. When they were both aboard, and the darky's head and person all well covered up by an apron and large splash leather, the major drove at full speed through alleys and cross-streets out of town, and by country roads reached a flag station of the E. &. T. H. R. R. Then with the Negro he boarded the north-going train for Terre Haute, just due, and at the latter named city, one hundred miles removed from the "dead line," he turned the prisoner over to the sheriff of Vigo County.

As soon as I knew that my bird was fairly out of reach of the mob I went among the crowd and announced that the African had safely escaped their clutches; and to convince them of the truth of my statement, I invited three of their number to accompany me into the jail. When satisfied that the game had flown they announced it on the outside, and the crowd cursed the sheriff long and deep, and grumblingly dispersed.

The mulatto (not a Negro, but nearly white), whose name was Oscar Shorter, carried in his skull, to the day of his death long years afterward, the bullet received from the white man's pistol that night; while the Kentuckian, who at the time of the shooting was supposed to have been mortally wounded, recovered his health in a short time.

Had I failed in my duty on that occasion, the city of Evansville, together with the state, would have been disgraced by the commission of a dastardly murder; doubly damnable, as the mulatto, by subsequent confession of the Kentuckian, was shown to have shot in self-defence only, after an unprovoked attack by the young Hotspur.

This same man Shorter had always been known as an industrious, submissive and orderly citizen; but in the eyes of a democratic mob he was guilty of the unpardonable sin of being a nigger and deserved to be hung at a lamp-post anyhow. All of which is held to be just and logical in the great republic which stands before all the countries of the world as the splendid Pharos of equal rights.

139

At the time when I was preparing to repulse the mob's expected attack on the life of my prisoner and the county's property, and while stationing the armed men under my command where they could best defend the entrance to the jail, I pictured to myself the arrival of the moment when, to check a rush attack of the mob, I should be compelled to give the command to fire. For one short second I closed my eyes and saw as the result of that order men staggering to the ground with ghastly bullet holes in their heads—men, moreover, whose faces I had known all my life, and as in fancied reality I heard the shriek of the widowed wife and the wail of the orphaned children. I shuddered, a sensation of undescribable horror crept through my fevered veins, and the thought that blood-stained faces of the dead should haunt my sleepless pillow from that time on made me distracted, and I have been truly thankful ever since that this bitter cup was permitted to pass my lips.

Subsequent to the above-described occurrence, and only a few years ago, a similar riot in the same county necessitated the calling out of the state militia and the shooting to death of a number of the mob. By prompt, intelligent action and manly courage of the sheriff, this dire catastrophe might have been averted and the sacrifice of life avoided.

5.-7. Rotten Apples in Posey County and What to Do with Them (1879)

5. We Will Do unto You. . .

A cantankerous farmer who lives a short distance from our city refuses to close the gates to his farm lot. Now and then neighboring cows stray onto his property through these inviting gates. In a short time this man has killed the cow of widow Truempi, and severely injured the cows of farmers Tischendorf, Hoge, Nussel, and of the widow Blosfeld. Recently this farmer received an anonymous letter which stated, "We will do unto you as you have done unto the cows."

6. Shame on You, Neumeyer!

This town has several known "never-do-wells". One of them, however, was of help to Watchman Jones in trapping the counterfitter Neumeyer at his moneymaking machine in the basement room of a house near the depot. U.S. Marshal Wunderlich of Evansville took Neumeyer to a federal prison.

7. Mount Vernon Cleaning up

It is rumored that a vigilante committee is being formed at secret meetings. Perhaps the time has come for the sneaking thieves, idle beggars and rowdy fist throwers to find new locations to pester decent people. Mount Vernon is cleaning up, not only streets, but also its population.

8. Frontier Justice

At the turn of the century, Ernst D. Hoeltke, his wife Katharina, their seven children and his widowed mother Sophia were living on the farm his parents had homesteaded west of Columbus, Indiana. There were several German farm families in the neighborhood, some of them relatives of the Hoeltkes. These men and women were known as hardworking and responsible people who lived sensibly and took care of their families. Particularly irritating to most of them, then, was a certain father in the area. His wife and children went without even the most basic of necessities, to the extent that the children sometimes appeared at their neighbors' doors asking for food. Every Saturday, however, their father would head for town to spend every cent he had at the local taverns. Thoroughly loaded he would then head home late at night after decent folk had long gone to bed, because they would be milking cows and going to church the next morning. As often as not he would run his horse and wagon into the ditch, then sit and yell until someone came and pulled him out.

After this had happened a number of times, two of Ernst's neighboring relatives declared that they had pulled that man out of the ditch for the last time. He could just sit there until morning. Maybe he would be sober by then.

Not long after, Ernst was awakened by the man yelling at the top of his lungs outside his own house. Angered by the drunk's disturbing of the peace and neglect of his family, Ernst got dressed and went out to confront him. Seizing the buggy whip, Ernst proceeded to give him a thrashing with his own whip. Perhaps thinking better of it the next morning, Ernst decided he had better report the incident to the authorities. After telling the sheriff what he had done, he was heartily congratulated by everyone who heard the story. Public and family responsibilities were taken seriously in those days.

9. The Stolen Ham

An old couple had a ham stolen from their smoke house. Said the woman to her husband, "Let's not tell anybody about it."

Weeks later, a neighbor came to visit them. He said, "I heard you had a ham stolen." The old woman said, "And you are the one who stole it."

10. Wheelbarrow Talk

Two men were out that night to steal some more turnips. As they sneaked toward the turnip patch with their wheelbarrow and kind o' slow, the wheelbarrow, in a low voice, went, *"Rue-ba ho-la, Rue-ba ho-la, Rue-ba ho-la"* ("get-tin' tur-nips, get-tin' tur-nips, get-tin' tur-nips"). But before they pulled the first turnip, the farmer, who had been waiting for them, peppered them with some birdshot which made them run—ouch, so fast!—into the night with their wheelbarrow. And guess what the wheelbarrow screamed at a very fast pace? *"KaRuebagseh-kaRuebagseh-kaRuebagseh"* ("seennoturnip-seennoturnip-seennoturnip")!

11. The Alibi

In court a man was testifying to establish an alibi for the defendant. His statement: "As I's drivin' down the road I seen 'im a settin' on the verandy and I knowed I knewed him, so I retched out my arm and wove at him."

XVI.

CIVIL WAR DAYS

"Moaning in the kitchen" (XVI.8.)

1. Morgan's Raiders and the Rev. Peter Glenn

General John Morgan and his men had crossed over the Ohio River from Kentucky into Mauckport, Indiana. On the way to Corydon they decided to stop first at the Rev. Peter Glenn home. Why did they want to stop there first? The (Lutheran) Rev. Glenn and a Rev. Abbott, a United Brethren minister, were known as "circuit riders" and had preached at a number of places in Kentucky and northern Tennessee. In their sermons these two ministers bitterly denounced slavery which displeased slave owners. It is reported that some of these men were with Morgan, and they had these two ministers marked and had decided to kill them.

Hearing that the Rebels were coming, the Rev. Glenn and the Rev. Abbott hid in the hills back of the Glenn home. The Rebels searched the hillside but failed to find their hiding places. And they began yelling that they would set fire to the Glenn house and buildings. The Rebels had already shot and wounded the Rev. Glenn's son, John. When the Rebels had come up to the house, John shouldered his gun and went out to meet them. When John learned that it was Morgan's men he started to run back. They called for him to halt, and when he failed to do so, they opened fire and shot him in the hip. John still ran and was shot in the hip on the opposite side. He had five wounds which he carried to his grave. He crawled under a pig-pen and the Rebels lost track of him. His mother and his wife then took him first to the cellar, but figuring that the house would later be set on fire, they took him to the orchard and placed him in the shade of a tree.

The Rev. Glenn knew that his son was wounded and feared that the women folks were unable to take care of John. Besides, the Rebels had hoisted a white flag. So he decided to give himself up. Of course, that white flag was only a ruse on the part of the Rebels. The Rev. Abbott stayed in hiding.

Some of the Rebels had gathered in the living room. And as the Rev. Glenn came in, he said to them, "What will you have, gentlemen?" They asked for a drink of water. He went to the well and brought a bucket of water and a dipper and set the bucket on the floor before them. They told him to drink first. He did, and while the Rebels were drinking, one shot him in the bowels. After Rev. Glenn was shot he walked out. Passing John, who was lying under that shade tree, he said to him, "John, I am wounded too." And he went to another shade tree and laid down. The women folks rushed to his side, but he never spoke again, passing away in a few minutes.

2. Morgan's Troopers Raid Oldenburg

Four thousand cavalrymen under the Confederate Morgan were raiding Indiana! One bright Saturday afternoon in July of 1863, two of the men in grey cantered up to Kessing's smithy. "New irons for the hosses, Yank, make it snappy." Mr. Kessing fibbed sweetly about no new shoes (although there were rows of them on the rafters overhead) but agreed to shoe the soldiers' horses and bring them down to Kuntz's beer emporia (later George Stenger's grocery) where the men wanted to cool off.

When the horses were led over to the saloon, the southerners made a little curtsy and, vaulting into the saddle, comforted the empty-handed Mr. Kessing with some foolishness about the Quarter Master settling up accounts when they'd won the bloomin' war. Loping along out of town toward St. Mary's, they met Dominic Siefert astride his trusty steed. "Buddy, we all wants that hoss." Ah! But Dominic was the born actor! Working up an insidious little tear in his voice, Dominic held forth on the lot of the small farmer; how bloody needful was his horse, etc., etc. In the end they struck a bargain: Dominic was to keep the bridle and saddle, but the Greys got the horse, which, according to Dominic, "twaren't much of a critter nohow."

Oldenburg was indignant. Then and there the burghers got together and organized the "Oldenburg Home Guard." Mr. Schanz was posted on top of the Batesville hill with a heavy horse pistol to sound the warning if Morgan should show up. It wasn't long till he saw a cloud of dust far up the road. Wham! Wham! One slug clipped his horse's ear so his good beast flew into town on the double quick with Schanz yelling wildly about the whole blasted army of the rebels bearing down on the town. Men mustered grimly, and soon a bristle of muskets and shotguns flanked the road were it entered town . . . Just when everyone's hair was on the verge of turning white from suspense and kindred emotions, a jolly little rig came clattering over the hill bearing a wide-eyed farmer . . . the whole blasted army of the rebels had finally showed up.

At night when things were quiet a few of the Greys did ride into town to have their boots mended at Mr. Kleinmeyer's place on Water Street. Mrs. Anna Hunteman, a little tot at that time, was snug in bed while her dad and three workmen kept to their lasts far into the night. The troopers, as her dad related the next morning, said to charge the bill to good old Uncle Sam.

Thus did Oldenburg figure in Morgan's raid: two shots, no deaths, one horse ear.

3. Morgan's Raiders in New Alsace: You Never Can Tell

Monday, July 13, 1863, the famous Confederate General John Hunt Morgan led a force of approximately 2,500 cavalrymen through New Alsace. Philomena Young, whose parents had died, and who was cared for by an aunt, Elizabeth Vogelgesang, helped her aunt feed the soldiers at the tavern-blacksmith shop where they had stopped. Philomena served a pancake breakfast to the men. They were very polite and paid for their food.

In later years, Philomena's brother began searching for the members of his family who were scattered upon the death of the parents. He found that he was one of the Confederate soldiers actually served breakfast by his sister, although neither knew it at the time.

4. Foolin' Morgan's Raiders at St. Leon

When two scouting parties of Morgan's Raiders joined forces and began to advance on St. Leon in 1863, the citizens scared them off by firing a cannon and by exploding powder on an anvil. The powder was weighted down and then exploded, making a terrific noise. On hearing this artillery of St. Leon, the scouting party rejoined the main force at Dover. They then proceeded to Harrison, Ohio. The men responsible for using the anvil and the powder were John Frey, John Stenger, and Charles Wilhelm.

5. A *Teufelsecker* Bites the Bullet in Ferdinand

The customary religious joy on the feast of Corpus Christi was marred frightfully on Thursday, June 9, 1863. Herman Beckmann and Frank Kometscher, volunteers of the ninety-first Indiana Regiment, were home on furlough. They were encouraging others to enlist. This enraged some of those from the *Teufels Eck* that were said to belong to the Knights of the Golden Circle. It was after the great Corpus Christi procession through the town of Ferdinand. Herman Beckmann was in his father's store, when Victor Drach, twenty-one years of age and exceptionally strong, and several of his associates, who had imbibed freely and had not attended divine service, invaded the store and dragged Herman out into the street with the threat to "cut his throat." Somebody rushed to Frank Kometscher who was about a block away and told him that they were killing his comrade. Running up the street, Kometscher drew his service pistol and fired at the man who was menacingly bent over Beckmann. Victor Drach, though mortally wounded, threw himself upon Kometscher, bore him down, then collapsed. For the moment the associates of Victor were stunned, and Beckmann together with Kometscher hurried into the store and locked the doors. The father of Victor Drach, being informed, came down the street as fast as his limping gait permitted; with both hands holding his hat before him, he stood over his son and said mournfully: *"Victor, Victor, du armer Teufel!*—you poor devil!"

Soon the friends of the dead man rallied and threatened to break into the store to take vengeance. But the two soldiers by a ruse escaped from the house—some thought it was with the help of Father Chrysostom Foffa—and hurried to Troy, with their enemies in hot pursuit. The two beat their pursuers to the boat by half a block. There were enough other soldiers on board to turn the tide against the pursuers and to prevent further attempts at violence. Upon the advice of Father Chrysostom, Kometscher requested to be placed before a court martial. This court justified his action; military authorities even threatened that if there would be any more disturbances at Ferdinand, it would be put under martial law.

The comment of the people upon the tragedy was, "whiskey did it." Because Victor Drach had on that day notoriously not attended divine service and had started the broil which cost him his life and because, though mortally wounded, he showed no signs of repentance, Father Chrysostom denied him ecclesiastical burial.

6. Copperheads?

Once I asked my father if his folks were considered "Copperheads" during the Civil War. Copperheads were people sympathizing with the South. He didn't answer the question with a yes or no. What he said was, "Boy, let me tell you something, those Federal troops were awful hard on Southerners." He then told a story of an aunt living in Kentucky who had five sons, four of whom were in the Confederate forces, the fifth was too young and was at home. One day he was plowing a field when a squad of Union foragers came by. They steadied their guns on a rail fence and shot the boy as he plowed. Supposedly they said, "That's one Rebel we don't have to worry about." My father said his aunt always cried when she told the story.

7. This'll Change Your Mind about Skunks

When my grandfather was in the Civil War, he was a scout and was on scout duty in a big woods in the south. A southern soldier was also scouting and hunting him. He was out of ammunition and saw a big, hollow log that was down. He managed to crawl most of him into one end, and pulled some leaves and debris over him. The southern soldier came to the other end and poked his bayonet in that end. There was a skunk in there that let loose. All three ran in different directions. My grandfather said he would have been killed—had it not been for the skunk.

8. Moaning in the Kitchen

My great-grandma, Elizabeth Stumpf, had her house full. There were her eight children and the eight children of her sister-in-law who had just lost her husband. He had hitched his horses for the first spring plowing, but they started running around a tree, strapped him around the trunk, and squeezed him to death.

One night shortly thereafter, it was during the Civil War, Great-Grandma was awakened in their two-story log cabin by some moaning that came from downstairs. She wanted to find out what that was. So she got up, lit a candle, and went down to the kitchen. Everything looked fine. But suddenly there was that moaning again, and it kept coming right out from the pantry where she had put the loafs of bread she had baked that day. Oh, she was a pioneer woman, not afraid of anything. She went right to the pantry door and opened it. That stopped the moaning. With her candlelight she saw that the loafs and everything else was still there. After a while she went back to bed. Great-Grampa woke up and asked her what she was up to there in the middle of the night. She told him what she had heard and that the moaning had now stopped. She never told what Great-Grampa said 'bout that, but we can guess . . .

When the war was finally over, their nephew George Rau, who had lived with them, came home and told them about his experience in Southern captivity. Food had been in such short supply, and more than one time they had none at all, neither the prisoners nor the guards. And one night, as he was lying on his cot, weak and hungry, his wishful thinking carried him to the pantry of his aunt, and he could almost smell her freshly baked bread that was always there in good supply. And as he fell asleep he took one of these beautiful loafs into his dream, and he ate it all.

After George had told his story, Great-Grandma asked him if he could pinpoint the date of his dream. Just as he had not forgotten the dream, he had not forgotten the date either: it was the very same night that Great-Grandma had heard the moaning in the kitchen.

XVII.

THE GERMAN-AMERICAN TRAGEDY: WORLD WAR I

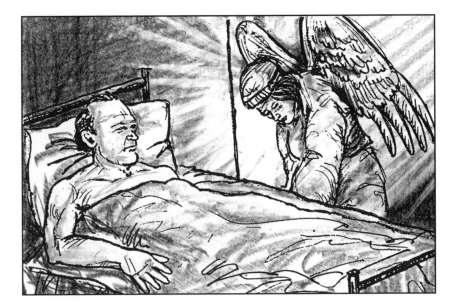

". . . and were being ministered to by angels." (XVII.10.)

1. My Friend Ethel and the "Lusitania"

Ethel and I were only ten years old when the "Lusitania" was sunk by a German submarine. The newspapers carried stories, and people were awfully shocked about the incident. My father, Albert James Roath, with his English background was real mad at the Germans. The next morning I met my friend Ethel Behrmann as usual at the corner on our way to school. I told Ethel what my father had said about these terrible Germans, and that I also thought that they were bad. Ethel came right back at me:

"You've got it all wrong. You know what my grandfather said? He said it serves them just right. Why did they run that ship back and forth to England, Germany's enemy, if it were not for guns and ammunition? And he said that the Germans had warned them several times."

I didn't take that from Ethel. "No," I said, "they've done us wrong and they are bad!" "Oh, shut up," she replied angrily, "my grandfather knows better than your father." Now I got mad, too: "No, *you* better shut up! My family has been in this country longer than yours." She screamed at me: "How do I care, if you don't think that I am right I won't talk with you anymore!" That was too much. I screamed right back: "No, I don't!" And that was the last time we spoke to each other for months.

One day, when I told my mother about our broken friendship, she said: "Child, this war is a terrible thing, and remember that my father, your grandfather, also came from Germany, like Ethel's grandfather. And let me tell you something else, it just isn't right that you girls have your own little private war. Why don't you talk with Ethel that you want to be friends again."

The next morning I saw Ethel at the corner and said: "Why don't we end our little war, 'cause I still like you." Ethel was glad that I had broken the ice. Our friendship was as nice as before the "Lusitania"—and it lasted until the end of Ethel's life in 1985.

2. The Spirit of Mars

It was in June, 1917. A glorious morning in a glorious month. The air was balmy. Patches of deep blue sky were sending their greetings from above the tall buildings down to the busy people rushing along the streets in their daily routine of dollar chasing.

Observing the men and women coming and going to and fro, one could not help noticing a certain nervousness in their behaviour, a more vivid tempo in their walk and a marked alertness in greeting acquaintances. From many buildings flags were fluttering in the breeze, streamers were stretched across the streets telling you to "do your bit."

The people were bewitched by the first ecstasy of war. The country was at war with a nation across the Atlantic, 3,300 miles away from Indiana's capital, at war with Germany, from whence so many thousands of her sons had come and founded a new home, and in the hour of darkness had helped to nominate and elect Abraham Lincoln and fought and died to preserve the Union.

The enchanting beauty of Dame Nature in her June bridal dress had lost its charm for the restless mortal. The spirit of war polluted the air. A centrifugal force had spread frenzied, hysterical patriotism over the land. On that June morning a mixed crowd gathered at the intersection of Market and Pennsylvania Streets; young men and old men, boys and girls, colored folk and white people. A number of young women clad in trim khaki uniforms mingled with the crowd. They knew that they looked alluring in their attire. Many of them had hoped to speed up the cardiac valve of some young fellow's heart. This was the time of adventure, of daring, because two months earlier America had joined the other twenty-five nations of the world to destroy Germany.

A band arrived playing martial airs. The crowd formed a circle from curb to curb and sang the new war songs with gusto. All were sincerely patriotic and naturally quite noisy. On the outside of the circle, newly made soldiers from Fort Harrison were scouting around, anxious to find some chance to display their newly acquired military spirit.

The crowd sang "Over There" and other songs again and again, the musicians exercised their lungs, the drummer pounded his calfskin with youthful energy.

Nothing happened.

At the corner of Pennsylvania Street a street car stopped. An old man stepped off carefully. A market basket hung in his left arm, in his right hand he carried a hickory cane that fifty years before he had brought with him from Tennessee.

Slowly he walked along the Lemcke Building, his head bent forward in deep thought; he was trying to remember all the instructions the old lady had given him as he left home. He was to get radishes at the third stand from the market corner, potatoes at about the middle of the block, parsnips near the side entrance to the hall, and then he was to count the change carefully that the potato woman might hand him. Only a married man can fully realize what a large assortment of duties and advice can quickly be heaped upon him by his spouse as she is closing the front door.

154

While our friend was peacefully walking towards the market, thinking of the blissfulness of matrimony, he was suddenly stopped by a boisterous mob in khaki. They seemed ready to lynch him. Deep in thought, he had forgotten to take off his hat before the numerous American flags carried by the crowd.

A bank clerk, who had observed the whole performance from his office window, rushed to the assistance of the victim of the mob spirit and succeeded in rescuing him by pushing him through the entrance door of the Peoples State Bank.

The crowd calmed down and soon dispersed after having enjoyed an exciting moment.

The clerk accompanied the old man to the market. On the way he said: "I am seventy-five years old, I served two years in the Union Army during the Civil War, we did a lot of real fighting, but never made such noise about the flag. I reckon times have changed," and saying this, he stopped at the third stand from the market corner to buy his radishes.

3. The Alien

Herman Wind was only nine when his mother died back in Germany in 1870. The family had planned to emigrate to America, and his father Heinrich decided to go even after his wife's death.

Life wasn't easy in the New World for Herman and his five brothers and sisters. They also lost their father after a couple of years, leaving them orphans with no money to support them. But Herman was an exceptionally hard worker. By middle age he had acquired a number of pieces of property, most of them small tracts bought one at a time from his savings from numerous jobs.

He had two great interests: reading and politics. He read books and magazines whenever he could, and he was a loyal Democrat. He held county jobs, such as seeing that the roads in his township were kept in good repair, and he also drove the "school hack" for the children of the neighborhood. When his son Henry, later to be county commissioner, got old enough to take the school route, the job was passed on to him. On the evening of every election day, Herman would drive his wife and children into Columbus and park at the courthouse. There they would sit and watch the election returns as they were posted outside for interested citizens, and he was certainly one of them.

Imagine then, the shock of finding himself suspect by the authorities when the U S. entered the War in 1917. As far as he was concerned, he had become a citizen years ago. He had gone to the courthouse and gone through the citizenship process, hadn't he? Hadn't he always voted? But something had gone wrong. Some mistake had been made somewhere. Perhaps the papers had never been filed properly. As far as the U.S. government was concerned, he was an enemy alien. There was no avoiding it, he must be photographed, fingerprinted, and registered as such.

The picture still exists, and those who knew him say that he looks absolutely furious.

4.-5. "Huns" and the Stars and Stripes in Columbus

4. Give Me a Kiss, Hun!

In 1988, at a restaurant in Columbus, Indiana, a group of women were overheard mentioning events from World War I. At one point the conversation turned to their recollections of how they, as children of German ancestry, reacted to the state of war.

"Until the war," one woman said, "all our family spoke German at home. But when we went to town after the war began, father gave us strict orders not to speak German on the streets. I remember being shaken to my senses once downtown for asking something of my mother in German."

Another lady broke in, "I always hated it when the boys yelled, 'Hun!' at me on the way home from school. They would say, 'How about a date, Hun! You are really cute, Hun! Give me a kiss, Hun!'"

5. Theophil J. Koch—Enemy or Patriot?

These women may or may not have been pupils at St. Peter's Lutheran School in Columbus during WW I when one of the teachers, the brilliant pianist T. J. Koch, had his own problems with the populace. Teacher Koch had been born in Germany and still felt a bond with his native land. Sensing this, some of the town leaders invited Koch to carry the American flag in all the local patriotic parades. Others, however, still questioned where Koch's sentiments lay.

One day, several men showed up at the door of Koch's classroom. Their intent did not seem friendly. Koch explained that the children were in music class and that he would talk with the men after the class was over. After several more songs were sung and just before the class period ended, Koch sat down at the piano and directed the children in a rousing chorus of THE STAR-SPANGLED BANNER. After the pupils filed out of the classroom for recess, the men told Koch that they had come to question his motives, but after hearing the national anthem so superbly sung, they were sure that Koch was a patriotic American.

6. Black Hands at the Cleaner's in Muncie

Conrad Charles Leitshuh—or you can spell it Konrad Karl Leitschuh—had immigrated in the 1890s. By 1900 he established a large drycleaning plant at the corner of Main and Madison Streets, and business was great. One night, after the war broke out, Leitshuh's "French Steam Dye Works"—as they were called—were visited by some super patriotic God-knows-who. When the sun came up, there were black hands painted all over the place. Whether Conrad said "damn" or "*verdammt*" we'll never know. But we know for sure that he was quick to remedy the insult—after all, it was his business to keep Muncie clean! Then he went out and bought several American flags and hung them all over the building. The Muncie paper reported the incident.

Conrad's 11-year-old boy, George, didn't look forward to going to school that day and face the kids. Was he glad when nothing happened there. But inside the Leitshuh home something changed for good: George didn't hear and speak a word of German anymore, and the old German customs his parents had observed were no longer followed— even at Christmas time. All because of the black hands of an awful war.

7. Monks of St. Meinrad Naturalized

Nearly fifty percent of the monks (50 of 105) were foreign-born; of these 37 had emigrated from Germany. When World War I commenced some of the lay brothers were found without full naturalization papers. Indiana passed a law requiring *second papers,* i. e. full citizenship with voting privileges, for all immigrants. Some of the brothers possessed only *first papers* which had until this time sufficed for some voting privileges, but not full citizenship. At the Abbot's request, Father Columban gave these men a full course in civics and brought them before a judge in Rockport to be examined by Federal agents.

Nearly all the brothers passed the first test, but a few had to learn more civics before receiving second papers. These interrogations produced a few light moments and some genuine irony. Brother Philip

Ketterer, both well-informed and intelligent, a chef in the monastic kitchen, was routinely asked, "Where does the Governor of the State reside?" "Ordinarily in Indianapolis, the State Capital," he replied, "but at the present time he is residing in the Federal penitentiary in Atlanta, Georgia." The examiner, smiling, turned to the man on his right and remarked, "Pretty good, eh?" The fact was: the governor had been found guilty of embezzlement of state funds and had been sentenced to prison as punishment.

To the question: "What is the function of the judge?" one brother, somewhat befuddled by the correct answer (to *interpret* the law) because of poor English, replied to the amusement of all assembled, "The judge is supposed to *know* the law." The examining U.S. agent turned to the judge with a smile, "Your Honor, is the answer correct?" The judge, likewise grinning, said, "He is supposed to, but I don't know if he does."

8.-9. Pretty Rough in Fort Wayne

8. Right in the Eye

Two middle-aged women of a highly respectable and wealthy German-American family in Fort Wayne were speaking German to one another while riding on a streetcar when an "English" woman came up shaking her finger at them and either inadvertantly or purposely stuck her finger in one speaker's eye.

9. The German Spy

In December, 1917, a number of citizens became excited when they saw a man walking around the alleys of downtown Fort Wayne making sketches of buildings. The police, flooded with calls, quickly arrested the man on the charge of being a German spy.

A crowd gathered outside the police department demanding that the arrested man be turned over to them for immediate retribution. Mayor William Hosey quickly had the alleged spy brought to his office for a hearing. The bewildered and frightened man explained that he was employed by the Sanford Fire Map Company of Chicago and was working to map out several buildings for use by fire insurance companies that utilized his firms findings in establishing premiums and coverage. The crowd which had gathered was calmed by the mayor who praised its members for their patriotic action and encouraged them to continue to be on their guard.

10. The Angel on the Battlefield

It was a long way from the farm in Bartholomew County to the Argonne Forest in France, and Alma Finke probably never imagined that she would end up in such a place when she persuaded her parents to let her enroll in nurse's training at Deaconess Hospital in Fort Wayne. When the U. S. entered the war in 1917, she and other young women at Deaconess were recruited as a unit and sent to train as army nurses at Fort Lewis, Washington.

As the war progressed, however, Alma and the other nurses were sent to France. Because these nurses were virtually all from German Lutheran homes and had grown up speaking German, they were put in charge of prisoners of war that were brought in to the field hospitals. By this time the war had bogged down in the trenches and was going badly, especially for the Germans. Many of the prisoners were barely more than boys and were very badly wounded in most cases. Frequently unconscious or delirious when brought in, often the first thing they would see when coming to was a young woman in white standing over them. After the horrors of the battlefield and hearing the figure speak German to them, many of the young men sincerely believed they had died and were being ministered to by angels.

XVIII.

POLITICKS AND POLITICKIN'

"Then, with a thud, a big onion struck him between the eyes . . ." (XVIII.1.)

1. "Gus" Lemcke and the Freemont Campaign of 1856 in a Democratic Neighborhood

The excitement incident to the Freemont campaign in 1856, and the strife, with its warlike alarums, attending the formation of a new political party, appealed strongly to those of us who were then young and enthusiastic.

When, in October of that year, one of my friends, a disciple of Coke and Blackstone, determined to do some missionary and crusading work in the "out counties," I made up my mind to accompany him on a trip into Warrick, Spencer and Dubois, then the darkest part of the Sudan of democracy in Indiana.

At that time I was bookkeeper and teller in the Canal Bank of Evansville, one of the "free" or so-called "wildcat" monetary institutions of our state. The directors of the bank, former whigs, had, with the Lecompton and Bleeding Kansas troubles, drifted on the current into the newly formed republican party, and in their zeal for "free soil" and its success, willingly granted a vacation.

My friend and I, provided with a wheezy old horse and the buggy stuffed full of anti-slave tracts and free-soil literature, buoyantly made our start on this trip of knight errantry into the enemy's country. At Boonville, Rockport, Ferdinand and other points in the then first congressional district, we met with but sorry success. The democratic dervishes, even through the back door of their understanding, could not be reached. Expounding to them the gospel of "free soil" threw them into fits, and maddened them as the red rag does the bull. No eggs, we learned, were too old for the anointing of black republicans and abolitionists. Slavery was yet looked upon as a God-given institution, supported by the pulpit and authorized by the Bible.

When we reached Jasper, county seat of Dubois, where we had an appointment by "early candle-light," we found the rostrum in the courtroom occupied by the democratic candidate for congress, holding spellbound a goodly crowd of the "unterrified." One banner among the decorations of the room, conspicuously surrounded by young ladies in white, bore in fat letters the devise: "Fathers, save us from nigger husbands!" The atmosphere within we found surcharged with protest and hostility. The heated pulpiteer "chopped logic," and by innuendo and open attacks damned all abolitionists and Yankee nigger-stealers, until it became apparent that it would not be long ere in that perspiring, superheated crowd "something would be doing." Presently, in response to an especial and personally insulting lambasting from the rostrum, my nervous companion, in a challenging manner, sprang to his feet to hurl back the lie.

Then, with a thud, a big onion struck him between the eyes, while the juice of an aged egg trickled down his nose upon his mustache, whereupon,

> He smole a sickly smile
> As he lay upon the floor,
> And the subsequent proceedings
> Interested him no more.

In the meantime I also had received my share of shots from the basket of foul and funky hen fruit, and while the speaker in his arduous ranting had burst both suspenders, the crowd was in a hilarious tumult, from which we were thankful to escape without additional chromos. On reaching the security of a chamber under the clapboard roof of the Waldorf Astoria of the place, it occurred to me that the banister of the stairs to fame is full of splinters, and "he who slides down the said banister will be filled with much tribulation and great pain."

On our arrival next day in Huntingburg, where we were billed for a daylight meeting, we found a big crowd assembled—such a one as usually attends a lynching. We were advised to keep shady, but the spirit of the crusader was within and gave us no rest.

Having hurried through a dinner of jowls and greens we sallied forth toward the school-house yard, where, from the top of a dry-goods box, the speaking was to take place. The rostrum, however, had already been usurped by a man with a moth-eaten beard whom the crowd greeted as "Old Cheezum," and who at fever heat "pointed with pride and viewed with alarm." This old linsey-woolsey imposter, we afterwards learned, lay claim to being an astrologer and a fortune-teller, and pretended to know

> When the moon 's in fittest mood
> For cutting corns, or letting blood;
> When for annointing scabs and itches,
> Or to the back applying leeches,
> When sows or bitches may be spay'd,
> And in what time best cider 's made.
> Whether the wane be, or increase,
> Best to set garlic or sow peas.

It was not until after his vocabulary had been exhausted, and he had viciously basted us and our nigger-loving party, that he gave way to repeated protests from us and yielded the floor.

I had hardly unpacked the documents and mounted the box to announce that I could not, but that the gentleman in the white necktie could and would make them a speech, such a speech as had not been heard from the days of Cicero to Mirabeau, and which would throw

Daniel Webster into a jaundice of yellow envy, when a suspicious commotion in the outer edge of the crowd made itself known. A fellow from behind the school-house, tricked out like a clown, led into the thickest part of the crowd, right up to the store box on which I was standing, a mule, whose hair, stiff with tar, was all standing on end. This the clown announced to be Freemont's "woolly horse." The crowd, like a newly-opened gas well, now became uncontrollable, and when someone tickled the mule under the tail, his first kick knocked the rostrum out from under my feet and sent me like a rocket flying head foremost into the boisterously delighted and uproarious pack. From the melee which followed we were glad to disentangle ourselves and, *sans* political tracts or republican platform, we hastily rang the bell and transferred to another car.

After supper, nothing daunted, we determined, notwithstanding the discouraging outlook, to make another attempt at preaching the gospel of freedom and equal rights to the democratic heathen. The school-house had been lighted for us with two tallow dips, which produced a brilliant illumination. The hilarity and frolic of the afternoon had started the unterrified to drinking, and some of the younger fellows especially had shipped up enough booze to put them in an ugly fighting temper. In this state of mind they had resolved to have a little additional fun with the two nigger-stealers from the seaport of the Ohio, and had armed themselves with clubs, ax-handles and corn-knives.

My oratorical companion, who had thus far not found an opportunity to unload any of his eloquence, had no sooner begun with a promising preamble than the door flew open with a bang, disclosing to sight a detachment of boys, closely followed by the "ax-handle brigade," a drunken rabble of men. While antiquated eggs in one's hair and whiskers are not altogether pleasant, and contact with the heel of a kicking mule is undesirable, the possibility of having one's throat cut with gleaming corn-knives or brains scattered in a cornfield by ax-handles, could not be considered with equanimity. Therefore, unostentatiously, abandoning hats, collars and neckties, and without ceremony, we tumbled out of the back window of the school-house into a potato patch.

Then commenced a lively race through the cornfields and over stake and ridered fences, we leading and the rabble chasing like a swift pack in hot cry. We, however, fleeter of foot, outwinded them, and eventually ran to cover in a widow's house, whose door happened to be open. Mother Blemker, the charitable old lady, promptly tumbled us on to her couch, threw a feather-bed on top, locked the door and put out the light .

The next morning we bestirred ourselves uncommonly early, fished both the hind wheels of our buggy out of the mill pond, hitched up the Rosinante, and without hats, stomachs empty, but noddles well filled with experience, we left for home. On parting with Mother Blemker she bade us forgive our persecutors. Therefore, not to be ungrateful for the protection the good soul had so hospitably given to us, we assented, but only with the mental reservation that we would not forgive them until after they were hanged! Cervantes' Knight de la Mancha in his fight with the wind-mills was badly worsted, and so were we. With grumbling gizzards, the hind wheels of the vehicle hamstrung, minus hats, neckties and collars, a buggy-rug and a whip gone, we hobbled along over a rocky road with gratifying emotions of no common description, and with Ralpho soliloquized:

> If he that in the field is slain
> Be in the bed of honor lain,
> He that is beaten may be said
> To lie in honor's trundle-bed.

The autumn coloring of the forest that season, green, intermingled with all shades of Roman gold, ruby and burnished brass, was unusually brilliant, and the gorgeous panorama presented from elevated points along the way was so entrancingly beautiful that youthful buoyancy returned ere long, and a clearer view showed us the ridiculously quixotic situation of our past experience in a new light and afforded much amusement the rest of the way home. We, like the King of France with forty thousand men, had "marched up the hill just to march down again."

A month later election returns from Dubois brought proof that our raid in the interest of the Pathfinder had been absolutely without result. Not half a dozen votes from that county were returned for free soil and the "woolly horse."

To us two crusaders nothing gratifying was left but the satisfaction of having bearded the lion in his den and the discovery of the wisdom of Aesop, when in his fable of "The Dogs and the Hides," he points out the moral: "Never attempt impossibilities!"

2. A Good Man with Two Faults

Cecilia had an uncle who lived on the Ohio River below Evansville. He was a big, husky, good natured man and operated a country store. Once when I spent the night with him I asked about a man in Mount Vernon upon whom I would call the next day. Uncle Pacific—he was named after the biggest steamboat on the river—he said, "Oh, he is a fine man, honest, a good businessman. But he does have two faults. He is a Democrat and a Catholic."

3. Puppies and Politics

A little boy was selling puppies and a man asked, "What kind of puppies are they?" And the boy said, "Republican puppies and the price is $2.00."

A week later the man came by again and the boy had a sign, "Democratic puppies $5.00." The man said, "I thought you said Republican for $2.00." "Yes," the little feller said, "but they have their eyes open now."

4. "Sister Sophie is a Republican"

In the 1870s following the Civil War there were very few members of the Republican party in our community of Oldenburg. Anyone who was knowledgeable about politics could just about name all of them. They were not held in high repute. So it was quite understandable that the following incident took place.

Sr. Sophia was teaching the upper grades at Holy Family School. She was a good, no-nonsense sort of a teacher and well able to keep the older boys in line. But one of the boys was consistently giving her trouble. He had often felt corrective measures taken to his hand and backside, such as he had even that morning. He schemed somehow to get even.

So at recess time when the room was empty he sneaked in and proceeded to write on the blackboard what he thought was the *nastiest* thing he could think off to call his teacher. He wrote in large letters the following:

"::: SISTER SOPHIE IS A REPUBLICAN ! :::"

Then he wondered what punishment might be in store for him now. But not to worry, for when the good Sister saw it, she laughed most heartily. She recognized a good joke when she saw one.

5. To Count or not to Count the Ballots? (1888)

The day following the presidential election of 1888, the returns were brought from St. Meinrad, also a Democratic center in Spencer County, to the county seat. When the inspector arrived he was informed that since the Democratic party had lost by a large majority, it would not be necessary to take care of his ballots. No doubt somewhat surprised, he replied: "Has the vote from Ferdinand Township been heard from?"

167

6. Grandfather Wampler and Women's Rights

My grandfather Wampler expected the women folk to move, and fast, when he spoke. My mother used to complain that as far as her father was concerned she never grew up.

Grandfather once said, "This country doomed itself to disaster when women were granted the vote."

XIX.

SURPRISE

". . . zmoking two zigarettes at ze zame time!" (XIX.10.)

"The Garrison Marching Out." Captain Helm's surrender at Vincennes
(XI.1.). *Source:* J. P. Dunn, *Indiana and Indianans* (1919), Vol. 1.

1. The Defender of Ft. Vincennes: Captain Leonard Helm

Ft. Vincennes . . . was built in 1727. In the wake of the soldiers came tradesmen, and Ft. Vincennes became a thriving French village and subsequently the first capital of Indiana. Among the early inhabitants we find men with German names, evidently Germans from Alsace Lorraine , who had immigrated with the French. When the English tried to seize this wild country in which the Indians were still on the warpath, Virginia sent General George Rogers Clark with an army west over the Ohio to take possession of it for the United States. Among his troops there were many German-Americans, one of whom, Captain Leonard Helm, was appointed commander of Ft. Vincennes and agent for the Indians of the Wabash valley.

. . .An English force under Colonel Hamilton came south to recapture Vincennes . . . Captain Helm, at the approach of the English, bravely placed a loaded cannon before the entrance of the fort and upon their coming within hailing distance, commanded them to halt, emphasizing his demand by brandishing a firebrand and shouting that he would shoot if they came nearer. Hereupon the English proposed a parley in which they agreed that Captain Helm and his men should have free passage from the fort with their arms. Imagine their surprise when Captain Helm, with his command of one man, stepped forward!

2. The Puzzle at the New Mill (1832)

The first mill in Scott Township, Vanderburgh County, Indiana, was erected about 1832 by Richard Browning. The first day they began to run the mill left an imprint. The grain was put in the hopper, the team started, the mill went round, but not the smallest particle of meal made its appearance. They were puzzled. They tried in vain to discover the reason and finally concluded they were beat. Mr. Browning decided to send for George Linxweiler who had experience with mills. In a few hours Linxweiler appeared. He looked at the arrangement and quietly informed them in his German idiom, that they had been trying to grind flour by running the mill backward.

3. Burglar Alarm at the Oldenburg Bank

. . .Who remembers, or better, who doesn't remember the bedlam that broke loose when the burglar alarm on the bank screamed out at 11 p.m. some years ago. My but the shooting was terrific—out of the back door! And the lady who started throwing flower pots out her upstairs window to scare off the burglars! And the awkward look on someone's face when he came hurrying down the street to explain that he must have forgot to set the alarm properly. And oh dear me! Father Hugh stalking the supposed intruder from behind the line of trees along the church, his shotgun finger waiting! And the cleric with him who kept repeating as in a litany, "They'll shoot to kill; Father, they'll shoot to kill."

4. Daniel Branstetter's Shoes

Lewis Fritch made shoes in the 1870s in Needmore, Brown County. A pair of shoes for Daniel were ready to be called for. Remember that Daniel was a large man and he had big feet. Lewis put on his cap, and a loafer in the shop asked him, "Are you going someplace?" Fritch said, "I thought I'd take a trip around Branstetter's shoes." At this point, Daniel happened to have opened the door and hear the remark. He did not call or pay for these shoes until his others were beyond wearing.

5. A King-sized Photograph (1890)

Henry O. Truebenbach of Fort Wayne served under the King of Saxony in the German Army. A few weeks ago he wrote to the king and asked for a photograph of the old commander. To his great joy, the request was granted, and the two and one-half foot high photograph, housed in a gold frame and bearing the king's signature, has arrived. Truebenbach gave the picture to the German Veterans Association of Fort Wayne.

6.-7. How Tales Get Taller (and Smaller)

6. The Memory Expander

Herr Stoltz was noted for telling tales about his life in the army. The older he got the bigger the tales became.

One day, one of his friends said, "Herr Stoltz, how come that the more you tell your tales, the bigger they get?"

Herr Stoltz thought a minute and said, "Well, you know, the thing is this, my memory just keeps getting better and better as I grow older."

7. A Tall Tale Correction

There was a man who always told big tales. One day his wife scolded him and told him that he should not stretch the truth. He promised that he would be more careful from now on.

Soon after this the man started telling a story to his friends. He said, "There was a man who built himself a new barn. It was *one hundred foot* long"—here he was interrupted by his wife—so the man went on, "and *one foot* wide."

8. The Mule in the Canyon

This doctor in Auburn, Ind., a friend of the family, had a son with a mental condition, probably retarded. My mother was visiting Herr Doktor's wife, and a bridge party was in progress. The boy came into the room and he started a story about the Grand Canyon in Arizona. It seems that a mule got too close to the edge of the canyon wall and fell straight down for a mile. The boy said, "The mule landed right on its head on a very sharp spire of rock and if the rock had gone in an inch further it would have hit a red corpuscle and killed him."

9. Indiana's 130 Germans

A student at IU had to give a report on the Vereins affiliated with the German-American Alliance of Indiana before World War I. He came out with 133 all told. The "P.S." on the handout he had prepared for the class read as follows: "Study of German population of Indiana: If you have *one* German, you have *one* Verein; if you have *two* Germans, you have *two* Vereins. Therefore, there were about 130 Germans in Indiana (excluding double membership)."

10. Professor Harry Velten and His Cigarettes

More often than not, Harry was engulfed in a blue cloud. And with his cigarettes he was just as discriminating as he was with the raw materials for his superb Martini. It had to be none other than a certain imported Turkish fag—the smell of which we won't talk about.

One day in a graduate seminar on Old High German, puffing away in his usual manner, he wanted to illustrate a point at the blackboard. So up he got from his chair, but not without taking his lighter and an extra cigarette which he managed to light before he reached the blackboard. There he paused and—looking at his left hand and at his right hand—he finally shook his head in utter disbelief and said, "For heaven'z zake, what am I doingk, zmoking two zigarettes at ze zame time!"

11. "Schafskopf" with an Earthy Sound

As long as Grandpa Fleck lived we went over there and played Schafskopf—sheepshead, a card game still popular in Dubois County. And one night, Grandpa really let one loose. Everybody laughed and he retorted, *"Besser in die weite Welt als in dem engen Bauch"* (Better out into the wide world than kept in the crowded belly).

12. The Apple Tree

Eric and Alma Domroese came to Indianapolis around 1908. Eventually they built a house on Brookside Parkway North Drive. In the late 1940s, the Park Department planted oak trees on the grass strip between the sidewalk and the street. Pop kept telling the neighbors that they had oak trees but he had an apple tree. Even though he had been a gardner in Germany, we all just laughed at him.

After dark one night, he went out and hung at least a dozen big, red apples from that poor-little-skinny oak tree. The next morning he told all the neighbors, "See, you have oak, I have apples." From then until the day he died, everyone asked him if he was planning on planting more apple trees.

13. Ridin' the Elevator

An elderly man and his grandson were on the elevator, when on came a pretty young lady. All of a sudden she slapped the gentleman's face. She happened to get off on the next floor. Grandpa said, "Boy, I'm glad she's getting off. I sure don't like her." The grandson said, "Me neither. She stepped on my toes, so I pinched her."

XX.

THE AUTOMOBILE COMETH

"I blowed my horn first!!!" (XX.8.)

1. The Preacher and His First Car (ca. 1910)

One day this preacher in Jackson County decided that it was time for him to have a car. So he told Frau Pastor that he was going to town to buy him one. A couple of hours later he came back with his new machine, but he didn't stop the thing. He just kept on driving around the house in circles. Frau Pastor got all upset after a spell and hollered, "Honey, what are you doing?" The preacher shouted back, *"Ich kann das Auto starte, but ich kann's net stoppe!"*

2. What Color Is the Light?

I dearly loved my father-in-law, the Rev. William John George Bockstahler. He was an old-time fire and brimstone preacher and a man of enormous physical strength which he demonstrated once when fire consumed the White Creek Methodist Church—but not before he had pulled out the pews by hand.

In 1940, the hardy Hoosier had just turned 77, and I was visiting him. When it was time for me to get back home, he said he would drive me to the Greyhound depot in Evansville. When we came to the first traffic light he asked me what color it was. "Why, ah, red," I said, "you better stop!" "Will you tell me when the light turns green?" he responded. At this point I felt that my beloved father-in-law and preacher had perhaps just a little bit too much faith, and I asked him, "Well then, how do you manage when you're driving alone, Grandpa?"—I always called him Grandpa. His answer, though, had not much to do with his faith in the Almighty. "Oh," he smiled back, "I just watch and go when the other cars do."

3. Two Nuns out o' Gas

Two nuns were assigned to a mission in a farming community. With their van all loaded up and headin' down the highway they had the misfortune of runnin' out o' gas. So they called on a resident nearby for a little gasoline to get them to the next filling station. "Yeah, I could spare some gas," he said, "if I had something to put it in." One of the nuns pulled a bed pan from their loaded van. Nearby stood a minister observing all this, and he said, "I'm gonna see if she'll start from this, and if she starts, I'm gonna change my religion."

4.-5. Asking Directions in Old Dubois County

4. To "Chasper"

One motorist—obviously "un-Dutch"—wanted to get to Jasper. What he heard from that man at that service station way out in the county sounded like this, "Vell, now, you go tree miles dis vay, den turn right und go on till you get to Chasper."

5. "Vell, less see now"

Here's the way another lost motorist got the "right kind" of directions in Dubois County. "Vell, less see now," said the man at the station, while scratching his head first on the left side and then on the other. "Less see now," he repeated and scratched his head some more. After a while he had it all figured out and said, "Gosh, I don't tink you can get dere from here."

6. The Farmer on the Interstate

A farmer was just getting his first experience in driving on the near-by Interstate. So he drove slowly, whereupon a cop came alongside of his car to offer some advice. The cop said, "Sir, I guess you know why I stopped you." The farmer quickly replied, "Sure, I'm the only one you could catch."

7. Parking Preference

In the (very) old days—when you parked your car most folks would do it at an angle rather than parallel. When parallel parking became more or less standard, one conservative German lady said she didn't like the new parking plan, she preferred "di gut old uncle parken."

8. John Wachtel and the First Stoplight in Indy

When the first stoplight was installed in Indy, everybody wanted to see it, so did John Wachtel with his car. But somehow he plowed right through the intersection only to bump into another car that was probably also under the distracting influence of the beautiful stoplight. Now who had the right-o-way??? John made it crystal clear: "I blowed my horn first!!!"

XXI.

"PROSIT!" TOO MUCH "PROSIT!" "ANTI-PROSIT!"

"Ein Prosit der Gemütlichkeit!"

1. A Little Homesick (ca. 1860)

Erinnerung der Alsenborner Kirchweihe

Was ein Unterschied ist heute
Zwischen diesem Ocean:
Draussen Alles voller Freude,
Hier nur Temperancenwahn.
O! wir moecht'n nur einge Stunden
Euren Rheinwein heute munden;
Und der Mutter ihre Kuchen
Moechten wir gern auch versuchen.—
Weil es aber nicht kann sein,
Fueg'n wir uns geduldig drein,
Schenken anstatt Euren Wein
Dafuer ein Glas Bier uns ein.

Remembering the Alsenborner Church Anniversary Fest

What a difference there is
'tween this and that side of the Ocean:
There—it's joyfulness, so gay,
Here—temperance nuts are on their way.
Oh! just an hour or so 'd be fine
Together with you and wine from th' Rhine,
And Mother's cakes we sure would savor.
But now since all this cannot be,
We'll simply bear it patiently
And substitute for your good wine
A glass of beer—that'll do us fine.

W. Hofmann
Th. Hofmann

2. The Raid on the Taverns

Wanna hear a "wacky" story? You do? Okay! Then there goes. Listen, my children, and you shall hear of the midnight raid on Sterling beer!

If you had been in Dubois County and been on or near Main Street in the heart of downtown St. Henry on a hot afternoon in June of 1885, you might have observed a scholarly looking 26-year-old graduate of Innsbruck, Austria, approaching from the direction of the teeming metropolis of Ferdinand, astride a young black mare whose only claim to fame lay in the fact that she was now carrying on her broad back the first resident diocesan pastor of St. Henry Parish, Father William Wack.

Father is described as having been talented and pious, possessing many priestly virtues, and having high ideals. In fact, he told one of the Benedictine Fathers at St. Meinrad that he was going to make a Saint out of everyone of the St. Henry parishioners. This, of course, is the aim of every pastor, but Father Wack was determined to get that job done overnight, at once, right now, immediately, if not sooner! And therein lies our story.

The first step, as he saw it, was to eliminate the three taverns that did a thriving business in town, two of which flourished in the shadow of the church steeple, or would have if the steeple had been on the other end of the church.

Now, when I say "thriving" business, I mean thriving business. Let me explain. At that time the "Johnsburg Station" on the Southern Railroad was doing a booming business, and the men to the east of St. Henry (toward Ferdinand) hauled a tremendous amount of produce by wagon through St. Henry to this Johnsburg Station.

Now this road was no I-64. In fact, it was more of an I-sore! In dry weather it was chokingly dusty, and when it rained the dirt road became the bottomless pit, and wagons sank to their axles in the shapeless mud, especially in the area to the east of town known as the "flats."

It took the patience of Job to make the backbreaking trip with a load of heavy produce, and, since many of these hardy pioneers had not the patience of Job, they were accustomed to fortify that patience at one of the local pubs, and then continue their exhausting journey.

One of the real "old timers" told me that he remembers coming through the town as a very little boy and seeing the teams and wagons lined up on both sides of Main Street from one end of town to the other, the drivers all inside fortifying their patience!

To put these three taverns out of business seemed to the youthful and zealous pastor a matter of absolute and immediate necessity, but how to do it without causing crushing financial disaster to the owners presented a rather thorny problem. But, in very short order, the good padre came up with a novel solution.

The parish would simply purchase all three taverns and then, as the new owners, would close all three! Simple! If he could get the men behind the plan, they could easily purchase the controlling stock and bonds.

So Father Wack called a meeting of the men, proposed the plan to them, and suggested they go out at once and buy up all the stock, but he evidently neglected to explain exactly what he meant by "stock,"—for the men proceeded to buy up all the "stock"—bottle by bottle, and would you believe that, to this very day, the "stock" has never been exhausted!

And that is the story of the midnight raid on Sterling beer, as engineered by Father Wack. Now ain't that a "wacky" story?

3. Confession Postponed

Old Frank was going to confession, and had several glasses of homemade wine before he left home. As he got into the confessional, Father said, "Frank, you were too close to the wine barrel again, come back next week."

Frank went across the street to the saloon and said to his old friend, "I was going to confession and it was a fizzle."

4. The Saloon Urinal in Jasonville, Greene County

Saloons in those days were rough places and not frequented by "nice" people. I have been told that the mining town of Jasonville, Greene County, had a saloon with a urinal running the length of the bar on the customers' side so they wouldn't need to interrupt the serious business of drinking.

5. Bartender's Luck in New Harmony

While tending bar at Peter Hackmann's Tavern in New Harmony, Karl Wehr was attempting to repair a rifle. The gun accidentally discharged into the barroom filled with customers. Fortunately the only casualty was a whiskey glass.

6. An Easy Job for Daniel

Daniel Branstetter and a relative one evening came back to this relative's house after a little outing. The relative's wife said to Daniel, "You've let him drink too much again."

Daniel said, "That wasn't hard to do."

7. Beer vs. Coca Cola

After a hard day's work at The Starr (Starr's Piano Company in Richmond), Jacob Kellner returned home with an empty lunch pail, actually about a two-quart bucket. Exhausted from his ten hours at the factory he rested in his easy chair while supper was cooking. His custom was to drop a dime in the bottom of the empty bucket and send his young son, Lee, to Adolph Blickwedel's saloon two blocks away for a bucket full of beer. Lee remembers running these errands when he could barely reach the bar . . .

Lee also remembers *Coca Cola for 5 cents* signs at Blickwedel's. One day, Lee was lucky enough to come by a nickel, and headed to Blickwedel's for his first coke. He reached up to the bar and placed his nickel there. When he ordered his coke, Adolph replied: "You don't want that stuff, son, it's no good for you. Wait a minute, I'll draw you a small glass of beer, that's much better for you."—Lee never did drink a Coca Cola until he was a teenager.

8. No, Thanks

One day a stranger came to town to see if he could find a distributor for a new soft drink. My father turned down the proposition. He said, "No one around here will drink that sort of slop."

The new beverage was called *Coca Cola*.

9.-10. Talent for Trouble: The Rev. Schifterling in Dubois County

9. Treatment from the Doctor

Dr. L. Weinert and Rev. Schifterling, the preacher who created so much difficulty in a Lutheran congregation in Col(umbia) Twp. some time ago, got merry and then mad over their wine at Ulrich's garden, and the doctor thrashed the preacher . . .(1870).

10. With Horse n' Buggy

Rev. Mr. Schifterling got drunk last Sunday, and let the horses run away with him in a buggy, throwing him out on the road, and breaking the buggy and injuring the horses some. The worst of it is: the horses and the buggy didn't belong to him . . .(1872).

11. How Many Puppies in the Basket?

At the turn of the century, Andy Isenbarger, an old German cabinet maker of the Howe Sewing Machine Company in Peru, was already in full bloom when he came into the Barrel House, John Coyle's saloon, which sold whiskey for 5 cents a drink. Herr Andy put a basket on the bar and said, "If anyone can guess, oops, how many puppies I've got in the, oops, basket, I'll give 'em to you, oops, both of 'em, oops."

12. When It Is Too Early for a Drink

"Let's stop in the saloon for a drink."
"Isn't it a little early in the day for a drink? It's so bright."
"So squint a little."

13. A Prohibitionist "Off Duty" (1871)

Yesterday, we happened to spot an eager beaver of the temperance disciples. His swaying gait revealed that it wasn't exactly cold water with which he had whet his whistle.

14. Temperance Crusade in Evansville (1880)

Look out, Evansville! The ladies of the Women's Christian Temperance Union have declared war on all taverns in that city. Their main target at this time is Albecker's Apollo Garden.

15. Yearnings (1907)

They stood on Patoka bridge at twilight
While the moon looked down from above.
The breezes blew soft and balmy—
'T was time for sighs and love.
They silently gazed at the water

And thought of things held dear.
She longed for an ice cream soda,
He yearned for a glass of beer!!

> It was Sunday and the lid was on in Jasper <

16. Prohibition Days in Dubois County

Our area was a hot "manufacturing" spot for the making of whiskey, home brew, wine, and cider. Prohibition didn't bother the folks much. Distillers always had spies in town to watch for Revenue Officers and talk them into telling them whose names were on the list for a raid. Then they spent the next few hours telephoning and warning the "manufacturers" to hide their products. For it was too bad if the stills were going when the officers came around unannounced. When a still was going full blast, you couldn't cool it down easily.

One bootlegger sold his products in Louisville. On one trip he had two ten gallon pottery jugs strapped to the outside of his automobile, on the running board. He had no other way to convey them. After sealing the corks, he poured a bit of country molasses over the corks and down the sides of the jugs. On the way, a policeman stopped him. When he saw the jugs, he told the driver that his sorghum was escaping. Looking out of the window at the jugs, the bootlegger said, "Yeah—I guess they're gettin' too hot." The policeman grinned and waved him on. Whew! that was close. But listen, for many of these poor farmers—and town folks—bootlegging was the only way to keep food on the table and clothes on their backs.

17. Moonshinin' in Spencer County

When the dry spell of prohibition hit the country and folks were squeezed so bad by the Great Depression, many a man in my neck of the woods took to moonshinin' as the only way out. Stills were owned jointly by rings numbering about twelve members. And they rotated these stills hoping that this maneuvering would confuse the neighbors and, of course, the police. Their customers came down from Chicago in highpowered automobiles that could easily outrun the police cars. Those "gentlemen"—two to a car and with Tommy guns between 'em—were none other than members of the Al Capone gang that was a heavyweight in the booze business. When the liquor was loaded into these cars, guards from both sides stood by with their guns ready for instant action.

One night things weren't going right. All of a sudden a gun-shot rang out and one of Capone's men was struggling on the ground. Not a word was spoken. But the loading speeded up and soon the cars were on their way back to Chicagoland—leaving a dead man behind. First the fellers didn't know what to do. Then they got some shovels and dug the man under at the edge of the woods, unhallowed and unknown.

18. Professor Harry Velten and His Martini

Professor Harry Velten guided many a graduate student at IU through the thickets of the early forms of the Germanic languages. He was a quiet sort of a man who—in his non-academic pursuits—had developed the art of making a Martini to the greatest degree of perfection. Mind you, there is unanimous agreement among the lucky few privileged to have enjoyed Harry's divine drink that nobody, but nobody, will ever be able to put one together like he did—and we mean it. To tell the truth, we never actually saw him mix one, because he did believe in "long-range planning" and always had a quart in his icebox ready to go. But don't you think now, especially if you are of the temperance variety, that Harry had any need to join the A.A. Far from it. It was only for very exceptional reasons that he suspended his policy not to drink one before 5 P.M.

Those afternoons when some of us regularly met at his house to make the class schedule for the next semester did become the exception. One time, we had been working away at it for quite a while and we were all coffee'd out and really ready for some "medicinal" break, somebody came right to the point and said, "Harry, don't you agree that this would be a good time to start with a little spiritual rejuvenation?" "Well," said Harry, as he looked at his pocket watch, "it iz actually a bit too early for dat." But as he squeezed his bushy eyebrows you could just see that his mind was still occupied with the tempting suggestion. Then he said, "What de heck, it iz alreddy pasht five o' clock in Scotland, we might as well."

19. James Heppner's Budget for a Trip to Germany

One night, mug in hand at the Rathskeller of the Deutsche Haus-Athenaeum in Indy, James said it would take him about five thousand dollars to go to Germany for a couple of weeks. Questioned about that high a price tag—even with a low 1990 dollar, he said, "Looky here, it's about $1,000 for transportation, hotel, and stuff, and $4,000 for the beer!"

Well, *Prosit!*

XXII.

ARTISTS

. . . 'cause his cow was poisoned by paint. (XXII.2.)

1. Theodore Stempfel Worried about Sculptor Rudolf Schwarz and the Gov. Morton Statue

The Indiana Legislature of 1905 appropriated thirty-five thousand dollars "for the purpose of erecting an heroic statue of enduring material to perpetuate the name, memory and service of Oliver Perry Morton, the great war governor of Indiana, the eminent senator, the courageous patriot." Later in the year, Governor Frank Hanly appointed five Civil War veterans as Commissioners for the Morton Monument. I happened to be personally acquainted with two of them. Immediately, Carl Lieber and I set to work on behalf of Rudolf Schwarz. I wrote letters to former members of the Pingree Monument Commission of Detroit. Their replies, as to Schwarz's ability as a sculptor, were uniformly complimentary. Then I submitted the whole correspondence to the Morton Commission. The Commission publicly invited sculptors to submit designs or models for the proposed monument and fixed ten o'clock A.M. on January 1, 1906, as the hour for the selection of the winner of the contest. The day before Carl and I went to the State House. Many artists had sent designs or models and many more monument and tombstone firms, samples, but the Schwarz model was missing.

In the evening, New Year's Eve was celebrated at the German House (Athenaeum) in the usual elaborate style. As soon as I saw Schwarz entering the hall I rushed up to him, impatiently asking about his model for the Morton Monument. *"Das werden wir schon machen"* (We'll get that done alright), he said dryly, admitted however that he had not yet begun with it. New Year arrived, the "Happy New Year" greetings and the clinking of the glasses resounded through the big hall. Schwarz had the time of his life. The hour was two o'clock. *"Das werden wir schon machen,"* he answered mischievously, raising his wine glass with a *"Prosit Neujahr!"* At last, near three o'clock, Schwarz left the hall for his studio. Clad in his festive evening suit he worked the rest of the night on his clay model. It was finished and delivered at the State House shortly before the appointed hour.

Schwarz had modeled a simple, but beautifully graceful shaft, mounted by the allegorical figure of a woman, representing peace and prosperity. Under the cornice of the shaft he had inserted a medallion for a relief reproduction of Morton's head. As there was already a life-size bronze figure of Governor Morton standing on the south side of the circle, Schwarz correctly chose the medallion form.

While the Commission was in session, Schwarz, still in his dress suit—he hadn't been to bed—Carl Lieber and I marched up and down the corridors of the State House, just as young husbands walk the floors of a hospital anxiously awaiting the announcement of the baby's arrival. Schwarz was optimistic as to the outcome, because his model was in depth of feeling and expression far superior to the models of his competitors. But in dealing with men who are experts in the game of politics, one is never sure of the coveted prize until it is actually delivered. After we had marched for over an hour, the door of the session room opened, the Commissioners came out solemnly and congratulated Schwarz on his election as the sculptor of the Morton Monument.

Already on the next morning a member of the Commission, a jovial politician of the glad-hand-shaking and bloody-shirt-waving type came to see me. "We selected Schwarz," he said, "not on account of his model, but upon your and your friend's recommendation and because he is an Indiana citizen. I don't doubt at all that he knows his business. One of our members even said that Schwarz's model was the work of a real artist; but after talking the matter over in our meeting we all agreed that Schwarz has not the slightest idea of our point of view. We don't want any of that symbolical stuff, we are old soldiers, we want to see a statue of Governor Morton as near life-like as possible at the time the Civil War broke out. We want Union soldiers, as many as Schwarz can put around Morton's statue. I am coming to you as a committee of one to ask you to send Schwarz to us. We'll drive the fluffy ideas out of his noodle and tell him what we expect of him in building the Morton Monument." I was disarmed from the start. It would have been folly to run up against the proverbial stone wall.

At the meeting of the Commissioners, Schwarz succeeded in having the number of soldiers at the base of the monument reduced to two, but Morton's full-sized figure was insisted upon by the Commission, so Indianapolis has the distinction of having within a stone's throw two monuments, similar in character, commemorating the same hero . . .

2.-7. Artists, Natives, and the Rest in the Hills O' Brown

2. Painters and Farmers

Carl Graf and Miss Goth called at the old Barnes cabin on West Owl Creek and wanted to paint the place but they were halted by a female voice who gave them to understand that they paid good money for the spot and if Graf wanted to paint it they would want money for it. They knew that artists got money for their canvases. The artists decided to pull their car up to the lane near a gate and paint therefrom and when the trio in the potato patch saw they were outdone they all went to the porch and sat down. Jim Yoder said he wasn't going to allow any artist on his place either as he said he had a valuable cow to die and when it was dissected by a veterinarian he claimed it was poisoned by paint.

3. The Hanging Committee in the Gallery

. . . Dale (Bessire) and Carl Graf comprised the hanging committee for a seasonal showing at the gallery. In making up the show they had come across a painting by the artist Glen Henshaw, a relatively new member of the group. The painting had been placed in a frame the corners of which were not square, and could not be hung to look straight, thus looking somewhat out of place. After wrestling with it for several minutes, and still undecided what to do about the matter, Carl finally said, "Dale, let's just get the horizontal right and let the vertical go to hell." And so the picture hung throughout the show.

4. How Carl Graf Caught Geese

Wild geese flew over the village (Nashville) Tuesday evening about dusk and many of them lit on the old Chautauqua building. Others flew loud over the post office. The jokers said Carl Graf just reached up and pulled down a few.

5. Gus Baumann's Nashville Flood Blues

When Gus Baumann (also a famous early Brown County artist) found that the flood had hemmed him into Nashville he got desperate and smoked up all the cigars he had saved as gifts from friends. He never smoked before and really wished to do something desperate—he got sick—of course.

6. Frank Hohenberger Warning His Brown County Readers

You Don't Have to Read These Items if You Don't Want to

Did you ever notice that some people have been in this county too long and others not long enough?

Brown County Publicity: . . . the scenery. . . it never belonged to us in the first place—the Good Lord entrusted it to our care and we certainly have been CARE-LESS with it.

7. Hohenberger Liked this Sign at the Town Pump

PLeas. DO. NOT
HaLL. WaTer
FROM. THIS WEL
DOURING DROUTH
       MaRShal

XXIII.

MUSIC AND CELEBRATION

"Musik, Musik ueber alles"

1. The Favorite Hymn in the Leininger Family

"Alone, yet not alone am I,
Though in this solitude so drear,
I feel my savior always nigh;
He comes the weary hours to cheer,
I am alone and He with me—
E'en here alone I cannot be."

This hymn, famous in the Leininger family legendry, is the hymn the mother of Barbara and Regina Leininger sang to them when they were young children. In 1755, Barbara and Regina were captured by Indians. Their father and brother were killed. Ten years later, the mother, searching for Regina among freed captives, raised her voice in song, singing this hymn and the two were united. Family legend assumes Barbara and the mother were also reunited. Barbara's and Regina's ancestors settled in the Blue Mountain area of Pennsylvania in 1682.

2. Auf Wiedersehen

One vivid memory of my father's childhood was this: A boy cousin, newly married, and his wife left Hendricksville for a farm near Washington, Daviess County—a distance of about 50 miles. But to this small community that was going to the end of the world or wherever Washington might be. At dawn, with their wagon and belongings, the couple departed amid much lamentation. As the wagon went down the road, family and friends sang songs, the last one being "God Be With You Till We Meet Again."

3. Songfests in Knox County

The first phone lines were all interconnected so that everyone could hear each other. One neighbor would call another and they would begin to sing. As people picked up their phones, more and more singers would join in. Families would gather around the phone and a songfest would take place all over the party line.

4.-6. Mt. Vernon Editor Leffel as Music(ians') Critic (1879/80)

4. And the Band Did not Play on in New Harmony

At a wedding there last week, a band of hired musicians were getting intensely joyful about the occasion to which they were called to perform and demanded far more than their share of the free-flowing drinks. When it appeared that they were becoming unmanageable, the bridegroom quietly slipped some purgatives into their beverages and soon they were observed leaving one by one.

5. The Brass Band 's Got Comp'tition

The Mt. Vernon canine population is not happy with the practice sessions of the brass band. Their barking and howling in competition with the band produces some very strange music.

6. A "Critical" Duet

A Frenchman visiting in New York wrote about his impressions of America to his friends back home. "American music," he said, "sounds like the crying of a Parisian cat whose tail had been pinched by a clothespin." We are glad this gentleman did not visit our vicinity, for we are afraid to think what he would have called the sounds produced by our local musicians.

7. "Musik, Musik ueber alles . . ."

Arthur Monninger (b.1882) didn't want to follow his father's foot steps and eventually take over the Gottfried Monninger Cafe in Indianapolis. He had his heart in music and wanted to become a pianist. Period. One day, when he was practicing the piano, as usual, his father came in and, without saying a word, reached out in anger and knocked him off the bench with a blow that left the boy unconscious on the floor.

Gottfried Monninger was so shocked and so ashamed of himself, but he began to see the light. If that boy really wanted to become a pianist, he figured, then only the best possible education would be good enough.

When Arthur graduated from high school, his father sent him to Germany, to the Berlin Conservatory. Arthur studied there for some four years or more, and he became a concert pianist.

After his return to America he concertized for some time before settling down in his hometown to teach piano and harmony at the Indianapolis College of Music and Fine Arts.

He had hardly been back to Indy when he walked by a Southside tavern from which some fine piano playing could be heard. That aroused his professional curiosity. He went in and saw a young lady tickle the keys with considerable technique that he stayed and listened to her for a beer's length or two. No doubt in his mind, there was a young talent of real promise.

A little later he had himself introduced to Amelia Kroeckle and asked her if she was at all considering the serious study of classical music. Of course, she wanted to. Arthur told her about his Berlin experience and suggested that she do likewise. But she told him that this was out of the question given her financial situation. Then Arthur said he knew exactly how much it cost, and if she wanted to go to Berlin he would send her a check every month. Amelia could hardly believe it, but she accepted the generous offer.

When she came back from Europe, an accomplished concert pianist, Arthur met her in New York. This time he proposed, and Amelia happily accepted again.

For many years the twosome ran their private music studio and taught at the Metropolitan School of Music and at the Jordan College of Music, which is now part of Butler University. Amelia also was the Maennerchor's accompanist for fifteen years. And you can imagine how proud Arthur was when she became the first pianist of the new Indianapolis Symphony Orchestra which she and six other musicians founded in 1930.

After Arthur's death she eventually remarried and became Mrs. William E. Mendell. She went on teaching piano in Indy for many, many years. And she was still playing the piano in her mid-nineties—you can ask Mayor Hudnut. He proclaimed April 20, 1985 Amelia Mendell Day, and she played for him when he visited the Pendleton nursing home where she spent her last weeks before she joined the heavenly band in 1987.

But wait a minute. Her mortal remains were not laid to rest in the Mendell grave. You see, before Amelia remarried, she and William Mendell made a prenuptial pledge that they would both be buried alongside their first spouses. And so Amelia is together with Arthur again.

8. The First Christmas Tree in Fort Wayne (1840)

The first home in Fort Wayne to be graced by the presence of a Christmas tree was that of Dr. Charles A. Schmitz, in 1840. . . . In June of 1840 Dr. Schmitz arranged for the shipment of the tree from Cincinnati to Fort Wayne via the canal. On Christmas Eve, this tree, glittering with candles and brilliant ornaments and decorations, was viewed by a company of invited guests. An infant daughter of Dr. and Mrs. Schmitz was placed in a basket beneath the tree, and the guests, including a number of Indians, were admitted. The beautiful tree brought exclamations of delight from the red men, but it is recorded that they found the baby a more lasting object of admiration.

9. "Merry Christmas, Mt. Vernon!" (1879)

Due to the extremely cold temperatures the holidays have been very quiet thus far. If the rickety bridge across Fourth Street doesn't cause a calamity, Christmas celebrations will continue with a joyful spirit in most households. There is no snow on the ground, only an occasional flake can be seen driven about by a very strong northwest wind which is blowing into town across Mill Creek. All streets and roads are frozen hard. The clanking of the horses' hoofs and the rattling of wagon wheels can be heard along with the happy voices of the neighborhood children who are out playing with their new toys.

On Christmas Eve, after the stores and businesses finally closed, a quiet hush settled over our town. There were no fights or quarrels on the streets; the few drunks were safely locked away in jail.

The German traditions of Christmas were observed by many of our town's families. For days the smell of cookies and candies spread from many kitchens. Even the newspaper office became a sampling place for all kinds of Christmas treats, from lebkuchen to pfeffernuts and gingerdrops.

Several area churches conducted special Christmas services. The traditional tree decoration service was held at the Evangelical Trinity Church on the night of Christmas Day. Each member brought and lit his own candle and hung a star on the beautiful tree. A manger scene was erected in front of the tree by a group of the young people. Late comers kept filing in and soon all seats were taken; many stood along the walls and in the aisles of the church. A strong wind kept blowing the door open and caused the lamps and candles to flicker. Two elderly sisters, both nearly deaf, whispered loudly into each others ears. They were disturbed by the leaves and brush which blew into the church each time the door opened, and in turn their whispers agitated those near them. Pastor Schneider delivered his sermon and left the spellbound crowd of worshipers with no doubt as to the origin of the biblical Holy Night. As the Schneider girls mixed their lovely voices in a Christmas duet, people dropped to their knees one by one.

A check into all parts of town showed that, due to the careful attention of our churches and ladies organizations, there was not one hungry person in Mt. Vernon.

10. The First Fourth-of-July Celebration in Indianapolis (1822)

Early Indianapolis was a proud city, boisterous and exuberant—and it loved to celebrate, particularly the Fourth of July.

The hoopla started in 1822. That year, the city fathers advertised for a special participant for their platform committee—a veteran of the American War of Independence. It seemed an unlikely feat, because few veterans were still alive—and fewer still lived on the sparsely populated frontier.

Nevertheless, one aged gentleman stepped forth, and, in the accent most associated with Pennsylvania's Germans, announced he was indeed a veteran. Instantly, he became the hero of the hour—until one celebrant asked, "What was your unit?"

The veteran proudly replied, "Why, I fought mit der Hessians."

The city fathers quickly agreed the veteran had seen the light and become a hardworking citizen, and the crowd cheerfully allowed him to keep his honored place on the platform.

11. The Hoosier Fourth-of-July Champion (1876)

George W. Dietz of New Albany thought that a feller ought to do something special for the Nation's One Hundredth Birthday. So he decided to go to Philadelphia, where it all began and where the big World Exposition 1876 was taking place. He started his special trip on May 1. Every day, except Sundays, he marched some 27 miles at a clip of about 2.5 miles per hour toward his destination that was more than 700 miles away. His total marching time was 298 hours. A healthy feller he was, and he arrived in Philly in good shape—and that included, to a lesser degree, his shoes, the only pair he used. They were put on display as a relic at the Indiana Pavillion. The hickory cane, his only travel companion, he had cut as a boy and at a spot that later was to become downtown New Albany. This cane, too, became a show piece at the pavillion. During his long hike, Herr Dietz stayed only in hotels. That accounts for the fact that it cost him three times more than if he had gone by train. But, of course, that was not the point. Everywhere he stopped on his way they gave him a hearty welcome. While in Philadelphia, he was spending his time at the Indiana headquarters of the World Exposition and helped make this place quite an attraction, because he was also a good talker and story teller at his tender age of—seventy-nine.

12. St. Joseph's Day in St. Leon, Dearborn County (1849)

In the dark days, when the dreaded cholera claimed its heavy toll of human lives in Southeastern Indiana, the men of the parish voluntarily gathered within the humble walls of their log church and, in a body, solemnly promised to keep St. Joseph's Day—March 19—the Patron Fest of the church as a Holy Day ever afterward, if they and their families would be spared the ravages of this fatal disease. This must have been in 1849. It is recorded that not one single death from cholera happened in this parish, although numerous cases existed in the vicinity.

The promise has been kept faithfully to this day.

13. The Best Speech of Herman B Wells (1951)

IU's most beloved president, the one and only Herman B Wells—a great-grandson of a *Bauer* by name of Harting from Klein Bokern near Osnabrueck—can be counted among the ardent admirers of the Forty-Eighters and the Turner movement. The Turners invited him to Indianapolis to give a banquet speech. The occasion was the 100th Anniversary of the Athenaeum Turners, celebrated on George Washington's Birthday, February 22, 1951.

The culinary delights, the toasts, the freely flowing libations, the music, and all the other what-have-yous at such round-figure fests were such that the clock slipped just about toward midnight before Herman B was finally on with his banquet speech. He had prepared it carefully, notes and all, and a clean seven-page manuscript. But with his judgment unimpaired by the aforesaid hoopla, he kept the manuscript in his pocket. He simply congratulated the turned-on Turners, thanked them for their hospitality and said, "This has been a rich feast of food and drink, and a rich feast of wit, wisdom, and oratory. In fact, after all that has been said by my predecessors, there is little left to say." Roaring applause. Of course.

When he sat down again, his neighbor at the table, Governor Henry Schricker—who had learned Bavarian German from his immigrant parents before he knew English—said, with a grin, "Herman, that's the best damned speech you ever made!"

Herman B didn't exactly recall at what hour of the morning they finally went home.

14. Picking the Date for the Evansville Volksfest (1975)

Gus Felker is so successful at picking rain-free days for the Germania Maennerchor Volksfest that one Evansville woman called the club last March hoping that if she planned her daughter's wedding for the same weekend it wouldn't rain. Felker, who is the secretary for the club, has been choosing the date for the 13 years the club has been holding the festival and he's yet to be rained out . . .

Felker who picks the dates months in advance said there is no secret to his long-range forecasting. "I simply use an almanac and choose the weekend in August that is closest to the full moon."

XXIV.

ALL KINDS OF NATIONALITY

1.-2. The Jackson County Dutch

1. Salutin' the Dutch Butchers

> Hurray for the Dutch!
> They're cleaning out the guts!

2. Nationality Tests "D" and "K" (take either or both)

The "D" Test:
If you ain't Dutch,
you ain't much.

The "K" Test:
If you ain't Kraut,
you're out.

P.S. Don't worry if you didn't pass the tests, that's no sin. Of course, it isn't nice either.

3. What's a "Hoosier German"? A (Nasty) Def'nishn from KY

A Hoosier German is a German who had to make a livin' in Indiana, 'cause his wagon broke down on the way from Kentucky to Chicago.

4. A Hoosier German Grandma Draws the Line—in the Water

Grandma: Child, thank God for rivers!
Grandchild Kari: Why, Grandma?
Grandma: 'cause if it wasn't for the Ohio there'd be nothin' to separate us from Kentucky!

5.-6. Watch Your Tongue in Mt. Vernon (1879/80)

5. Should a Kentuckian Ever Boast in Mt. Vernon?

Here is one that did, but alas . . . This thirsty neighbor from across the river arrived in our city Saturday night and promptly began to sample the quality of the bartenders' products. After visiting the fourth saloon and getting fuller and louder with each stopover he boldly proclaimed, "Nobody in this town can touch me!" Our brave jailer Ed Hayes did.

Monday morning, after paying a fine of $7.80 and having been "touched," our daring visitor returned to his native Kentucky.

6. Same Goes for Evansvilleites, too

A fight of considerable proportion took place between Gus Uri of Evansville and Charles Davis. After Uri made several derogatory comments about Mt. Vernon, Davis thought to defend his home town with blows and bruises and thereby convey an unwelcome to other like-minded Evansvilleites.

7. Hoosier or Texan? Dat's de Queshtshn

Gosh, were they happy, Claude and Martina Eckert, when they heard from their son Stan, who practices medicine down in Austin, Texas, that he and Brenda would bring their first child home to Jasper to be baptized. While they were visiting in good old Dubois County the question of "nationality" came up. Martina wanted to know if the young'ns considered little Megan to be a Hoosier or a Texan. Stan said, "Well, Mom, Megan was born in Texas—that makes her a Texan, don't it?" "Not necessarily so," said Martina. "Supposing your cat had kittens in the oven, would you call them *biscuits?*"

They all had a big laugh and Stan reconsidered calling Megan a Hoosier.

8. How the Irish of Ireland, Dubois County, Became "Cherman"

In Dubois County, north of "Deitsch" Jasper, there is a little town that goes by the name of Ireland. There you can get a glass of green beer on St. Patrick's Day. One day, a reporter from an Evansville paper was trying to get a good Hoosier-flavored story for St. Patrick's Day. So he went to Ireland and asked a woman for an interview. "Tell me," he said, "are all the people here of Irish stock?" Mimicking a German accent, the woman replied, *"Ach, nein—ve are all Cherman."*

9. "Naturonality"

Until my twelfth year I didn't know that Austrians were not exactly Germans. Only one thing had disturbed me immensely as a child: when my father spoke Austrian in public instead of the dialect of my hometown, Stuttgart. I was so embarrassed because he didn't speak *Schwaebisch.*

One day, in 1938, our teacher said, "Everybody stand up, except Eberhard!" My God, why was he singling me out? What had I done? He started speaking to us about a triumphant Hitler entering Vienna and bringing Austria "home into the Reich." And then he said,"This long awaited day is also a great day for our class, because our own Eberhard is now, finally, also a *real* German, a citizen of the Reich. Let's all congratulate him!"

I think I went from red to pale and red again, and I was thoroughly confused and ashamed when they all shook my hand. What had I been yesterday? Not a German? Not the right kind of German? A wrong kind of German? Yes, that was it, like my father, sort of half-German—a damn Austrian-German.

When I got home, my mother said she was glad that father didn't have to go to the police anymore to have his residence permit renewed ever so often. At times she had feared that some day he would come back from the police registry without a renewal and that he, and perhaps the whole family, would be deported to Austria. Strangely, my father had no comment at all on the *Anschluss.*

Now let's jump seven years. In August of 1945, when I came home from the war, I went to the police registry to get an ID card. I filled out the form. The clerk checked my entries against the records. "Ja, Herr Reichmann," he said, "you made one error, you are now no longer a German citizen, you are Austrian again." "Says who?" I wanted to know. "The Military Government," he said. "See that dirty uniform I'm wearing?" I responded, "that's not Austrian, that's German. And see the ruins out there. These are the ruins of *my* hometown, and if I ever wanted to be *German,* I want to be it *now* in this hellishly hopeless year of 1945." He said he couldn't help me, he had to stick to the laws of the Military Government, and I should be glad to be Austrian, for as a "foreigner" I'd be getting a somewhat larger food ration than "the Germans." I assured him that I didn't want any preferential treatment. He just shook his head. I told him that my uncle was the new state prosecutor. That impressed him somewhat, "So, so, Herr Zais is your uncle, but not even he can help you in this case." I left the place with a new ID card and a new-and-old nationality: Austrian.

Now let's jump six years. In 1951 I had chance to spend a year in America. The U. S. Office of Education had initiated a program for young German teachers to experience the famed "American Way of Life." That was for me. I was accepted. I wrote to the Austrian Consulate in Munich that I needed a passport. When I read their reply, I had the financial shock of my life. The fee was 42 German marks or $10. My net salary was something like 175 marks a month—with which I could, usually, survive the first three weeks. And they wanted 42 marks! That was impossible, and having been raised in the old German cash-only tradition, borrowing seemed out of the question. I talked to a friend who had just been abroad. He said he paid 2.50 marks for his German passport. That sounded more like it, and it gave me an idea. I went to the county office, told them—in the thickest local *schwaebisch* dialect—that I was offered a year in America, and that I needed a passport. "How exciting," the clerk *schwaebisched* back at me. Then came the personalia:

"Born?" "December 8, 1926."

"Where?" "In Schtuagert" (Stuttgart).

"Occupation, yeah, teacher." "Yeah, poorly paid."

"Religion?" "Catholic, but not really practicing."

"Makes no diff'rence. Still Catholic." "I suppose."

"Nationality—ha, ha, naturally." "Yeah, ha, ha—naturally."

"And that will be two marks and fifty pfennigs." "Gladly."

Now take onother jump with me, twelve years, to 1963. Eugene and Norma Bristow had invited Ruth and me to a cocktail party in Bloomington, and, prompted by my accent, the inevitable three-part question came up:

"How long have you been in America?" "Ten years."

"How do you like it over here?" "I like it very much."

"Do you plan to become an American citizen?" "No." Surely, the man had not expected my "no" answer, for he nearly dropped his dentures in his martini. I felt I owed him an explanation. Meanwhile, our host drummed up everybody to hear why I would want to forego the blessings of U.S. citizenship. So here goes:

"I am now a first-class citizen of second-class country. I don't see any sense in becoming a second-class citizen of a first-class country."

"What do you mean by first and second-class citizen?"

"If I try hard enough, I can become president or chancellor of the Federal Republic. But no matter how good I'd be here, I could never become president of the USA, because I'd always be a foreign-born, naturalized citizen, and thus disqualified for the highest office, hence *second class*."

The first comments were twofold. A minority held that "Eb has a point there." The majority, though, felt that this was such a hypothetical case and, after all, "Who'd be crazy enough and wanna be president, anyway?" Our gracious host waited patiently until all had their say. But then, appropriate for the advanced cocktail mood, Gene lambasted everybody, "Wrong, wrong, wrong! Shame on all of you! You don't know how our Constitution works! If we want Eb to be the next president of the United States, we will amend the Constitution." We all drank to that, and I said, "I have a question for Gene and Norma: Will you two act as citizenship sponsors for Ruth and me?" Of course, they agreed. And one day in 1964, the two "natives" drove the two "foreigners" to the swearing-in ceremony in Indianapolis, and on the way back there were four Americans in the car.

P.S. *Naturally,* in the meantime I've dropped the idea of running for president, 'cause that wouldn't leave me no time anymore for them old Hoosier Germans.

XXV.

"... these damned stubborn mules would stop right on the railroad tracks ..."
(XXV.6.)

1. *Der Grundsau*

Einmol hat da Ed Meyer eine neue Flint' g'kriegt fir sein Geburtstag. Und da hat da Ed zu die Frau, die Frau hat Josie g'heisse', er hat g'sagt: "Josie, ich geh amol die Flint' ausprobiere." Und ist da Ed in da Busch g'gange und ist a bisstel ins Feld rumg'lofe. Uf einmol dort hinne der Baum hat a Grundsau rum da Baum g'guckt. Und da hat amol da Ed die Flint' g'nomme und hat amol g'schosse. Und der Grundsau hat wiede um da Baum g'guckt. Da hat da Ed wiede abgelade. Und dann hat der Grundsau wiede um da Baum g'guckt. Da hat da Ed amol ufgezielt und hat ord'lich abgelade. Es war nimme lang, hat der Grundsau wiede rum g'guckt.

Und weisst du was? Dreiadreissig mol hat der Grundsau rum der Baum g'guckt. Und dreiadreissig mol hat da Ed g'schosse. Uf einmol ist da Grundsau nimme um da Baum g'komme und hat da Ed g'sagt: "Ja, jetzt ist's los." Da ist da Ed rum da Baum g'lofe und hat g'guckt. Und weisst du was? Dort ware dreiadreissig tote Grundsai g'lege.

The Groundhog

Once Ed Meyer got a new gun for his birthday. Then Ed said to his wife, she's called Josie, "Josie, I'm gonna try out my new gun. So Ed went into the woods and walked around in his field a little. All of a sudden a groundhog stuck its head around a large sycamore tree. So Ed shot at it. Again, it peeped around the tree. Again, Ed shot, this time taking better aim. When the groundhog stuck its head around the tree again, Ed shot again, giving it the very best aim he had. Again and again he shot—the groundhog sticking its head out time and time again. And do you know what? Thirty-three times the groundhog looked around the tree, and thirty-three times Ed shot until, finally, the groundhog appeared no more. Then Ed wondered what was wrong. So he walked around the tree to see. And do you know what? There lay thirty-three dead groundhogs.

2. *Spatzies*

Einmol hat de Ed Meyer und die Josie, die ware auf die vornest Porch g'sesse und wollte schock'le. Und die Spatzies ware so schlimm, dass sie h'en net auf die Porch sitze koenne. Es hat Spatziedreck iber alles g'gebe.

Da hat de Ed g'sagt: "Josie, mir koenne net dohaus sitze da ganze Sommer, wo da Spatziedreck und alles ist." Dann hat die Josie g'sagt: "Ja, ja. Was gehst tue?" Er hat g'sagt: "Ich hab an Idea." Da ist er mol ins Haus g'ganga und hat amol sein Pfeif g'holt und hat amol die Pfeif ordlich ufg'lade mit das staerkste

Tubak, was er g'habt hat und hat amol unte da Baum g'gange. Da hat er amol
ordlich g'schmockt und g'schmockt. Er hat about zwei Stund g'schmockt. Und die
Josie hat g'sagt: "Was tust, Ed? Das tut kei' gut." Und de Ed hat g'sagt: "Geb mich
just zehn mehr Minute." Und da hat die Josie g'watched. Und uf einmol hat's
Spatzies g'regnet. Und weisst du was? Es hat Spatzies g'regnet fir drei Tage.

Sparrows

Once Ed Meyer and Josie were sitting on the front porch rocking.
The spatzies were so bad that they could not sit on the porch. There were
spatzie droppings everywhere.

Ed said to Josie, "We cannot sit out here the whole summer with
these spatzie droppings and all." Then Josie said, "Well, what are you
going to do?" He said, "I have an idea." So he went into the house and
fetched his pipe. He filled his pipe full with the strongest tobacco he had.
Then he sat under the tree. There he smoked and smoked. He smoked
about two hours. Josie said, "What are you doing, Ed? That isn't helping
any." Ed said, "Just give me ten more minutes." So Josie watched. All of a
sudden it began to rain spatzies. And do you know what? It rained spatzies
for three days.

3. *Da Sturm*

Einmol hat da Ed Meyer dieselbe neie Flint g'nomme, die er fir sein
Geburtstag g'hat hat, und hat er die Josie g'sagt: "Ich geh amol in die Nordverzig
laufe mit der Flint." Und da Ed ist gerad so ungekimmert durchs Weizefeld gelofe.
Uf einmol gerad aus a nirgend ist a ordliche Sturm ufg'komme. Es hat da Ed so
verschrocke. Und da Ed hat g'sagt: "Was kann ich tue?" Es hat geblitzt, weisst. Da
Ed ist amol in da Weizeschock g'jumpt. Und es hat da vorne geblitzt und dadriebe
geblitzt und dohieber geblitzt und dahinne geblitzt und als geblitzt.

Da Ed hat amol der Weizeschock ufg'macht und hat amol 'naus g'guckt. Er
hat sich mol gepetzt, mol senne, ob er noch lebendig ist. Und es hat wieder geblitzt
und dorieber geblitzt und dohieber geblitzt und dohinne geblitzt. Und dann hat da
Ed wieder der Weizestock ufg'macht und hat amol a Faust g'macht und in der
Himmel geguckt und hat g'sagt: "Dohieber bin ich!"

The Storm

Once Ed Meyer took the same new gun, which he had received for
his birthday. He said to Josie, "I'm goin' walkin' in the North Forty with
my gun." And Ed walked so unconcernedly through the wheat field. All of

a sudden out of nowhere a tremendous storm arose. It frightened Ed. And Ed said, "What can I do?" It was lightening, you know. So Ed jumped into a wheat shock. It lightened in front of him, to the left of him, to the right of him, and in back of him. It lightened everywhere.

Ed opened the wheat shock and looked out. Then he pinched himself to see if he was still alive. And it lightened again here, there and everywhere. Then Ed opened the wheat shock again, made a fist, and looked up to heaven and said, "I'm over here!"

4. *Brunne Digge*

Einmol hat da Ed Meyer—seine Frau hat g'sagt: "Ed, mir h'en kei Wasser. Was geh'n mir tue?" Da hat da Ed g'sagt: "Ich hab a Idea." Dann hat da Ed amol seine Stiefele ang'tan und ist amol 'naus zum Peach Baum g'ganga und hat amol a Ast abg'haue. Und die Josie hat g'sagt: "Was gehst tue?" "Ich geh Wasser finde." Und dann hat er der Peaches Ast g'nomme und ist 'naus g'gange und hat der Peaches Ast g'used Wasser auszufiehle. Ausgefiehlt und ausgefiehlt hat er und uf einmol ist der Ast gerad in da Bode g'gange. Und es war so stark, er hat ihn beinoh ab seine Fiess gepullt. Und dann hat er amol ang'halte und hat g'sagt: "Josie, gerad do geh'n mir der Brunne digge." Uf einmol ist der Peaches Ast abgebroche. Und dann ist da Ed in das Haus g'sprunge und hat der Schaufel g'holt und hat amol g'schaufelt, weisst. Und er hat gediggt und g'schaufelt und gediggt und g'schaufelt. Und weisst du was? Er war verzig Fuss im Bode und hat noch kei' Wasser g'troffe. Und auf einmol hat er a bissel mehr g'schaufelt und g'schaufelt und uf einmol hat er Wasser g'troffe. Er hat das Loch 'nauf g'guckt und hat g'sagt: "Josie, hol die Leiter! G'schwind! Mach schnell!"

Dann ist die Josie abg'doppt und ist g'sprunge und hat die Leiter g'holt und hat sie amol ins Loch g'stosse. Und da Ed ist uf die Leiter g'krabbelt. Und weisst du was? Er ist gerad uf die oberst Stepp g'komme und ist das Wasse in dem sei Schuh g'lofe.

Diggin' a Well

Once Ed Meyer's wife said, "Ed, we have no water. What are we going to do?" Ed thought briefly, then he said, "I have an idea." Then he put on his hip boots, went out to the peach tree and chopped off a branch. And Josie said, "What are you going to do.?" "I am going to find water," Ed said. So he took his peach branch, went out and used the peach branch to divine for water. He divined and divined and suddenly the branch went right into the ground. It was so strong, it almost pulled him off his feet. But he held tight and said, "Josie, right here we are going to dig the well." Suddenly the peach branch broke off. Ed then ran into the house and fetched the shovel, you know. He digged and shoveled, and digged and shoveled, and do you know what? He was forty feet in the ground and still had not hit water. All of a sudden he shoveled and shoveled again and then he hit water. He looked up out of the hole and said, "Josie, get the ladder, quick, hurry!"

Josie stumbled away and ran and got the ladder. She shoved it in the hole. Ed scrambled onto the ladder. And do you know what? He was just on the top rung when the water ran into his boots.

5. *De Wageraede*

Einmol hat de Ed Meyer a solche schobliche Wage g'hat. Und jedesmol, wo er rund das rechte Eck g'gange ist, ist das linke vornest Wagerad abg'falle. Und es hat de Ed so verzornt. Er hat net g'wisst, was tue. So ein Sonntagmorge ist de Ed in d'Kirch g'gange. Er ist rum das linke Eck g'komme wieder und uf einmal sind alle vier Wageraede—sie sind abg'falle. Und es hat de Ed so verdammt falsch g'macht. Er ist ab de Wage g'jumpt und hat die Haend uf die Hifte getan und hat amol gebrummelt und geknurrt und hat g'sagt, "God damn!"

Und dort iber die Stross war das Pfarrhaus und der Pfarrer war unter die Tir g'stanne und hat g'sagt, "Aber, aber, Ed, das ist a 'no, no'. Du musst sage, 'Gelobt sei Jesus Christus, jetzt und in Ewigkeit. Amen.'"

Aber de Ed wollt das net heere. Er hat als geknurrt und gebrummelt und hat die Wageraede g'fixt, weisst. Und er ist uf de Wage g'jumpt und ist fort g'fahre. Und de naechst Sonntag ist das same Ding passiert. Er ist rum das Eck g'fahre und alle vier Wageraede sind wieder abg'falle. Und de Ed ist ab de Wage g'jumpt und hat die Haende uf die Hifte getan und hat g'sagt, "Gelobt sei Jesus Christus, jetzt und in Ewigkeit. Amen."

Und weisst du was? Die vier Wageraede sind g'rad so scheen von 'leinig ufg'stanne und haben sich selbe g'fixt. Und de Ed ist uf de Wage g'jumpt, hat g'pfeift und ist fort g'fahre. Und iber die Stross war der Pfarrer g'stanne in die Tir und hat die Haend uf die Hifte g'tan und hat g'sagt, "God damn!"

The Wagon Wheels

Once Ed Meyer had a very delapidated wagon. And each time he went around the right corner, the left front wheel fell off. It made Ed very angry. He didn't know what to do. So one Sunday morning Ed went to church. He came around the left corner again. Then suddenly all four wagon wheels fell off. It made him damned mad. He jumped off the wagon, put his hands on his hips, grumbled and growled and said, "God damn!"

And there across the street was the rectory. The priest was standing in the doorway. He said, "Uhhh, uhhh, uhhh, Ed, that's a no-no! You should say, 'Praised be Jesus Christ, now and forever. Amen.'"

But Ed didn't want to hear that. He continued to grumble and growl and fixed the wheels, you know. Then he jumped on the wagon and drove away. The following Sunday the same thing happened. He drove around the corner and all four wagon wheels fell off again. Ed jumped off the wagon, put his hands on his hips and said, 'Praised be Jesus Christ, now and forever. Amen."

And do you know what? All four wheels got up by themselves and fixed themselves. Ed jumped on the wagon, whistled and drove away. There across the street stood the priest in the doorway. He put his hands on his hips and said, "God damn!"

6. *Die Esel*

Einmol da hat da Ed Meyer solche stobliche Esel g'hat und jedesmol, wo er in die Stadt g'komme ist, sind die verdammte, stobliche Esel gerad uf die Railroad Tracks g'stopt. Es hat da Ed so verzornt, er hat net g'wisst, was tue.

Einmol am Samstag Morge ist da Ed in die Stadt g'komme und gerad uf die Railroad Tracks sind die stobliche Esele g'stopt. Es hat da Ed ganz falsch g'macht. Einmol hat da Ed da Choo-Choo-Train-Whistle geheert. Es ist wiede "choo-choo" g'gange. Da Ed hat g'sagt: "Ich muss was tue. Ich hab a Idea!" Da ist da Ed von sei Wage g'jumpt und ist hinne da Wage g'gange und hat a ordliche armvoll Holz g'holt. Da hat er amol a ordliche Feuer unne die verdammte, stobliche Esele g'macht. Und weisst du was? Die verdammte Esele sind just weit genug gemoved, dass da Wage verbrennt ist.

The Mules

Once Ed Meyer had such stubborn mules. Each time he went into town these damned stubborn mules would stop right on the railroad tracks. It made Ed so angry, he didn't know what to do.

One Saturday morning as Ed came into town and just as he was on the railroad tracks the mules stopped again. This made Ed so angry. Suddenly Ed heard the choo choo whistle. It went choo choo again. Then Ed said, "I must do something. I have an idea." Ed jumped off the wagon, went behind it, and gathered a large armful of wood. Then he built a tremendous fire under the damned stubborn mules. And do you know what? Those damned stubborn mules moved just far enough so that the wagon burned up.

7. In's Bett

Ed Meyer hat amol zuviel g'hat zu trinke. Er hat amol a ord'liche Kisch g'hat. Er ist heim g'komme in die Middle die Nacht. Die vornest Tir war g'schlosse und die hinterst Tir war g'schlosse. Uf einmol hat er die Kiche Fenster ufgemacht und is amol 'neing'krabblet. Er ist ganz iber sich g'falle, weisst. Und er hat die Schuh abg'nomme und hat amol ganz tip tee, weisst, 'nein in die Bettstub g'gange. Und dann hat die Josie sich ins Bett g'movt, weisst. Und dann is da Ed zum Schockel g'sprunge und hat amol hart g'schockelt. Und die Josie hat g'sagt: "Ed, was tust du dort driebe?" Da hat da Ed g'sagt: "Josie, ich tu's Baby schockele." Die Josie hat g'sagt: "Ach, Ed, komm ins Bett. Ich hab das Baby mit mich scho zwei Stund g'hat."

Into Bed

Ed Meyer once had too much to drink. He had tied on a good one. He came home in the middle of the night. The front door was locked, and the back door was locked. But then he got to open the kitchen window and climbed in. He fell all over himself, you know. He took off his shoes and went quite tip toe in the bedroom. Then Josie moved in bed, you know. Then Ed jumped to the cradle and rocked it hard. Josie said, "Ed, what are you doing over there?" Then Ed said, "Josie, I'm rocking the baby." Josie said, "Oh, Ed, come to bed. The baby 's been with me for two hours already."

8. Da Sorg

Da Ed Meyer hat amol zuviel g'hat zu trinke. Und seine Verein hat g'sagt: "Mir geh'n da Ed lerne, dass er nimme zuviel sauft. Das ist a Suend und a Schand."

So h'en sie ihn nunne g'nomme zum Undertaker und h'en ihn in a Sorg g'tun. Und sie h'en ihn ufgefixt und h'en Blume um ihn g'fixt, weisst. Und sie h'en dort g'stanne und ware g'wacht. Und da Ed ist net ufgewacht. Sechs Stunde' war er dort gelege, hat net ufgewacht, weisst.

Und dann h'en sie g'sagt: "Ja, ich wett, der ist g'storbe." Da hat da ein' ihn g'nomme und hat ihn a bisstel g'schittelt, weisst. Und da ist da Ed ufgejumpt und hat amol rumgeguckt. Dann hat da Ed g'sagt: "Wenn ich in a Sorg bin, soll ich tot sei'. Aber wenn ich tot bin, wie kommt's, dass ich brunse' muss?"

The Coffin

Once Ed Meyer had too much to drink. And his friends said, "We are going to teach Ed never to drink so much again. That is a sin and a shame."

So they took him down to the undertaker and put him in a coffin. They fixed him up and put flowers around him, you know. Then they stood there and watched. But Ed did not wake up. For six hours he lay there and did not awake.

Then they said, "I bet he is dead." Then one of them took him and shook him a little, you know. Then Ed jumped up and looked around. Ed said, "If I am in a coffin, I should be dead. But if I am dead, why do I have to pee?"

9. *Des neie Waschzimmer*

Eimol hat der Ed Meyer wieder so ne ordliche Kischt ghatt un er hat wirklich der Arsch voll ghatt. Un da hat der Ed zu de vornest Dier kumme un er hat die vornest Dier brobiert un es war gschlosse un er is hinder ganga un hat de hinnerst Dier brobiert un es war gschlosse un da hat der Ed gsagt, "Was kann ich du?" Un da hat der Ed gsagt, "Ich hab en Idea!" Un er is zu de Kichefenster gange un er hat das Kichefenster brobiert un es war uf. Er hat's Fenster nufgeschowe un is naigegrawwelt. Un grad da hat er misse zum Waschzimmer. Dreiundreissig Johr wars 'outside' un hen sie's naigegrickt ins Haus zwei Woche vordes.

Des neie Waschzimmer war zwei Woche alt un die Josie hat net gwisst wie's butze. Un dann hat die Josie emol gsagt, "Ja, ich glaub, ich weiss was du." Da is sie nausgange—des war bevor der Ed heimkumme is—un sie is nausgange un hat emol a bissel nafta-gas grickt. Sie hat e bissel gas naigerirt un hat's ufgerirt un das war grad about zwei Stund 'vor der Ed heimkumme is un er hat misse gehe, weischte? Un der Ed hat emol iber des Hauwe gsesse un hat e Cigarette geschmookt, weischt? Un er hat des Cigarette ins Hauwe gworfe un es is gange Hwiii! Un die Josie is ufjumpt un hat gsagt, "Ed! Ed! Was war des Lerme? Hat des Lerme net de Ohre wehgedaun?" Un hat der Ed gsagt, "Josie, bekimmer dich net uf des Lerme un uf de Ohre! Des hat halwes mei Schwantz weggegrickt!"

The New Bathroom

Once again Ed Meyer had really tied one on. This time he'd really gotten loaded. And he got home to the front door and tried it but it was locked. So he went to the rear and tried the back door but it was locked. Then Ed said, "What am I to do?" And then he said, "I've got an idea!" He went to the kitchen window, tried it, and it was open. He pushed the window up and crawled in. And right then he had to go to the bathroom. It had been outside for thirty-three years and they had gotten one inside the house two weeks before.

The new bathroom was two weeks old and Josie didn't know how to clean it. And then Josie said, "Yeah, I believe, I know what to do." Then she went out—that was before Ed came home—and she got a little kerosene gas. She poured a little gas into the toilet bowl and stirred it up and that was about two hours before Ed came home. He had to go (to the bathroom), understand? And Ed sat over the bowl and was smoking a cigarette. Then he tossed the cigarette into the bowl and it went Hwooof! And Josie jumped up and said, "Ed! Ed! What was that noise? Didn't it hurt your ears?" And Ed said, "Josie, don't you worry 'bout the noise and the ears! It's blown away half my tail!"

10. *Wie Ed Meyer gheiret hat*

Eimol, wo der Ed Meyer e junger Kerl war, is er in de Steddel kumme. Er wollt e paar Sache kaufe un er wollt auch sei Liewe senne. Josie war ihr Name un sie war der Mann sei Dochter, wo de Schtor hat ghat. Ed wolt des Maedel heire, aber der Vadder war dagege und er hat immer "nein" gsagt. Josie hat der Ed auch heire wolle, aber ihr Vadder wollt es net erlaube. Der Ed konnt die Josie nur sehe in de Kirch un in de Schtor.

Der Ed is in de Schtor kumme un der Vadder war da. Der Mann hat gsagt: "Gude Morge, Ed, was wilsch du heit?" Un der Ed hat gsagt: "Ich will e paar Sache kaufe un ich will dei Dochter Josie heire." Des hat de Vadder arig bees gemacht, wenn er des wieder gheert hat un er hat gsagt: "Ed, des is des letschte Mol, wo du des sagscht. Wenn ich des wieder heer von dich, dann loss ich dich nimols wieder nai in mei Schtor!" Dann is die Josie drunner kumme in de Schtor un hat de Ed griest. Un dann hat der Ed zu sich selbst gedenkt: "Ich hab en Idea!" Un er hat gsagt: "Ich muss dei Dochter heire, ich muss sie hawe." Der Vadder hat geantwort: "Was meinschte, du musch sie hawe?" Un der Ed hat gsagt: "Ich muss dei Dochter hawe, because ich hab sie schon ghatt." Die Josie hat gschrien: "No, no, Ed! Des sollschte net sage!" Der Vadder hat sie beide angeguckt, er war so verzornt un er hat gsagt: "Aweg mit eich beidi! Fort aus mei Schtor! Fort aus mei Haus!

Raus! Raus!" Der Ed un die Josie sin gschwind naus gsprunge, auf de Wage jumpt un sin weider fahre. Un die naechste Woch hen sie gheiret.

How Ed Meyer Got Married

Once, when Ed Meyer was a young man, he was coming into town. He was going to buy a few things and he also wanted to see his sweetheart. Josie was her name and she was the daughter of the man who owned the store. Ed wanted to marry the girl, but the father was against it and he kept saying "no!" Josie also wanted to marry Ed, but her father would not allow it. Ed could see Josie only in church and in her father's store.

Ed came into the store and the father was there. The man said, "Good morning, Ed, what will you have today?" And Ed said, "I want to buy a few things, and I want to marry your daughter." That made the father really angry when he heard that again. And he said, "Ed, this is the last time you say that. If I hear that again from you, I'll never let you step in my store again!" Then Josie came down into the store and greeted Ed. And then Ed thought to himself, "I have an idea!" And he said, "I have to marry your daughter, I have to have her." The father answered, "What do you mean, you have to have her?" And Ed said, "I have to have your daughter because I've already had her." Josie cried out, "No, no, Ed! You shouldn't tell!" The father looked at both of them. He was so angered, and he said, "Away with both of you! Out of my store! Out of my house! Out! Out!" Ed and Josie ran out quickly, jumped on the wagon, and rode off. And the following week they got married.

XXVI.

THE OLD FOLKS BACK HOME IN INDIANA

"Thirty-five years ago I sat on this rock when I took my Dad to the poorhouse"
(XXVI.9.)

1. Go-Mom and Go-Pop

Anna Marie Vetter learned to walk on the ship that brought her and her parents to New York harbor in 1865. From that time on she stood on her own feet. As Mary Wint, she was a traditional farm wife in many ways. But she was also a modern woman in her own way. Her father was a carpenter and she was always handy with a hammer, fixing things herself when they needed fixing. She raised sweet corn and other produce for the local grocery store to make extra money for the family. She was known in the neighborhood as a capable lady who was always there to help her neighbors when needed.

By the time Mary and her husband Herman decided to sell the farm to the daughter's family and retire to a house on the edge of Columbus, Mary was known to her grandchildren as "Go-Mom." It seems one little grandson was unable to say *Oma*, German for "Grandma," so Mary and Herman became "Go-Mom" and "Go-Pop."

Go-Mom decided that the new house should have some of the conveniences they had lacked on the farm. She proceeded to have the house wired for electricity and had a phone put in. Go-Pop, a more old-fashioned person, thought this was all an unnecessary expense. Every evening Go-Pop would light the oil lantern, as he had done for so many years. Later, Go-Mom would enter the room and flip the light switch. This went on for about a week, until Go-Pop gave up lighting the lantern. He knew there was no point fighting it any longer.

Some years later, Go-Pop passed away. Go-Mom decided that her children, who for many years had driven them to church and wherever they needed to go, were too busy to be bothered all the time driving her around. She didn't want to be dependent on them. So she bought a small Ford and learned to drive it. She was sixty-five.

2. Mama Having Problems with the Bible

During her childhood Mama got a lot of Bible exposure in the *Sonntags-Schule* (Sunday school) at Zion's Kirche in Indianapolis. She learned her verses not so much for fear of the Lord but rather of the stern German minister who didn't appreciate any mistakes in reciting *Bibelverse*. But then, for some reason or other, she didn't touch a Bible until the last year of her life. Now she wanted to read it in English and she did so every night before she went to sleep. After a number of days she came to breakfast one morning and all red in her face—a sure sign that she was quite upset with something. I asked her what was bugging her.

She said, "Oh, those awful old Jews! They begot and begot and begot and begot and they had two wives or more!" What could I do to calm her down? I told her, "Mama, that's very simple, they lived up to God's command. He didn't tell them to *add*, He definitely told them to *multiply*."

3.-6. My Father

3. A Quiet Man

He was a very quiet man, my father, with little to say. His reasoning? "The more you say, the more you have to take back."

4. A Philosopher

He used to say, his was the kind of luck that when soup was served, all he had was a fork.

5. A Man of Faith

Once I found that a person was stealing in the business my father operated. I told him of the situation. But he said:

"If he has done me wrong he need not settle with me—but with his Maker."

6. His Rules for School

1. If we got a spanking at school—we would get a spanking at home.
2. If we started a fight in the school yard—that would result in another spanking.
3. If a fight was forced upon us and we didn't fight back—you guessed it.

7. A Roger Pfingston Favorite: "Of Stories Fathers Tell"

Of stories fathers tell repeatedly,
as most men love the word
in their own way, poet or not,

there is one about a nose my father tells
of his Uncle John Lewis Pfingston
who some fifty years ago lunged over table
and chairs to settle a card dispute
while travelling the Ohio on a riverboat.

It seems the man with whom he fought
was orally inclined, having locked his teeth
on Uncle John's ear. Uncle John, just as mean,
and while delivering other blows, opened wide
and bit the nose off Lark Fitzgerald
at a cost of one thousand dollars, out of court.

John's mangled ear and Lark's flat face
have long since ceased to matter,
but I'd like to think that in their
current form of travel they might be amused,
even flattered, and rush to be there
when my father laughs to set the mood
and says again he had an uncle once
who did the damndest thing, years ago . . .

8. The Night Hunter

It was a cold November night in the year 1978. My dad, the two
dogs, and I were walking down an old wagon road. As we walked, we
talked about the family tradition of coon hunting. My father told me
about how it was when he was a boy. As he was talking, I could see his eyes
shine from the lantern's light. I could tell he was enjoying the experience
as much as I was. I also noticed by his trembling hands that he was very
weak from the short walk. My dad had suffered from two small strokes,
which disabled him from work eight years earlier, about the time I was
born.

By this time, my dad had caught my fullest interest and humor. I
must have looked like a zombie staring into that old man's eyes. But his
stories always amazed me. I may have been only eight years old, but I listened and observed his story like a senior in college. I never missed a
word he was saying. He told me about the old log cabin he, his mother,
and two brothers lived in. "It was a simple place," he explained. "The
floor was dirt and the cracks in the old log walls were filled with mud and
straw. This was to keep the insects and the rodents out. However, the
upstairs of the old cabin was as cozy and dry as a new home."

It had gotten quiet for a moment. I broke the silence. Maybe I shouldn't have because I could tell my dad was having a wonderful time reminiscing in his thoughts. I had to learn more, though. I could just shut my eyes and see myself doing the things my father had done. He must have had a funfilled childhood.

"Dad," I asked him, "is there anything funny, like maybe a prank or something you did when you were a boy?" I knew he would think of something, and I knew I would have probably heard it before, but I love to hear his stories. They never get old.

"Well, I'll tell ya boy. There was this one time. You see, because our house was small, my brother and I had to stay in the same room. We would be awake at night and think of things to do, just to be mean. Where we lived at this time, there weren't too many people to pick on. Our mother, however, had just gotten married again. Sam was his name. He wasn't too good at talking because of his tongue. It just wouldn't move at times. Anyway, my brother and me were lying in bed one night when my brother, Emmett, came up with this hilarious idea."

"Well, ya see, old Sam was a very protective person and would shoot someone for trespassing on his land. At first he might fire a warning shot, but if you didn't leave—hey, you were shot."

"During this time there had been someone or something stealing our chicken from the hen house. Well, we waited until it was good and dark one evening. My brother ran down to the neighbor's corn patch and stole their scarecrow. I quietly slipped into the house and down the small hallway to Mom and Sam's room. I slowly moved my hand to grab Sam's hat off the rack. The old floor squeeked when you walked on it. So, I had to really take my time getting out of their room. But once I hit the porch, I was getting with it. I ran out to the chicken house. My brother waited excitedly for me to appear with Sam's hat. We sat the scarecrow upright beside the chicken house."

The old pile of straw and sticks might scare crows off, but it wouldn't scare Sam. Somehow we needed more—something to make it more official. I slid back to the house like a thieve in the night. This time I got Sam's new jacket. I had no worries this time because old Sam was snoring like a chain saw. I chuckled to myself a little bit, then ran back to the hen house. I threw the jacket on the scarecrow. All was ready now. We planned our escape route. We were going to run into the chicken house and out the side door and up under the house. From there we would be safe from any harmful acts that old Sam might pull. My brother went first and I followed. We jerked open the chicken house door and ran screaming and jumping through the feathers and out the side door we ran. Up under the house we went."

"Boy, those chickens were flocking and the feathers were flying. We watched and waited. Then suddenly, there was old Sam. 'Get out of here you tat gumb, son of a buck!' he yelled. 'I'm gonna shoot,' he said. 'Blam!' the old single shot gun went off. Sam quickly reloaded. 'I told you once to get out of here. All right, that does it.'"

"Sam took good aim and 'Blam!' the gun went off again. This time he hit his target, but the object he was shooting at just stood there. Sam shot again, this time the hat went sailing off the scarecrow. Sam ran up to the object. He had full intentions of wrestling the thing to the ground. When he had gotten close enough to it, he realized he had been tricked into actually destroying his hat and jacket with his own gun. 'Damn!' he exclaimed. 'Them tat damn boys done made me shoot my own hat.' By this time we were laughing so hard we were about ready to be sick. Well, the next day we both got a good lickin', but it was well worth it."

My father's story inspired me to the point that still today I can remember it. I think we finally ended up getting a coon that night. It wasn't the coons I was hunting for, it was the togetherness. I love my father very much. I guess the reason I do is because he was unable to do anything with me. He has been sick all my life, so I cherish the good things about him, not the bad.

In some cases, however, it might do kids good to learn the responsibility of an adult at the age of twelve. It did me. I still yearn to be able to do something with the sweet old man. That one very special trip was my first and last hunting trip with my dad. He has been getting worse and worse each year. Somehow I can't help but think that he must have known that would be the last.

Rest in peace, Pop. You sure earned it.
May the sky be forever blue
And the roses forever sweet
Like the picture in my mind.
Someday again we will meet.

9. Taking Dad to the Poor House

Sixty years ago my Dad told me that a young man in his 30s was walking his father over the hills to put him in the county poor house. As they got near, they sat down on a big rock overlooking the poor house, and the old man started to cry and said, "Thirty-five years ago I sat on this same rock when I took my Dad to the poor house."

The young man looked at his watch and said, "Pop, if we hurry, we can make it home for dinner."

10. Pop's Last Words

A friend of mine told me this one—a true story: Pop and I farmed for several years. Each had a span of mules. I went to the army and when I came home, I farmed again with him till he died. I was with him, and the last words he said to me were, "Son, I guess we just worked those mules too hard"—and he died.

11. The Best Things in Life (According to Uncle Carl)

Uncle Carl had a good long life. He got to be 92 or 93. Beginning with his 75th birthday he was given a big party every five years. On his 75th, he was asked what he considered to be the best things in life at that age. He answered, "Good food and good sex." On his 80th the same question was put to him. His answer? "Good food and good sex."

At the party on his 85th birthday—you guessed it—the same question came up again. Uncle Carl replied, "I have learned to keep my mouth shut."

12. Grandpa's Exactitude

One day, my dad was still a little fellow, he was lying in the grass and looking at the clouds in the sky. His mother came by and she said to his father, "You better find him something to do." He sure did. And while they were working together the following exchange took place:

Grandpa: How wide is this?
Dad: I reckon about three foot.
Grandpa: Damned, I don't want any *abouts!*

13. Why Guido Schloot Wanted to Outlive His Wife

A year before my father died he said, "Son, I want to outlive Mama—so I can take care of her." When Mama died, she was 89, Dad passed away two months later.

14. George Schricker's "Grandfather Song"

His laughter raised my spirits,
And he let my mind run free,
He made me ask the question
About what it means to be.
He had a gentle nature,
A light within his eyes,
That gave me reassurance
And taught me to survive.

Chorus
Some said he was a giant
Who walked in steps of gold.
Some say he was a legend
Of whom stories are still told.
But to me he was just my grandpa,
White hat, cigar in hand,
I didn't know the governor,
I knew a wise old man.

He let me climb the pine trees
That dad had planted behind the house,
I'd go up into the branches
And bring those pine cones down.
He'd gather them in a basket,
And that night by the fireside,
He'd throw them into the lapping flames
And we'd watch the colors rise.

His backyard was full of wonder,
Grape arbor, plum, and pine,
And in the front stood a giant oak
Which still brings this to mind.
One day he held an acorn
In his outstretched gentle hand,
And said, "Herein's a lesson
I hope you come to understand.

Each person has a purpose
That is up to them to find,
And if you trust your intuition

You'll find a peace of mind.
It may not be real easy
To take your life in hand,
But I know you'll feel the difference
When you've grown to be a man."

Chorus
Some said he was a giant
Who walked in steps of gold.
Some say he was a legend
Of whom stories are still told.
But to me he was just my grandpa,
White hat, cigar in hand,
I didn't know the governor,
I knew a wise old man.

15. When Old Friends Die

At the service for one of his last friends at Flanner and Buchanan, an Indianapolis funeral home, Franklin Vonnegut remained seated after the conclusion of the proceedings. To an attendant who finally inquired if he was feeling well, Vonnegut—well in his nineties—replied, "Oh, yes, I was just wondering whether it's worth the trouble to go home or not."

16. Back to the Old Country?

After my great-grandfather, Hermann Dryer, had passed away, Dryer relatives over in the old country asked his widow, Elizabeth, if she would now come back from America. She answered, *"Ach, nein! Ein Dryer ist mir genug!"* ("Oh, no! One Dryer is enough for me!").

236

XXVII.

DOORS TO THE PAST

1. Theodore Stein, the Lucky Historian of *Our Old School* (1913/14)

When Theodore Stein, a former student of the German-English Independent School of Indianapolis (1860-1882) set out to write the history of his beloved Alma Mater, he was seriously hampered in his work for a long time owing to his inability to procure from the members of the Schulverein the records of the school. He almost despaired of ever gaining access to the books, when one day the "purveyor" at the German House, "Joe," accosted him about as follows:

"Say, Mister Stein, sind Sie ein Mitglied vom Schulverein? (Are you a member of the School Association?). Not willing to commit himself to Joe, the latter continued, "I know you are a member, for I've seen your name on bills of sale, and when I saw it I put these papers aside to give them to you, that is: if you want them; if not, I throw them out or sell 'em, for I am sick and tired of dusting them again and again."

So let it go on record that the original records of the old school were saved for posterity, because the author's name on an abstract of title was the only one which "Joe" could read.

2. A (Bullet?) Hole in the Family History

There is a cemetery a couple of miles out of Linton, Greene County, called the German Methodist Cemetery, with numerous German names on the gravestones. No doubt, many of the men were coalminers. The story goes, though, that these mining Dutchmen were not very popular. And Saturday nights could get rough, including gunfights.

My father had an uncle of whom one was never to speak. So I even don't know his name. I tried to find out the story—but no one would ever tell. When my aunt Nora was on her deathbed, so told a daughter, she said, "If Henry wants the story he should go to Jasonville." I never did go to that old coalminer's town. But I have a relative, Dorothy Hamm, who followed another lead, namely to Hendricksville (where the family did all the pottery), to talk to an old man. When he came to the door she identified herself and asked if he could help in this Jasonville story of "Uncle X." He said, "Let the dead rest in peace." And he slammed the door in her face. Both of us are now more curious than ever.

3. Adding Diversity to the Genes

No one knows better than Dorothy Hamm—with her tremendous genealogy files—how many times in those days relative married relative. She tells the story of a daughter who married to Wyoming. Despite the distance from the Greene County home, Dorothy was pleased when the daughter decided to marry there, since that would add some diversity to the genes.

Guess what. The young man was a distant relative with Greene County genes.

P.S. I ain't gonna tell you anything about *my* family.

4. Was Editor Leffel Making Fun of Genealogists? (1879)

Hier ist die originale deutsche Version:
"Wenn die Mutter deiner Mutter die Tante von der Schwester meiner Mutter ist, wie ist dann der Neffe vom Onkel deines Urgrossvaters verwandt mit dem Schwager der Cousine meines aeltesten Bruders?"

Here is the English translation:
"If the mother of your mother is the aunt of the sister of my mother, how then is the nephew of your great-grandfather's uncle related to the son-in-law of the cousin of my oldest brother?"

5. How Ralph Ruppel Got into Family History

My interest started back in 1958 when Uncle Sam sent me a nice little notice that I had to spend two years in the service. Well, shortly after basic training I was headed for Germany, the land of my ancestry, which I found very exciting.

After being there a couple months, on one Sunday afternoon, lying on my bunk reading the *Stars and Stripes* newspaper and as I was glancing thru it and looking at the various pictures, one in particular caught my attention. I thought to myself, "damn, that looks like my uncle Frank Ruppel back in the states."

And Lo & Be Ho, this man's name was Professor Dr. Alois Ruppel. The caption went on to say that he was the Director of the Gutenberg Museum located in Mainz, Germany, where they have the first printing press and the first printed Bible of the world, the Gutenberg Bible.

So that evening I wrote him a letter and got an immediate reply—in German, which I had to have deciphered as I don't read or speak German.

In his letter he asked if I would like to come and visit his family. I immediately wrote him back telling him yes, and before I knew it, I was on the train heading for Mainz.

Upon arriving I got a hotel room and then by cab to the museum. His secretary met me at the door, took me into his office to meet this gray-headed gentleman. He sure had the Ruppel look, no doubt about it.

He could not speak English, but his secretary acted as our interpreter. We talked for a while, then he asked me where I was staying, I told him, and before I knew it his secretary sent for my things and we headed for his home. She had cancelled my hotel room and said I was to stay with his family. After meeting his family he went into another room and hurriedly came back with an old newspaper. It was the *Chicago Times*, dated 1933. He was pointing out the picture on the front page, which was himself. All excited, he told me all about coming to America in 1933 to Chicago at the World Fair as a representative of the German Government. His country was displaying the Gutenberg Bible and the first printing press. He just went on and on about America.

The next day he took me to meet the Lord Mayor of Mainz and other officials of the city and then to see all the historical points of interest. Later that day he said, he wanted me to meet his son-in-law who was colonel in the German Army, who he said, could speak English.

That evening the Colonel and his wife took me out for dinner and as the evening went on, the Colonel kept bringing up things about America he knew, which surprised me for a foreigner to know that much about our country. He kept calling it "God's country" and that he had the greatest admiration for the American people.

I asked him how he knew so much about America? He said he first encountered Americans during the war and was captured by them early in the war. He said when he was captured, the American soldiers immediately took all his possessions, his watch, billfold, everything he had, which he naturally expected. There was this one thing, though, that he really wanted back, and that was his watch, which had been handed down from generation to generation. Before being put on the POW truck, he begged and begged and asked every American soldier he saw, that he wanted his watch back, but to no avail, so he finally gave up.

Later, as he was climbing on the truck to go to POW camp, an American soldier walked by and slipped something into his coat pocket. He didn't reach into his pocket right away as he was afraid someone else might see him, so he waited for the right moment, reached in and discovered that it was his watch. This really impressed him.

Shortly after arriving at the POW camp, he found out to his surprise that they would be shipped to a prison camp in America. This really excited him.

After arriving in America he couldn't believe the good food and plenty of it, the living conditions and the way they were treated. He said they had daily movies and he even got paid for working.

I asked him where in the states he was at, and he said Kentucky. I told him that wasn't too far from where I lived in Indiana. He said he knew where Indiana was, because he worked there picking up corn on an abandoned airfield. He said they called it gleaning corn. These farmers had a new picking machine and it would miss a lot of ears especially if the wind had blown down the corn. He said these farmers would come down to Kentucky and hire them from the government and they would go up there to this field and pick up this corn and throw it into their wagons.

I asked him if he rememberd where this airfield was, and he said it was in southern Indiana, they called it St. Thomas. It had one little school, church and a country store.

He said he remembered, everytime they would go up to this field, there would always be that little bunch of kids, who would just stare and watch them for a while, and all at once they would run off to this little country store and in a while would come back with some bottles of Coca Cola for them to drink. He understood that the lady at the the store gave it to them. He thought is was very generous of her, and said it was the next best thing to beer.

Folks, that lady was my Aunt Mary Bono, those kids were my brothers and sisters, and those farmers were my Dad and my uncles. I thought that was quite a coincidence to run into one another like that, not really knowing it.

I visited these people several times after that and got aquainted with several other families, and before heading home, they gave to me, for the Ruppels in America, a printed page of the Gutenberg Bible and a printer's casting key. We never did get our relation confirmed because most of the records were destroyed during the war and so we just called each other name cousins.

My grandparents came over to America in 1858. Another coincidence, they came over on a ship named *Bremen*, and exactly 100 years later in 1958 I went over to Germany on a ship named *Bremen*. That's the reason I became interested in family heritage.

Folks I'm proud of my family heritage and I'm sure you are too—or you wouldn't be here at this Vincennes German Heritage Dinner.

6. Oh, Them Good Old Days (1880)

On this hot summer day, Friday, August 13, 1880, J. C. Leffel, the publisher and editor of the weekly *Mt. Vernon Demokrat*, was faced with a number of unsettling problems. This caused him to look back to the "good old days" of 1780, and he penned his thoughts in a German poem, *Vor Hundert Jahren*.

One Hundred Years Ago (=1780)

One hundred years ago, it seems, 't was mostly like in our days.
Upon the poor and rich alike the sun was shining down his rays.
Honor among most men prevailed, justice proudly did her reign.
And always did the ground get wet, when clouds did send
The needed rain.

But some things, for us now old, were yet strange for them by far.
For instance, no one thought to ever see a railroad car.
Machines with steam they did not have, nor telegrams racing
Through the air,
And hardly ever would you see such finery upon the ladies fair.

One hundred years ago they only knew: with hands a man must
Sow and thresh.
Never one in government considered taking bribe or cash.
They had in America, 'tis true, their sauerkraut and spaetzel,
But nowhere in this fair land was there lager beer or pretzel.

The Colt revolver was not yet, nor "Old Dominion coffee pot."
The men who thought of things to come, had to invent still quite a lot.
No "likeness" on a photo then—your face on paper wasn't there,
Nor could a maiden with her beau visit a circus or the fair.

All of this, and more, they missed—a hundred years ago,
But then they had, what now we don't, more honest folks—it's so,
For whether poor the man—or rich, he always, sooner or later
Would come around and gladly pay what he owed for his newspaper.

7. Two Hundred Years from Now (=2106)

The Rev. J(oseph) Thie committed to print thirty-two pages bearing this unique title:

History of / St. Pius Parish, / Troy, ... / Here you have a hundred and one things thrown together for ev-/ery one to pick out what / suits him. / It is not expected that these pages will be of / much interest just now; but after being buried about 200 years / among the trash in some / historical library, / they will be all right.

Joseph A. Thie, / Rector of St. Pius Church / St. Joseph's Day, A.D. 1906.

8. Can You Hear "Ancestral Voices"? Listen with Hoosier Poet Norbert Krapf

Down the subway tunnels
of the family line
I hear muted voices
of relatives who were
buried back in Midwest
village cemeteries before
I was born. I see their
mustachioed German faces
paling in piety as ovalled
on Catholic memorial cards
my grandmother showed,
but remember their spirits
more fully fleshed in
boisterous country stories
my father told. If their
train could jump the tracks
between us, my ancestors
might pull up at this New
York station and cry out
the directions which would
light curves in the tunnel
leading up to myself.

NOTES

Notes, Chapter I

1. From: Norbert Krapf, *Finding the Grain: Pioneer Journals, Franconian Folktales, Ancestral Poems.* Jasper: Dubois County Historical Society and Herald Printing, Inc. (1977), 119.—New edition in preparation.

2. Sent by Dorothy Keiser Campbell, Center Point, Clay County, May 1991. The poem was written by Emmet Skelton. The trunk is now in the possession of a great-granddaughter of stowaway Harmon Henry Keiser (1822-1889), Monteen Bugher, Carmel, Ind.

3. From : *St. Joseph Parish* by Albert Kleber, O.S.B., St. Meinrad (1937), 20-21.

4. From notes on "What I Have Learned from my Mother," by Agnes Elizabeth Schafer Bufka (1981). Courtesy Norbert Bufka, Midland, MI.

5. From: B. J. Griswold, *The Pictorial History of Fort Wayne, Indiana* (Chicago, 1917), I, 357.

6. Told by Bernadette Stenger, St. Leon, Dearborn County, 1986; based on Leo M. Stadtmiller's Family Tree.

7. Told by Mrs. Ernest B. Miller, Edwardsport, Knox County, Sept. 1988.

8. Told by Ellen Klingman Pettay, Bloomington, July 1988.

9. Based on an account from Elizabeth Huemmer, as retold by her daughter, Justine Ziegler, Plymouth, Marshall County. Collected by James Ziegler, Plymouth, 1988.

10. From: *South Bend Tribune*, Aug. 1, 1881. Collected by James Ziegler, 1988.

11. From: Theodore Stempfel, *Ghosts of the Past*. Indianapolis (1936), 48-51; privately printed autobiographical sketches, published by Theodore Stempfel, Jr., shortly after the death of his father. Copy at Indiana Historical Society Library, Indianapolis.

12. *Ibid.*, 51-52.

13. From: *Huntingburg Signal*, the Dubois County German-language paper, April 8, 1897 (30th year!). Trans. by James Ziegler, 1988.

14. From: *Rockport Journal* , Oct. 5, 1894. Dr. Lester Bockstahler (b. 1895 in Santa Claus, Ind.), who supplied the story, writes, "As a boy I gathered ginseng and may apple roots and sold them to the good doctor. From these he made alcohol-herbal fusions, which were in vogue at the time as medical nostrums"(Aug. 10, 1988). Dr. Maslowsky (1845-1906) was the son of a Prussian officer. He came to America in 1870 and studied at the medical colleges of Louisville and Cincinnati. His medical practice at Mariah Hill spanned some 30 years. He eventually married a Hoosier German girl, Margaret Heichelbech (see *Rockport Democrat*, April 13, 1906).

15. From: Carol Burke, Ed., *Plain Talk*. West Lafeyette: Purdue University Press (1983), 3 (Esther Strasburger talking to Tom Flora).

16. Told by Frances Himes, Nashville, Brown County, 1990.

Notes, Chapter II

1. From: C. Earl East, *Relive It With C. Earl East. Stirring Stories Which Really Happened*. Bloomington (private printing, 1963), 6-7. Supplied by "Uncle" Henry Wahl, Bloomington.

2. From: Ronald L. Baker, *Hoosier Folk Legends*. Bloomington: Indiana University Press (1982), 192.

3. From: Linda Robertson, Ed. *Wabash County History, Bicentennial Edition 1976*. Marceline, MO: Walsworth Publishing Co. (1976), 478.

4.-5. The German Methodist founders of the hamlet were opposed to alcohol. This makes (4)—as cited by Ronald L. Baker and Marvin Carmony, *Indiana Place Names,* Bloomington: Indiana University Press (1975), 148—a bit less likely than (5), supplied by Bill and Pat Koch of Santa Claus, Sept. 1991. For a third, also child-inspired, version, *see* Baker's *Hoosier Folk Legends*, 190-191.

6. From: Wayne Guthrie, "Huntingburg Named For Good Hunting," in the column "Ringside in Hoosierland," *Indianapolis News*, Aug. 1976 (semi-ident. clipping), sent by Jim

Kleifgen, Indianapolis. Col. Geiger first called his town Huntingdon. Probably to avoid postal mix-up with Huntington, he later chose the name Huntingburg.

7. From: George F. Loehr, "The History of Holland," in: *125 Years Holland, Indiana (1859-1984)*. Holland (1984), 4-5.

8. I heard this story years ago but do not recall the source. *Ed*. Ronald L. Baker has a tragic "Nigger Hill" entry in his *Hoosier Folk Legends*, Nr. 228.

9. From: Ronald L. Baker, *Hoosier Folk Legends*, Nr. 210.

10.-11. From: Albert Kleber, O.S.B., *Ferdinand, Indiana, 1840-1940. A Bit of Cultural History*. St. Meinrad (1940), 210; 191.

Notes, Chapter III

1. Told by Emma Wallpe, Oldenburg, 1986.
2. Told by Ellen Klingman Pettay, Bloomington, July 1989.
3. From: Anton Scherrer, "Muellers Used to Get Mixed up—So They Took Names of Trades," in the *Indianapolis Times* column "Our Town"; undated clipping, provided by Indianapolis city historian William Selm.—Anton Scherrer was the son of Adolph Scherrer, Swiss-born architect, whose work included the completion of the State Capitol after the death of its first architect, Edwin May.
4. Told by Melvin H. and Jo Ann Roberts Sundermann, Anderson, Oct. 1990. The Krugers were among the early German pioneers in the Huntingburg area of Dubois County. Our Argonaut Kruger had 14 children from his first wife and 12 from his second.
5. From William Selm's interview with Corina Christian Wilhelm, Oldenburg, 1987.
6. Told by Ruth Noerr Scanland, Indianapolis, June 1988.
7. From: *A Historical Sketch of the Holy Family Church and Parish, Oldenburg, Indiana, 1837-1937*. Compiled by Robert Wilken, O.F.M. (1937), 82.
8. Told by Irvin ("Mugs") Waechter, Oldenburg, 1987 ("Mugs" was "a pet name given to him by his sister who knew of a ball player, Mugsie McGraw," says Emma Wallpe).

Notes, Chapter IV

1. From: *Huntingburg Signal*, Aug.15, 1895. Trans. by James Ziegler, Indiana University, 1988.
2. Told by "Uncle" Henry Wahl, Bloomington, 1989.
3. Heard from Elfrieda Lang, Bloomington, 1985.
4. From a letter (Nov. 11, 1985) by L.C. Rudolph, Bloomington.
5. Told by Ellen Klingman Pettay, Bloomington, July 1988.
6. From: Elfrieda Lang, "German Influence in the Churches and Schools of Dubois County, Indiana," *Indiana Magazine of History*, XLII (June 1946), 161. "My source was Albert Kleber, *St. Joseph Parish*. St. Meinrad (1937), 75." (E. L.).
7. Told by Louis Hoelker, Oldenburg, 1990.
8. Heard from "Uncle" Bill Hoelker, Oldenburg 1986.
9-10. Told by Leander C. Wollenmann, Ferdinand, Dubois County, 1989.
11. William Selm, Indianapolis, provided this sample of mixed language—often erroneously referred to as Pennsylvania Dutch (=Pennsylvania German) which is a German-American dialect with relatively few English ingredients.
12.-14. Told by Leander C. Wollenmann, 1989.
15. Told by "Uncle" Bill Hoelker, Aug. 1986. "I heard my father relate this story quite a few times" (B. H.).
16.-18. Told by "Uncle" Henry Wahl, 1985.
19. Told by Leander C. Wollenmann, 1989.

Notes, Chapter V

1.-4. All Father Ferneding selections from: Sister Dorothy Marie Bockhorst, O.S.F., "Growth and Development of the Western Missions of the Archdiocese of Cincinnati," unpubl. B.S. thesis in Education, Teachers College of the Athenaeum of Ohio, Cincinnati (1942), 13-14. The stories were related to her by Miss P. Fihe, great niece of Fr. Ferneding; she had heard them from her great aunt, Catherine, the sister of Fr. Ferneding.—In 1833 Fr. Joseph Ferneding was appointed missionary to all the German Catholics between Louisville, Vincennes and Indianapolis. New Alsace was the first big Catholic German settlement in southeastern Indiana. Fr. Ferneding, who had become their priest in 1833/34, still had a lot of traveling to do to see the other settlers in this huge area. The "circuit rider" practice, usually thought of as a Methodist specialty in frontier days, was common to all principal denominations.

5.-8. From: G. E. Hageman, *Friedrich Konrad Dietrich Wyneken, Pioneer Lutheran Missionary of the Nineteenth Century.* In: *Men and Missions* , Number III. St. Louis, MO: Concordia Publishing House (1926), 23; 28-29; 30; 24-28. Pastor Wyneken succeeded C. F. W. Walther as the second president of the Missouri Synod.

9. Told by Professor Antonius Holtmann, Universitaet Oldenburg, Oct., 1990, on the occasion of the St. John's Sesquicentennial.

10.-12. Told by the Rev. Wilford C. Butt, Harrison County, Aug. 1988.

13. From a mimeographed pamphlet by the Rev. and Mrs. Wilford C. Butt on the "History of the Mount Solomon Evangelical Lutheran Church, Harrison Township, Harrison County, Indiana" (1969), 5.— On Glenn's death *see* XVI. 1.

14.-15. From: Friedrich Albert Hoff, "Early History of the Santa Claus German Methodist Episcopal Church, Salem Congregation, Spencer County, Indiana." This history was written in German script by the Rev. Hoff while serving as minister to the congregation (1878-1881). The text was trans. by Lester I. Bockstahler (1977). Rev. Hoff's frank account suggests that life in Santa Claus had some rough edges. Preacher Severinghaus noted: "One evening in August 1874, M. Scherzinger had me arrested on charges of provocation. The investigation started at midnight, before the JP in Buffaloville. My opponent had a lawyer. I pled my own case. At one o'clock in the night I was set free. Then my accuser, Scherzinger, threatened to beat me up on my way home. I said to him, 'I will be there myself.' When we consider all these things, hatred for the Preacher and the early controversies, I wonder that any good work can take place in Santa Claus" (Bockstahler, trans., 15).

16.-17. From: Albert Kleber, O.S.B., *Ferdinand, Indiana, 1840-1940. A Bit of Cultural History.* St. Meinrad (1940), 113; 141-142.—Available again in reprint edition (1988) by Ferdinand Historical Society.

18. From: C. G. Schnell, *Celestine, Parish and Town, 1843-1968, Quasqui-Centennial,* 13-14. The Rev. Joseph Wirz(?) served German Catholics of Celestine from 1854 to 1856. The town and parish were founded by Fr. Joseph Kundek, the great Catholic pioneer priest and colonizer in Southern Indiana. He served this parish at various times between 1842 and 1847. The land was entered by Bernard Merkel and Boniface Fehr, both from Baden. They sold it to Fr. Kundek.

19. From: Albert Kleber, O.S.B., *St. Pius' Parish, Troy, Indiana, Centenary History, 1847-1947.* Troy, Ind. (1947), 52.— Beginning of text rephrased. *Ed.*

20.-23. Told by Martina Eckert, Jasper, 1988.—"A true story (#20). It was dramatized in St. Anthony Parish" (M. E.).

24. From: Agnes Elizabeth Schafer Bufka, "Grandma's Memories" (1979), 20.—Thanks to Norbert Bufka, Midland, MI.

Notes, Chapter VI

1.-15. Unlike Ed Meier, the other legendary Dubois County character (*see* XXV), Fr. Basil Heusler, O.S.B. (1860-1942) was very real. A native of the Canton of Berne, Switzerland, he served St. Joseph's parish in Jasper from 1898 to 1942. Stories #1-15 were told by Clarence Krapf, Dubois County, Aug. 20, 1978. Mary Jo Meuser transcribed the recordings and did most of the translating. Thanks to Norbert Krapf, Long Island University, for providing the stories.

16.-17. Collected at the "Schnitzelbank" during the Jasper Strassenfest, Aug. 1990, from Martina Wehr Eckert (16) and Jasper Mayor Jerome Alles (17).

Notes, Chapter VII

1. Told by Genevieve Langferman Waechter, Oldenburg, Franklin County, June 1988.— Elfrieda Lang recalls the same "two-houses" rule from her childhood in Posey County: *"Wenn du zwei Haeuser hast, kannst du beides drauf haben"* ("When you own two houses, you can have both on it").

2. Told by Eberhard Reichmann, Nashville, Brown County, 1988.

3. From: The Bloomington *Herald Telephone,* "Same Christmas Card exchanged for 50 years," Dec. 24, 1986, A-2, an AP News Feature.

4. Told by Marcia F. Schwenk, Hope, Bartholomew County, 1988.

5. Told by Nan Schenck Polley, Nashville, Brown County, March 1989.

6. Told by Mrs. G. M. Rodgers, Nashville, Brown County, 1988.

7.-11. From: *Mount Vernon Wochenblatt,* June 6 and July 4, 1879; June 18, 1880; June 27, 1879; June 11, 1880. Trans. by Ilse Horacek, Posey County Historical Society.—Leffler, a second-generation and perfectly bilingual German-American, was editor of this German-language weekly. He also published the English-language *Western Star.*

12. Albert Kleber, O.S.B., *Ferdinand, Indiana, 1840-1940, A Bit of Cultural History.* St. Meinrad, (1940), 218-21.

Notes, Chapter VIII

1. From: John H. Teder, *Teder's History of Dubois County* (1964), 143-144; author unknown.

2. From: Fred D. Cavinder, *The Indiana Book of Records, Firsts, and Fascinating Facts.* Bloomington: Indiana University Press (1985), 109.

3. Told by Joe Becher, Ferdinand, Dubois County, Oct. 1988.

4. From: Agnes Elizabeth Schafer Bufka, *Grandma's Memories.* Midland, MI (1979), 29-30.

5. Told by Joan Quante, Ferdinand, Dubois County, 1986.

6. From: Agnes Elizabeth Schafer Bufka, *Grandma's Memories,* 29.

7. From: Ellsworth Barnard, *Wendell Willkie, Fighter for Freedom.* Marquette, MI: Northern Michigan University Press (1966), 51.

Notes, Chapter IX

1. Told by Martina Eckert, Jasper, 1989.

2. Oldenburg Oral History Project, 1987. Emma Wallpe talking to William Selm, Indianapolis.

3. Told by Elfrieda Lang, Bloomington, 1989.

4. Oldenburg Oral History Project, 1987. John Bernard Flodder (b. 1907) talking to William Selm.

5. Bob Hoffman (b.1909), Jasper, talking to Marilyn Nathan, Aug. 1988.— A typical form of narration for older Hoosier Germans. Since the *Deutsch* has become rusty from disuse, story lines are presented in English, but punch lines of well remembered incidents from child-

hood are retained in the local Hoosier German dialect, just as much as stock phrases like *"danke"* (thank you), or *"dat wees ik nik"* (Low German for "that I don't know").

6. Told by Mrs. Ernest B. Miller, Edwardsport, Knox County, Sept. 1988.

7. From: *Wefel Across the USA, The Newsletter of the Wefel Family Association*, Vol. II, No. 2 (1989),

7. Address: 114 Fontana Dr., Oxnard, CA 93033. The Wefels have deep roots in Fort Wayne, and they are proud of "their" Wefel Street.

8. Told by Martina Eckert, Jasper, Sept. 1989.

9. From: Ellsworth Barnard, *Wendell Willkie, Fighter for Freedom.* Marquette, MI: Northern Michigan University Press (1966), 19.

10. Told by Joseph R. Gogel, Ferdinand, 1990.

11. Told by Dr. Elmer E. Peters, Brookville, Franklin County, 1986.

12. This poem was read by James Whitcomb Riley on Sept. 14, 1880, at Dickson's Grand Opera House, Indianapolis. The program for that evening lists it as "Dot Leedle Boy of Mine—German-English Dialect." It is included in Whitcomb's *Green Fields and Running Brooks.* Indianapolis (1893), 116-120.

Notes, Chapter X

1.- 4. From: Theodore Stein, *Our Old School. Historical Sketch of the German-English Independent School of Indianapolis.* Indianapolis (1913), 39, 42; 46-47; 140-14l.

5. From William Selm's oral history interview with Emma Wallpe, Oldenburg, 1987.

6. Told by Ellen Klingman Pettay, Bloomington, July 1989.

7. Told by Martina Eckert Jasper, 1989. "A true story!" (M. E.).

8.-10. "Uncle" Bill Hoelker from Oldenburg told the Ed Hoelker anecdotes in 1985; Genevieve Langferman Waechter from Oldenburg told the musician anecdote in 1987.

11. From: Herman Pattee, "Kewanna Characters and High Jinks," in: *Fulton County Historical Society Quarterly,* 62 (1986), 109-110.

12. Told by Lora Naffe, Jackson County, Feb. 1991.

13. Told by Louis Hoelker, Batesville, Ripley County, Sept. 1991.

14. Told by Martina Eckert, Oct. 1988.

15. From: *Mount Vernon Wochenblatt,* April 4, 1879. Trans. by Ilse Horacek, Posey County Historical Society.

Notes, Chapter XI

1. From: *Huntingburg Signal,* the German-language paper of Dubois County, March 16, 1893. Trans. by James Ziegler, Indiana University, 1988.

2. This note appeared in the Jasper *Courier,* Jan. 29, 1875. Our text is taken from the extensive *Courier* anthology volumes presently being compiled by Lillian Doane, Jasper. According to Doane, the "prolific" father had one more child.

3. Told by Martina Eckert, Jasper, Oct. 1988.

4.-14. From: *Mount Vernon Wochenblatt,* March 28, 1979; Nov. 15, 1878; Jan. 30, 1880; April 11, 1879; April 9, June 11, March 12, March 5, July 16, 1880; March 7, 1879; Aug. 27, 1880.—Trans. by Ilse Horacek. The *Wochenblatt,* an independent weekly (1875-1881), had a circulation of 960 copies (1880). Editor and publisher John C. Leffel, also published the English-language *Western Star.* He was assisted for a time by F. A. Willmann. It wasn't for lack of subscriptions that the *Wochenblatt* folded in 1881; Leffel just couldn't find a German printer.

15. From: Albert Kleber, O.S.B., *Ferdinand, Indiana, 1840-1940. A Bit of Cultural History.* St. Meinrad (1940), 214-218.

16. From: Lillian Doane's anthology manuscript of the Jasper *Courier,* Oct.30, 1868

Notes, Chapter XII

1. From: *Huntingburg Signal*, the Dubois County German-language paper, Jan. 13, 1898, Trans. by James Ziegler, Indiana University, 1988.
2.-4. Told by William Selm, Indianapolis (formerly of Brookville), June 1989. "Dr. Elmer Peters, Brookville, identified the three girls (in Nr.4): Catharine Kilgenstein, Frances Thalheimer and Eleonora Wissel" (W. S.).
5. Told by "Uncle" Henry Wahl, Bloomington, 1988.
6. Told by Evangeline C. Bockstahler, Nashville, Brown County, 1988.
7. Oldenburg Oral History Project, 1987. Emma Wallpe talking to William Selm, Indianapolis.
8. Told by Mrs. Ernest B. Miller, Edwardsport, Knox County, 1988.
9. Told by Lillian Doane, Jasper, Oct. 1988.
10. Told by Evangeline C. Bockstahler, Dec. 1989.
11. From: Albert Kleber, O.S.B., *St. Pius Parish, Troy, Ind., Centenary History, 1847-1947*. Troy, Ind. (1917), 52-53. The Rev. John B. Unverzagt of St. Maurice parish, Decatur County, had gradually become insane. He died in St. Louis, March 12, 1901.
12. Told by Eberhard Reichmann, Nashville, Brown County, 1989.

Notes, Chapter XIII

1.-12. Told by Sr. Adele Weyer, O.S.B., Ferdinand and Fort Wayne, Oct. 1989. "The two Ladies in Black were very frequent communicants, performed great acts of charity. The first lady also made large donations to the church and paid for a number of seminarians' education to the priesthood. What I can't understand is the people" (Sr. A. W.).
13. From: Ronald L. Baker, *Hoosier Folklegends*. Bloomington: Indiana University Press (1982), 108.
14.-16. Told by William Selm, Indianapolis, June 1989. He had the good fortune of having a story-telling grandmother, Gertrude Maria Clarissa Wissel Selm, b. in the German Catholic village of St. Peters in Franklin County.
17.-18. Told by Jeanne Melchior, Jasper, 1989. Her grandfather, John Gress (b. 1890 in Celestine, Dubois County) was "a great storyteller. He possibly inherited this talent from his grandfather, August Betz, an early settler in Dubois County whose journals have, in part, been translated and published" (J. M.). For the August Betz journals, *see* Norbert Krapf, *Finding the Grain: Pioneer Journals, Franconian Folktales, Ancestral Poems*. Jasper (1977), 35-46. An enlarged edition is planned for 1992/93.

Notes, Chapter XIV

1. Told by Phyllis Johanneman, Ferdinand, Dubois County, 1989.
2.-3. From: *Mount Vernon Wochenblatt*, July 18, 1879; June 1880. Trans. by Ilse Horacek, Posey County Historical Society.
4. Told by "Uncle" Henry Wahl, Bloomington, 1989.
5. From: *Mount Vernon Wochenblatt*, Feb. 20, 1880. Trans. by Ilse Horacek.
6. From: Anthony A. Fette, *History of New Alsace* (1951), 44-45.
7. From: *Huntingburg Signal*, May 8, 1890. Trans. by James Ziegler, Indiana University, 1988.
8. From: *The Columbus Republic*, Oct. 12, 1876.
9. From an undated, typed copy of an unidentified German-language paper text in the Wilhelm Hofmann files at the Indiana Historical Society Library. Trans. by Eberhard Reichmann.
10. From: Patricia Zimmerman, "Partners in Progress," in: Dorothy J. Clark, *Terre Haute, Wabash River City*, Chatsworth, CA: Windsor Publications, Inc. (1983), 102.—The reader

might be interested to know that Joseph Schlitz, founder of the famous brewery, also met his death on the boat to Europe.

11. From: Chris Betz, "A Sad Day in September: The Dangers of Digging a Well," in the forthcoming volume: *Backroads: A Legacy of Southeast Dubois County* , a local history project of Ferdinand's Forest Park High School, Rock Emmert, editor.— Chris's grandpa, Leo Betz, told the story.

Notes, Chapter XV

1. From: *Tales of Pioneers. History of Owen County*. Spencer: Owen Litho Service, Inc. (1962), Vol. I, 606.

2. From: *Huntingburg Signal*, May 14, 1870. Trans. by James Ziegler, Indiana University, 1988.

3. Told by Louis Hoelker, Batesville, Ripley County, 1990.

4. From: J(ulius) A(ugust) Lemcke, *Reminiscences of an Indianian. From the Sassafras Log behind the Barn in Posey County to Broader Fields*. Indianapolis: Hollenbeck Press (1905), 202-206. "Gus" Lemcke was born in Hamburg (1832) and died in Evansville (19ll). He held the office of State Auditor (1887-1891), but he declined a subsequent offer to become U.S. Secretary of the Treasury.

5.-7. From: *Mount Vernon Wochenblatt*, Oct. 3; Sept. 5; Nov. 28, 1879. Trans. by Ilse Horacek, Posey County Historical Society.

8. Told by Marcia F. Schwenk, Hope, Bartholomew County, 1988.

9. From: Agnes Elizabeth Schafer Bufka, *Grandma's Memories* (1979), 31.

10. Told by Evangeline C. Bockstahler, Nashville, Brown County, 1991.—"I can't ask my mother anymore, but the story may well have been brought over from the Palatinate in the 1900s" (E.B.).

11. Told by "Uncle" Henry Wahl, Bloomington, 1986.—"Sylvan Tackett, a local attorney, confirms this true story" (H. W.).

Notes, Chapter XVI

1. From a mimeographed pamphlet by the Rev. and Mrs. Wilford C. Butt on the "History of the Mount Solomon Evangelical Lutheran Church, Harrison Township, Harrison Co., Indiana" (1969), 6-7. Text slightly edited. *Ed.*

2. From: Robert Wilken, O.F.M., *A Historical Sketch of the Holy Family Church and Parish, Oldenburg, Indiana, 1837-1937* (1937), 80-81.

3. From: Maxine Klump, *A History of St. Paul's Parish, New Alsace, Indiana, 1833-1983* (1983), 37-38. (Text slightly edited). Philomena's aunt Elizabeth was the wife of the first village blacksmith, George Vogelgesang.

4. Told by Bernadette Stenger, West Harrison, Dearborn County, 1986. "This story has been verified by several old-timers, many years back" (B. St.).

5. From: Albert Kleber, O.S.B., *Ferdinand, Indiana, 1840-1940. A Bit of Cultural History*. St. Meinrad (1940), 213-214.

6. Told by "Uncle" Henry Wahl, Bloomington, 1985.

7. From: Lillian Doane, "My Happy Childhood on the Farm" (mimeographed, Jasper, 1986), ll.

8. Told by Evangeline C. Bockstahler, Nashville, Brown County, 1988.—"The George Stumpf farm was located on a quarter section at Three Notch Road, or, in today's terms, at S. Meridian and Troy Ave., Indianapolis. George, who had come to Indianapolis from Darmstadt, Germany, in 1830, helped cut down trees to make Washington Street. He also operated an underground railroad on his farm. His three-year-old daughter, Katharina—my grandmother —got the shock of her young life, when she tiptoed down to the kitchen and saw all these negroes being fed by her mother" (E. B.).

Notes, Chapter XVII

1. Told by Evangeline C. Bockstahler, Nashville, Brown County, 1988. The episode took place in Indianapolis after the sinking of the "Lusitania", May 7, 1915, by the German submarine U-20.
2. From: Theodore Stempfel, *Ghosts of the Past.* Indianapolis (1934), 98-99.
3. Told by Marcia F. Schwenk, Hope, Bartholomew County, 1988.
4.-5. The stories were related during the German Heritage Project in Bartholomew County, 1984 and l988; text by Betty Lou (Thralls) Randall, l988.
6. Told by Jane Leitshuh Harnett, La Porte, 1990.—George Leitshuh took over management of the plant until it closed in 1967.
7. From: Frank J. Feeney, "World War I German-American Sentiment at Saint Meinrad Abbey, Indiana." M. A. thesis, Dept. of Religion, Indiana University (1970), 55-56.—Feeney has also a slightly different ending for the Brother Philip anecdote: "After asking the question and listening to Brother Philip's reply, the court experienced *dead silence.* And the examiner passed him in a hurry and summoned another."
8.-9. From: Clifford H. Scott, "Fort Wayne Germans in World War I: A Cultural Flue Epidemic," *Old Fort News,* 40, No. 2 (1977), 3-17.
10. Told by Marcia F. Schwenk, 1988.

Notes, Chapter XVIII

1. From: Julius Augustus Lemcke, *Reminiscences of an Indianian. From the Sassafras Log behind the Barn in Posey County to Broader Fields.* Indianapolis: The Hollenbeck Press (1905), 195-205.— "Gus" Lemcke, b. in Hamburg, got his introduction to America at his uncle's farm in Posey County. He became sheriff in Evansville and served two terms as Indiana's state auditor.
2. Told by "Uncle" Henry Wahl, Bloomington, 1989.
3. Told by Irvin ("Mugs") Waechter, Oldenburg, Franklin County, 1988.
4. Told by Louis Hoelker, Batesville, Ripley County, Sept. 1991.
5. From: Elfrieda Lang, "The Germans of Dubois County _ _ _ ," *IndianaMagazine of History,* XLII (Sept. 1946), 239.
6. Told by "Uncle" Henry Wahl, 1985

Notes, Chapter XIX

1. From: Dr. William A. Fritsch, *German Settlers and German Settlements in Indiana.* Evansville (1915), 6-7. Reprint edition, with Index, by the Friends of Willard Library, Evansville (1979).
2. From: *History of Vanderburgh County, Indiana .* Madison, Wis. (1889), 581-582.
3. From: Robert Wilken, O.S.F., *A Historical Sketch of the Holy Family Church and Parish, Oldenburg, Indiana, 1837-1937* (1937), 83.
4. Told by Mrs. G. M. Rodgers, Brown County, Oct. 1988.
5. From: *Huntingburg Signal,* Jan. 9, 1890. Trans. by James Ziegler, Indiana University, 1988.
6.-7. Told by Mrs. Ernest B. Miller, Edwardsport, Knox County, Sept. 1988.—"These tales— also 'Mush, Mush, Mush' and 'The Skinned Horse'—were told by Grandpa Sam Miller all his life . . . I heard him tell them to his grandchildren (our children). He lived from 1860 to 1937" (Mrs. E. B. M.).
8. Told by "Uncle" Henry Wahl, Bloomington, 1985.
9. Told by Eberhard Reichmann, Nashville, Brown County, 1988.— The student was Charles Christian; the course at IU, Fall 1987, dealt with "The Hoosier Germans." What Charles didn't include in his "calculation" was the large number of non-affiliated Vereins, notably of the German churches.

10. Heard from graduate students at IU Bloomington in the 1960s. *Ed.*
11. Bob Hoffman talking to Marilyn Nathan, Jasper, Aug. 1988.
12. Told by Kay Smith, granddaughter of Eric Domroese, Indianapolis, Oct. 1989.
13. Told by Martina Eckert, Jasper, Oct. 1988.

Notes, Chapter XX

1. Told by Victor Baumgart, Harrison County, Oct. 1988.
2. Told by Evangeline C. Bockstahler, Nashville, Brown County, 1988.
3. Told by Martina Eckert, Jasper, Dec. 1989.
4.-5. Told by Sister Adele Weyer, O.S.B., Fort Wayne, 1989.
6. Told by Martina Eckert, Oct. 1988.
7. Told by "Uncle" Henry Wahl, Bloomington, 1985.
8. Told by Gerhard Klemm, Indianapolis, 1991.

Notes, Chapter XXI

1. One of several occasional poems from the Wilhelm Hofmann files at the Indiana Historical Society Library, trans. by Eberhard Reichmann.—Hofmann immigrated by way of Pennsylvania and settled in Posey County, where he married Catherine Wolf in 1856; (*see* also XIV, 9, "A Gruesome Accident in Posey County").
2. From: Fr. Lawrence Moll, Historian of the Catholic Diocese of Evansville; published in *The Message* (Oct. 19, 1973), 238.
3. Told by Irvin ("Mugs") Waechter, Oldenburg, Franklin County, Nov. 1988.
4. Told by "Uncle" Henry Wahl, Bloomington, 1989.
5. From: *Mount Vernon Wochenblatt,* Dec. 12, 1879. Trans. by Ilse Horacek, Posey County Historical Society.
6. Told by Mrs. G. M. Rodgers, Brown County, Oct. 1988.
7. From: Donald M. Royer, *The German-Amercian Contribution to Richmond's Development: 1833-1933.* Richmond: The Indiana German Heritage Society and The Richmond German Heritage Society (1989), 67.
8. Told by "Uncle" Henry Wahl, Bloomington, 1986.
9.-10. From: Jasper *Courier,* Aug. 12, 1870; Sept. 20, 1872. Text from Lillian Doane's comprehensive *Courier* anthology manuscript.
11. Told by C. R. Borneman, Peru, Miami County, Oct. 1989.
12. Told by Ray E. Hall, Bicknell, Knox County, Oct. 1988.
13. From: *Spottvogel*—Indiana's popular German-language weekend edition—Feb. 3, 1871. Trans. by Eberhard Reichmann.
14. From: *Mount Vernon Wochenblatt,* July 23, 1880. Trans. by Ilse Horacek.
15. From: Jasper *Courier,* June 7, 1907. Provided by Lillian Doane, Jasper.
16. Told by Sr. Adele Weyer, Fort Wayne, 1989.
17. Told by Charles E. Bockstahler, Dale, Spencer County, 1990.
18.-19.Told by Eberhard Reichmann, Nashville, Brown County, 1988; 1990.

Notes, Chapter XXII

1. From the privately printed memoirs of Theodore Stempfel, *Ghosts of the Past,* chapter on "Artist's Life, Rudolf Schwarz and Karl Bitter." Indianapolis (1936), 87-88.
2.-7. "Painters and Farmers"(2) is from an Aug. 1924 diary entry by photographer and columnist Frank Hohenberger. His column in the *Indianapolis Star,* "From Down in the Hills O' Brown County," was not appreciated by the "natives" but contributed greatly to

Nashville's attractiveness. Indiana University's Lilly Library has an excellent Hohenberger collection. Our text (2) is also found in Dillon Bustin's beautifully illustrated tribute to Hohenberger, *If You Don't Outdie Me, The Legacy of Brown County*, Bloomington: Indiana University Press (1982), 128.—"The Hanging Committee..."(3) is from Maurice V. Miller's recollection of "The Early Artists in Brown County," in *Brown County Remembers*, comp. and ed. by Dorothy Birney Bailey, Revere Press (1986), 152-153.—The wild goose tale about Graf (4)—the tallest of all Brown County painters—is found in Hohenberger's Notebook (Oct. 1925), 402.—The Baumann anecdote (5) dates from Oct. 1919, p. 128.—Hohenberger's "Warning" (6) is from a printed loose leaf, presumably from his 1955/56 monthly, *The Nasville Observer*, at the Brown County Public Library, which also has the unidentified newspaper clipping of the Hohenberger photo of the "Drouth"(7).

Notes, Chapter XXIII

1. From: Georgene (Leininger) Gallagher, *An American History of the 1837 Leininger Family*. Hinsdale, IL (1980), 20. "The legend comes from... *The Leininger Family* (1930), publ. by Sophia (Leininger) Bailer" (G. L. G.).—The settlement year of 1682—if indeed correct—makes the Leiningers one of the very oldest German-American families, for German group settlement in North America didn't begin until Oct. 6, 1683, with the Krefelders landing in Philadelphia and their subsequent founding of Germantown, PA. The Leiningers' Indiana branch is largely centered around Fort Wayne.
2. Told by "Uncle" Henry Wahl, Bloomington, 1988.
3. Told by Sheryl Schaefer, Bicknell, Knox County, 1987.
4.-6. From: *Mount Vernon Wochenblatt*, Nov. 21; Oct. 10, 1879; July 2, 1880. Trans. by Ilse Horacek, Posey County Historical Society.
7. Told by Evangeline Bockstahler (b.1905), Nashville, Brown County, 1988. Arthur was her favorite uncle. Apparently, he brought Amelia to tears a couple of times, when he insisted on *"noch mehr Gefuehl"* (still more feeling) in addition to her brilliant technique. For Amelia Mendell's obituary see *Indianapolis Star*, Oct. 20, l987.
8. From B. J. Griswold, *The Pictorial History of Fort Wayne, Indiana*. Chicago: Rob. O. Law Co. (1917), 358; picture of Dr. Schmitz, 335. He was also associated with the attempt to launch the first German-language newspaper in Fort Wayne; there are no extant copies.
9. From: *Mount Vernon Wochenblatt*, Dec. 26, 1879. Trans. by Ilse Horacek.
10. From: George W. Geib, Ed., *Indianapolis. Hoosiers' Circle City*. Continental Heritage Press, Inc. (1981), 13.
11. From: *The Huntingburgh Signal*, June 29, 1876. Trans. and retold by Eberhard Reichmann.
12. Told by Bernadette Stenger, West Harrison, Dearborn County, 1986.
13. This episode is based on Chancellor Wells's oral account to Elfrieda Lang and on copies of his notes and the speech he never gave. During his presidency of IU (1937-1962), the Normal College of the American Gymnastic Union, headquartered at the Deutsche Haus-Athenaeum, Indianapolis, became part of the IU School of Health, Physical Education, and Recreation.
14. From an unidentified clipping (Aug. 1975) of an Evansville paper in Fritz Bockstege's souvenir album of the Germania Maennerchor Volksfest in Evansville.

Notes, Chapter XXIV

1.-2. Collected by Arthur Schwenk, Hope, Bartholomew County, 1987. The origin of these ditties is unknown. The overweening stance of the "Test" ditties, though humorously expressed, may be interpreted as a reaction to the encroachments of nativism on "the damn'd Krauts'" ethnic culture, and as a simple reminder to "stick to your own."—P.S. Since *ditty* , according to Webster, may be "a little poem intended to be sung," try the *Blue Danube* melody, it works.

3. Told by Carl Eugen(e) Miller, Louisville, KY, Sept. 1989 (in New Harmony, on Hoosier territory!).

4. Told by Kari Points, Columbus, 1989. The advice is from Grandmother Schmitt-Geier.

5.-6. From: *Mount Vernon Wochenblatt* , May 7, 1880; Oct.3, 1879. Trans. by Ilse Horacek, Posey County Historical Society.

7. Heard from Martina Eckert, as she showed us a photo of her grandchild at the Dubois County Historical Society dinner in Jasper, March 1989.

8. Told by Sr. Adele Weyer, O.S.B., Fort Wayne, l989.

9. Told by Eberhard Reichmann, Nashville, Brown County, 1989.

Notes, Chapter XXV

1.-9. The Ed Meyer stories are based on versions told by Bob Steffe and Mary Joe Meuser of Jasper and recorded by Sabine Jordan (1981) and Peter Freeouf (1986-1987). The original versions are in Dubois County German dialect; the individual stories have not been standardized orthographically. The reader will find, e.g., *de Ed* as well as *da Ed* , both dialect versions of *der Ed*. Jasper's Bob Steffe is the grand master in presenting the stories orally.

10. Especially written for *Hoosier German Tales* by Peter Freeouf, Bloomington. His dissertation, "Religion and Dialect: Catholic and Lutheran Dialects in the German of Dubois County, Indiana," Indiana University (1989), provides the first linguistic description of the major Dubois County German dialects.

Notes, Chapter XXVI

1. Told by Marcia F. Schwenk, Hope, Bartholomew County, 1988.

2. Told by Evangeline C. Bockstahler, Nashville, Brown County, 1990.

3.-6. Told by "Uncle" Henry Wahl, Bloomington, 1985.

7. From Roger Pfingston, Bloomington. "Of Stories Fathers Tell" has been reprinted many times; it was first published by Sparrow Press in *Nesting* (1978).

8. Told by Scott Wiseman, Ferdinand, Dubois County. His father, Albert, passed away in 1989, a few days before Scott's graduation. This story is a part of *Backroads: A Legacy of Southeast Dubois County,* a collection of works by students at Ferdinand's Forest Park High School. "Publication expected early 1992" (Rock Emmert, editor).

9.-10. Told by Irvin ("Mugs") Waechter, Oldenburg, Franklin County, 1988.

11. Told by "Uncle" Henry Wahl, Bloomington, 1989.

12.-13. Told by James Schloot, Martinsville, Morgan County, 1991.

14. Original song by George Schricker, Jr., Plymouth, Marshall County. His grandfather, Henry F. Schricker—son of Bavarian immigrants—served twice as Governor of the State of Indiana (1940-1944; 1948-1952).

15. Historian James Madison, Bloomington, got this story from Eli Lilly who used it to illustrate his own predicament of outliving friends. However, according to Richard Vonnegut, Sr.—living encyclopedia on the Vonnegut family—the figure in the anecdote had to be Franklin Vonnegut rather than the Clemens Vonnegut of the James Madison version. Thank you, Richard.

16. Told by David Dryer, Indianapolis, Sept. 1991.

Notes, Chapter XXVII

1. From: Theodore Stein, *Our Old School. Historical Sketch of the German-English Independent School of Indianapolis.* Indianapolis (private printing 1913-1914), 14. First sentence of our version slightly modified; "Joe's" remarks are given in translation.

2.-3. Told by "Uncle" Henry Wahl, Bloomington, 1989.

4. From: *Mount Vernon Wochenblatt,* Sept. 26, 1879. Trans. by Ilse Horacek, Posey County Historical Society.

5. From Ralph Ruppel's talk at the German Heritage Dinner in Vincennes, Nov. 23, 1985.

6. From: *Mount Vernon Wochenblatt,* Aug. 13, 1880. Introduced and trans. by Ilse Horacek.

7. From: Albert Kleber, O.S.B., *St. Pius Parish, Troy, Ind.* (1947), "Introduction."

8. From: Norbert Krapf, "Ancestral Voices," in: *Finding the Grain: Pioneer Journals, Franconian Folktales, Ancestral Poems.* Jasper (1977), 101.

GERMAN-AMERICAN CENTER
and
INDIANA GERMAN HERITAGE SOCIETY
401 East Michigan Street, Indianapolis, Indiana 47204

PUBLICATIONS (Book Series)

VOLUME 1 (November 1989)

George Theodore Probst / Eberhard Reichmann:
The Germans in Indianapolis. 1840-1918
Revised and illustrated edition by Eberhard Reichmann. 200 + xii pp. Numerous illustrations and charts. Bibliography. Includes Vereins membership lists. Index by Elfrieda Lang.

VOLUME 2 (June 1991)

Theodore Stempfel's 1898 Festschrift:
Fuenfzig Jahre unermuedlichen Deutschen Strebens in Indianapolis/
Fifty Years of Unrelenting German Aspirations in Indianapolis 1848-1898
Bilingual Edition 1991. Translated and edited by Giles R. Hoyt, Claudia Grossmann, Elfrieda Lang and Eberhard Reichmann. 150 + VIII pp. Large 9 x 12 format. Illustrated. Includes Vereins membership lists. Index of Names. Historical advertisements.

VOLUME 3 (December 1991)

Eberhard Reichmann, Editor:
Hoosier German Tales — Small and Tall.
Some 333 German-American anecdotes, tales, legends, stories, memoirs, and jokes from all over Indiana, from oral history interviews, written submissions, church, school, town and county histories, newspapers, biographies and monographs. 258 + xx pp.
The biggest German-American story collection in the country! English-language version. All German texts rendered also in translation.